To Cheyenne

Love, Grampa

THE SCIENCE OF COLD CASE FILES®

THE SCIENCE OF

COLD CASE

FILES®

Katherine Ramsland

BERKLEY BOULEVARD BOOKS, NEW YORK

A Berkley Boulevard Book
Published by The Berkley Publishing Group
A division of Penguin Group (USA) Inc.
375 Hudson Street
New York, New York 10014

PRINTING HISTORY
Berkley Boulevard trade paperback edition: September 2004

Library of Congress Cataloging-in-Publication Data

Ramsland, Katherine M., date
   The science of cold case files / by Katherine Ramsland.
      p.   cm.
   "Reveals the absorbing true stories behind the pioneering A&E television series"—Cover.
   ISBN 0-425-19793-X
   1. Criminal investigation—Case studies.   2. Homicide investigation—Case studies.
3. Forensic sciences.   I. Cold case files (Television program)   II. Title.

HV8073.R326 2004
363.25'9523—dc22

                                                                            2004046317

PRINTED IN THE UNITED STATES OF AMERICA

10   9   8   7   6   5   4   3   2   1

To Dana DeVito and our
midnight discussions at the Ripper's Pub

and to Marilyn Bardsley,
who keeps me exposed to crimes new and old

and Kim Lionetti, for her "dark" inspiration

CONTENTS

Acknowledgments

While I have been exposed to many experts in the forensic world, I'd like to specifically thank those who assisted with this book in one form or another.

I've always been inspired by *Cold Case Files* host Bill Kurtis. I had been watching the television show since its first airing, so I was pleased to have the opportunity to fully immerse myself in the area of cold case investigations. I want to thank A&E for its production.

Gregg McCrary, my coauthor for *The Unknown Darkness,* spent hours over margaritas with me discussing cold case protocol.

Tracy Starrs and Sandra Anderson (and Eagle and Otter) showed me quite a bit about actual death investigations, as well as "forensic friendships," and I've learned a lot in discussions with Dr. Frank and Julie Saul, Dr. William Bass, and James E. Starrs.

My perspicacious editor, Kim Lionetti, is always an enthusiastic sounding board and source of encouragement, as well as clearheaded and skillful in her sense of a project's direction. We're in synch.

John Silbersack of Trident Media Group, good friend and agent, has been my main support for the vision and direction of my writing, and I'm deeply grateful that he is protective, innovative, and always there for me. That counts for much more than he may realize.

Furthermore, I'm indebted to the following people for comments, suggestions, interviews, brainstorming, research, friendship, and other forms of assistance: Marilyn Bardsley, Stacy Beers, Lorelei Brodskey, Jamie DiPasquo, Dana DeVito, Donna Johnston, Marie Gallagher, Big Mike Krajsa, Jackie Lageman, Barbara Martineau, Isadore Mihalakis, Ruth Osborne, Detective Rich Peffall, Detective Mike Santarelli, Dean Schaffer, Tiffany Souders, Al Sproule, Karen T. Taylor, John Timpane, Vicky Vavladellis, and Pelli Wheaton.

Introduction

"Wherever he steps, whatever he touches, whatever he leaves, even uncon-
sciously, will serve as silent witness against him. Not only his fingerprints or
his footprints, but his hair, the fibers from his clothing, the glass he breaks, the
tool mark he leaves, the paint he scratches, the blood or semen he deposits or
collects. All of these and more bear mute witness against him. This is evidence
that does not forget. . . . Only human failure to find it, study and understand it,
can diminish its value."

—Dr. Paul L. Kirk, *Crime Investigation*

Time is of the essence in criminal investigations, and those cases
that fail to generate substantial leads or solid evidence within the first
two days acquire a swiftly decreasing likelihood of getting solved. As
time passes, they grow cold. Coldness generally reminds us of death,
but in the forensic arena a cold case is not a dead case. That's because
such cases can still be heated up, and typically that heat comes from
the passion of an investigator, a victim, or a victim's relative or friend
who will not give up. Interest preserves memory.

In 1960, just over 9,000 homicides were recorded in the U.S.

After that, the murder rate steadily rose, with the greatest increase occurring during the 1980s. In 1985, the Department of Justice recorded 18,980 homicides. Serial killings also increased during this decade, and by 1993 the homicide count stood at 24,530. Even worse, the percentage of murders that were random in nature increased. In 1992, murders by strangers rose to 53 percent of recorded homicides, and it was much harder in such cases to assess motives and develop leads.

Thus, many major cities became overwhelmed with unsolved rapes and murders, and their investigative resources were taxed to the limit. When cases did not get solved quickly, they necessarily decreased in priority as new ones occurred, with better potential for investigation. By 1995, there were an unprecedented number of unsolved crimes on the books. The clearance rate had dropped from 91 percent in 1965 to 65 percent in 1992.

Yet by the mid-1990s, murder rates nationwide had declined. In 2003, most of the country's large cities logged their lowest murder rates since the late 1960s. This trend freed homicide detectives to open the files of historical cases for which they once had limited time and resources. With more time on their hands and with dramatic new developments in forensic science and technology, the solution to some of those cases looked more promising. A new breed of detective was acknowledged who relied as much on science as gumshoe, and cold case squads found success because of men and women with the peculiar tenacity to keep hope alive and foresee the day when the "unsolvable" case would be satisfactorily resolved.

In the past decade, the cold case units around the country have cleared hundreds of backlogged cases, putting behind bars killers and rapists who believed they'd escaped detection. Crimes up to several decades old—even half a century—have been addressed, using science to both exonerate innocent individuals and convict those who deserve it.

In solving cold cases, human beings are the key—people who care enough to go over and above what the job calls for, who are innovative, experienced, and resilient. They don't seek recognition or rewards. They want justice for the victim.

Relying on both new technology and old-fashioned police work, their methods present a study in perseverance. A&E's TV series *Cold Case Files*® is a visual textbook for how these specialized detectives work. The series examines how evidence, witnesses, critical logic, and teamwork pave the road that leads detectives to their killer.

Cold Case Files has broken new ground in the forensic detection documentary genre. Law enforcement agencies around the country have hailed the show and regularly use episodes as models for investigative technique in training seminars. They learn how tried and tested methods work on older cases, as well as what can happen when someone engages in innovative thinking, such as in the following case from one of the earliest episodes.

On a Navajo reservation in Leupp, Arizona, in 1969, Surette Clark, age four, disappeared. Years later the police in Phoenix were alerted to the possibility that Wayne Roberts had beaten the child to death, but the place where they believed Surette had been buried was now a parking lot. Detective Edward Reynolds knew that there were aerial maps of the area from different dates, so he searched for one from 1969 and found it. With the map, he located the trailer park where Wayne Roberts had lived and examined it for soil irregularities. One area looked like a grave. With support from medical records of injuries to the child, along with witnesses who had seen Roberts beat her, he was able to get Roberts extradited from Canada to stand trial. A jury convicted him of second-degree murder.

While the typical avenues of forensic science can solve cold cases, sometimes it requires a bit of ingenuity. In this case, Reynolds could not easily dig up a parking lot, bring in dogs, or use chemical detectors to find the child's body. By thinking outside the box, he came up with something unique that worked. Not only that, by going through the steps he took in that episode, he provided an inspiring role model for detectives everywhere who might see how well it worked.

But the show is not just about detectives. Sometimes a cold case is kept alive by family members or friends of a victim, or by victims themselves. Each time an episode offers a case that was finally resolved by the persistence of a caring person, others are inspired to keep up their own efforts. Hopefully this book, which offers both cases from the show as well as from my own research, will continue that tradition. Ordinary people often feel powerless until they see someone else like them stand up and fight for justice.

In 1983, eighteen-year-old Laura Newman was raped in her home by an intruder. The negative effects on her life were far-reaching. She feared getting close to people, which kept her from getting married or having children. Even her relationships with her family suffered. She said that her mother doubted her and other family members refused to discuss it. She felt that the experience was an emotional life sentence.

The police did little to solve the crime. They believed that Laura had been molested by an acquaintance. Yet she knew the truth: She had been forcefully raped by a stranger who had entered her home. She did not know that the case had been shelved. Time passed and she heard nothing from investigators.

Nineteen years later, in 2002, she read in the newspaper that over four thousand rape kits were sitting on shelves gathering dust. She realized that hers was one of them. She also learned that the police department was starting a cold case unit, so Laura called and got Detective Bernie Holdhouse, the lead investigator for the Baltimore Sex Crimes Unit. He and his partner agreed to look into her case.

They discovered that the rape kit was missing from Evidence Control, but they did have fingerprints collected at the time and they entered these into the state's fingerprint database. In less than an hour, they had a match. Within three days, they tracked the suspect down and confronted him. He admitted to the rape and was sentenced to fifteen years.

Laura then formed the Laura Newman Foundation to urge other rape victims to come forward on old cases to get them solved. Her dogged persistence convinced the detectives they had a real case and they went to work with the evidence at hand. Often, to close older cases, it just takes investigators with a new attitude and a different approach.

Gregg McCrary, a former member of the FBI's Behavioral Analysis Unit, assists with a weeklong cold case seminar held every year at the Henry C. Lee Institute in Connecticut. Before case presentations begin, he and other professionals teach those who attend how to organize a team for unsolved historical crimes and develop a viable plan for investigation.

"You prioritize by solvability factors," McCrary says, "such as having a suspect or available witnesses, or a relationship that was intact at the time that has since broken up. In some cases, new technologies can move a case up the solvability scale. Or you may try something that wasn't utilized in the original investigation, such as profiling or linkage analysis."

Top priority cases have well-developed suspects and evidence that has been preserved and on which a new technology can be used, such as biological evidence that can be tested with new techniques, or fingerprints that can be entered into databases that now have more prints than they had before. Cases with many unknowns or which may have high expenses with little payoff are relegated to the lowest priority.

Cold case squads or units often have access to outside resources in the FBI's National Center for the Analysis of Violent Crime, the U.S. Marshals Service, military investigative services, organized groups of retired personnel, and crime investigation volunteer groups that offer unique services. Cold case personnel can also benefit from the numerous seminars around the country that feature new techniques in criminalistics, medical investigation, crime reconstruction, and forensic science.

Cold case detectives are most interested in witnesses who were previously uncooperative or unknown. Some may have once felt intimidated by threats that are no longer in place, or may have left relationships and now feel bitter toward the person they once protected. They may have overheard a killer boast about his crime when his own inhibitions relaxed, or they may have heard something new since the last time they were questioned.

The arrest of a suspect renders a case *closed*, according to the

Bulletin for the Bureau of Justice Assistance, regardless of whether that person is brought to trial or convicted. It can also be administratively closed if the only viable suspect has died or is behind bars for life for other crimes. A case is considered *solved* when justice has clearly been done.

While solving cold cases reduces the case backlog, it can also have the effect of inspiring interest in other cold cases. Or it might get a killer or rapist off the streets who would otherwise commit another crime. Most of all, it can bring closure and a sense of justice to a family who has been waiting for it for a long time. They gain a renewed faith in investigators. As famed criminalist Henry Lee has said, "We have to learn the universal language: love and care."

The science of cold cases involves more than just the latest technologies available for solving older unsolved cases. It's also about historic incidents and inventions that have helped to develop specific aspects of a relevant discipline like ballistics or toxicology, or have gained ground in court for an increasingly more intelligent and just approach to crime investigation. Mistakes have been made along the way, but the general impetus of forensic science has been to improve crime scene processing, criminal investigation, and courtroom testimony.

Many of the cases I will highlight in this book are taken from the *Cold Case Files* archives, but some I discovered when they were mentioned by a police officer or jumped out from my research and seemed to nicely illustrate an investigative technique or scientific method. At other times I thought the scientific information would profit from a narrative gleaned from the history of forensic science, such as one that brought attention to the use of fingerprints or advanced the detection of poisons in the human body. Just as *Cold Case Files* uses a compelling context to present how a case was resolved, I follow that tradition with narratives that either support the procedure from a case featured on the show or bring out additional aspects that the show was unable to cover.

If you're fascinated by the forensic field, this book will provide in-depth information on the science and many of the cases it's helped to solve. If you're a fan of the show, each turn of the page will enhance your appreciation of the episodes you've seen. And if you're a reader who's less familiar with the subject, at the very least you'll come to admire the science and the people who continue to solve cold case files.

ONE

Death Investigation

1

On July 4, 1992, in Baraboo, Wisconsin, Chris Steiner, fourteen, disappeared from his home. He was not the type to run away, and what happened to him was told in an episode of *Cold Case Files* called "The Tortured Truth." Indications that he had been kidnapped included a shoe impression outside his bedroom window and muddy tracks inside. Five days after he disappeared, his body was found caught on a tree along a bank of the Wisconsin River. An autopsy was performed and the cause of death was attributed to drowning, but the manner of his death—accident or otherwise—remained undetermined.

One aspect of death investigation involves evaluating the cause, mechanism, and manner of death. A cause of death is whatever made death occur, such as strangulation, and the mechanism is what happens physiologically—e.g., oxygen deprivation. The manner of death, according to the NASH classification, places it on one of four categories: Natural, Accident, Suicide, or Homicide. If it cannot be classified, such as was the case with Chris Steiner, then its manner is considered undetermined. It is estimated that some 15–20 percent of deaths around the country occur in a manner that is undetermined.

With no clear leads or ideas about what had happened, the Steiner case went cold. No one in his family knew how Chris could have drowned, but since it was not clearly a murder, the police did not look for a perpetrator.

A year passed and another boy, Thad Phillips, was taken from his bed in the same town while he slept. But he survived to tell the story. He woke up to find himself a captive to an older teenager who called himself Joe. To Thad's astonishment, Joe grabbed and twisted one of his ankles until it broke. Though in agony, Thad still tried to escape, but Joe caught him, brought him back, and then broke his other ankle in the same manner as the first. He seemed satisfied that this would now keep his captive in place.

While it may appear that Joe was merely being practical by disabling his prisoner, he actually proved to have a sick obsession. He admitted to Thad that he liked to hear bones break. But he also liked to attend to them, and he wrapped Thad's injuries in socks and braces. Thad remained in Joe's bedroom for two days, but despite his physical distress he awaited an opportunity to make a second escape attempt. Finally it arrived. He managed to get to a phone and call the police, who surmised from earlier incidents that his captor was a seventeen-year-old named Joe Clark.

After the police rescued Thad, he told them that Joe had admitted to killing Chris Steiner. This came as a surprise, since the pathologist who had examined Steiner at the time had found no sign of an injury. Nevertheless, the case had been mysterious and the body had been bloated from being in the water; the pathologist could have overlooked something. Then investigators learned that no X-rays had been taken.

There was only one way to discover whether Chris Steiner had been subjected to the same bizarre treatment that Thad had endured, and thus to link the two crimes to a single perpetrator: They had to exhume Chris Steiner's remains. In other words, they had to reopen his grave, remove the casket in which he lay, open it up, and remove the body for a closer examination.

Once this was done, the forensic pathologist went over the small body once again, and this time, armed with more information, he identified four separate breaks in Chris Steiner's legs. It was apparent that had the boy been thrown into the water in this condition, he could not have used his legs to swim and could easily have drowned—as he actually did.

That discovery gave detectives probable cause to search Joe Clark's bedroom, where they found a notebook with three lists, all written in his handwriting, that included the names of eighteen local boys. Their headings were "Get to now," "Can wait," and "Leg thing."

Clark claimed to be innocent in Steiner's murder. His mother backed him up with an alibi. She said that if he had left home on the night Steiner was abducted, she would have known, because he'd have passed through her bedroom. However, it was shown that she was a heavy sleeper and that he'd managed to slip by her before. Thus, Joe Clark had no alibi. A jury found him guilty of Chris Steiner's murder, and this case was finally closed with a conviction.

Death investigation can take place above or below the ground. As such, it calls on a diverse range of scientific specialties, and the coordination of these approaches is most focused in the field known as taphonomy.

2

The science of forensic taphonomy is the discovery, recovery, and analysis of human remains in a context that has legal ramifications. The term *taphonomy* derives from the Greek words for burial, *taphos,* and laws, *nomos.* This discipline deals with the complex factors involved in the history after death of physical remains and the ways in which death-related processes have affected them. A corpse undergoes a series of changes, which influence how professionals may estimate time of death, the individual's identification, and the cause and manner of that person's death. These changes also affect the types of other creatures that are attracted to it, how the environment may impact it, and what alterations may occur under and around it, thus making the corpse the center of a micro-environment.

Different climates will affect decomposition rates, with cool temperatures having a greater preservative effect and thus a longer period for decomposing. Signs of early-stage decomposition are bloating, skin slippage, and bacterial discoloration under the skin. The corpse will discharge a foul odor, which grows worse. Eventually the expanding gasses inside burst through, the eyes and tongue bulge out, and the internal organs and fat begin to liquefy. Flies will lay eggs that will hatch into maggots, which feast on the tissues. As tissues are consumed, the remains become increasingly more skeletal and the head or limbs may become disarticulated.

Some researchers in taphonomy use the knowledge they collect to study ancient environments and some to understand human behavior in older civilizations. In other words, the study of human remains includes knowledge of the person's life history, sociocultural context, and any environmental variables related to the remains. To get a useful taphonomic reading requires the team effort of professionals from different disciplines, including biology, entomology, anthropology, and pathology, as well as botany and geology. It may even involve climatology—an analysis of the weather patterns, or an archaeological examination of soil layers in a grave.

In Britain in 1962, three-year-old Stephen Jennings vanished from home. There was a history of abuse to the boy, but the police could find nothing to implicate his father. They could not even find a body until 1988, when bones protruded from the ground near the boy's former home. A team of archaeologists, who could study soil disturbances to establish a time frame for burial, carefully excavated the grave, which indicated that the dead child had been placed under stones. Over the years, a wall of stones had fallen on top of his grave, adding another layer. A pathologist and

odontologist (dental specialist) determined that the remains were those of a boy about three to four years old, and damage to his bones coincided perfectly with medical records for Stephen Jennings. He appeared to have been punched or kicked to death during a bout of prolonged violence that had broken eight ribs. His father was arrested and convicted of the murder.

Taphonomy is primarily concerned with the death event, the soft tissue modification through decomposition, the subsequent bone exposure to external agents, and the event of discovery and collection. At that point, if there's been an injury to the bone, for example, it's crucial for the death investigator to decide whether it occurred prior to death (antemortem), during the immediate stage prior to death (perimortem), or after death (postmortem). That involves knowing the processes to which the bone was exposed, such as animal activity or weathering, and what specific types of damage look like in the bones of a living person versus the bones after death. The former generally contain moisture, the latter generally appear more brittle. In "The Tortured Truth," for example, the taphonomic investigation would involve knowledge about bodies in water, types of injuries that can occur, decomposition rates, marine life that may feed on flesh, and other factors specific to the area and to a drowning. In the case of the abused boy in Britain, anthropologists would need to know how to distinguish postmortem damage from soil and falling rocks from actual abuse to the boy while he was still alive.

The deceased will contribute his or her own individual features to all taphonomic calculation, e.g., height, weight, type of clothing worn (or not), the presence of illness, the use of drugs, ethnicity, and the physical properties of the individual's bones. The type of burial rituals adopted by the person's culture, such as embalming methods, burial procedures, and whether or not autopsies were permitted, can also influence the findings. Whether a body is found on the ground, submerged in water, buried under dirt or sand, locked in a trunk, dismembered, or exsanguinated (having lost blood) will result in diverse calculations. In one climate, a body can decompose to a skeleton in two weeks; in another it may take three years or longer—or be quite preserved for centuries. Death investigators concentrate on a multitude of factors to try to assess the time since death.

Even the clothing a corpse wears is studied. To understand what happens to clothing in soil, for example, a team of scientists buried different types of material in different types of soil. They recorded the rates of decay over a period of four years. Buried rayon and cotton were the quickest to disintegrate, with total deterioration within seventeen months. Silk and wool lasted longer, with destruction at thirty-five months. Leather and synthetic proved to be the most resistant. Wet soil broke cotton and rayon down faster than did dry clay or sand, yet that same moisture helped to preserve wool and silk. Warmer climates accelerated deterioration, especially above seventy degrees.

Death investigation can take many different forms:

- the search for a body when someone is missing and presumed dead

- the search for identity and clues about the manner of death when a body is found

- an autopsy to determine cause and manner of death

- the identification and analysis of skeletal remains

- an exhumation to find something that was missed the first time around, such as in the situation with Chris Steiner when no one caught the broken bones in his legs

The search for a body can be quite complicated. Anthropologist Doug Owsley is shown in his biography, *No Bone Unturned* by Jeff

Benedict, searching for four missing members of David Koresh's Branch Davidian compound after it went up in flames in 1993. A garbage-strewn landscape nearby had confused the cadaver dogs, so he pushed a long, thin rod around in the dirt until he found loose soil that told him it had recently been disturbed. Sure enough, the four bodies had been piled, one on top of another, in this makeshift grave shaft.

Quite often, such searches involve dogs trained in the detection of decomposition odors, but sometimes an investigation requires more sophisticated means, as depicted in the *Cold Case Files* episode "Portrait of a Killer." When photographer Michelle Wallace, twenty-five, turned up missing from Gunnison, Colorado, in 1974, the police suspected a drifter named Roy Melanson. It turned out that he had Michelle's camera, yet he insisted that she had been a casual acquaintance and had given it to him. Eventually some hikers found a clump of brown hair and a piece of human scalp, but a thorough investigation of the area turned up nothing more. The case went cold.

Eighteen years later, in 1992, a team of investigators known as NecroSearch went to Colorado to begin one last search for Michelle's body. Incorporated in 1991, NecroSearch International is a volunteer organization of victim advocates comprised of biologists, geologists, chemists, meteorologists, geophysicists, plant ecologists, anthropologists, and other specialists who use the most advanced technology to help solve unsolvable crimes and to find bodies in unusual places. They often work separately but in tandem to use different branches of science to look for the same thing—the time it takes a plant found on a murder victim to wilt, for example, compared to the developmental stages of insects on that body. Referred to as the "Pig People" because they use swine carcasses to demonstrate the effects of decay during burial in various circumstances, the NecroSearch team has been able to find both bodies and evidence that had once seemed hopelessly lost.

In the case of Michelle Wallace, twenty NecroSearch members mapped out a grid in the remote area where the hair had been found so they could cover it in a uniform manner. They aligned themselves roughly an arm's length apart, walking through the terrain and using their professional eye to look for anything out of place or indicative of human activity. If they could not find something in this manner, they would bring in the high-powered electronic equipment they had as well. But this time, they were lucky.

At one point when geologist Cecilia Travis stepped away for a break, she glanced down a hill and spotted what appeared to be a large, white mushroom. Then something near it glinted in the sun, and Travis knew they had a discovery: Michelle had had a gold molar. Travis went to investigate and the "mushroom" turned out to be a skull. Nearby, more bones were carefully excavated from the ground.

After eighteen years, investigators had enough evidence to try Roy Melanson, the original suspect, for the murder of Michelle Wallace. Found on the camera in his possession were pictures of hers that she had not developed. Melanson was found guilty and sentenced to a life term in prison. Michelle's father, who had lost his wife to suicide after Michelle had disappeared, could now lay his daughter to rest.

3

A body itself is a death scene. Sometimes it's also a crime scene.

The first known application of medical expertise to determine the cause and manner of death was in 44 B.C., when Roman physician Antistius announced which of the twenty-three stab wounds inflicted on Julius Caesar had actually killed him. He declared this to the governing body, and in *Corpse*, Jessica Snyder Sachs points out that this is the origin of the word *forensic*—"before the forum."

A death can often be analyzed by clues at the scene where the body is found, and the type of specialist utilized will depend on the condition of the remains: either a corpse in some stage of decomposition or a set of bones. We'll look at the corpse here and the science of bones in the following chapter.

When a corpse is discovered, a coroner or medical examiner is called to the scene (depending on the jurisdiction). A coroner will generally bring the body to a forensic pathologist for an autopsy, unless a doctor can be found to acknowledge that the individual was ill and the death was from natural causes not dangerous to the community. A medical examiner, who generally has more medical training than a coroner, may make a cursory examination at the death scene.

The next step is to identify the deceased. Sometimes a piece of ID is on the body (in a wallet or purse), but sometimes the body itself serves as the means for identification. Generally the teeth, which tend to last much longer on a body than soft tissue, offer a means for identification through the records a dentist may have from X-rays and previous dental work. If no records are available, sometimes a scar, distinctive mole, or tattoo can assist. A forensic artist may also make a drawing or sculpture of the face to be photographed and publicized. At the very least, a DNA profile can be extracted from tissues via biological techniques in a lab.

Even while the process of identification is going on, the time of death must be established as soon as possible, because it can place victims with a suspect at a certain time, eliminate suspects via alibis, or break alibis altogether. Such an investigation might arrive at a postmortem interval (PMI) with the line of reasoning used in the *Cold Case Files* episode "The Unluckiest Man."

Following four fires that had been associated with John Veysey during the 1990s and for which he had been paid off heavily in insurance money, the Bureau of Alcohol, Tobacco and Firearms investigators determined that the latest one in 1997 in Illinois had definitely been arson. They then looked into the 1995 death of Veysey's first wife, Patricia, from a supposed heart attack. He'd collected nicely from that incident as well. A closer look at the autopsy report indicated that while Patricia had been discovered lying on her back, she'd had a nasty bruise, or contusion, on her head, above her eye. She could not have hit her head falling forward, as was erroneously surmised in the report, so it seemed likely that someone had hit her.

Prosecutors asked experts in pathology for a good fix on the time when Patricia Veysey had died. They went over the crime reports and learned that when the first responders arrived on the scene, Patricia had already shown signs of rigor mortis in her jaw and tongue, and at 4:08 P.M., she was cold. The pathologist had determined that she had been dead approximately two hours. That put her time of death at approximately 2:00 P.M., at least forty-five minutes before John Veysey was believed to have left the house that afternoon. He had no alibi and he clearly had a motive. John Veysey was not tried specifically for the murder of his wife. However, a jury implicitly found that he had caused his wife's death: He was convicted of committing mail and wire fraud against his insurance company, based on the fact that he had "caused the death of Patricia Veysey and then filed a fraudulent insurance claim, concealing his role in her death." For his conviction on this charge and related arson charges, a court sentenced him to 110 years in federal prison.

While time-since-death estimates can be difficult to determine, and while experienced medical examiners can totally disagree, it's generally the case that the sooner after death the time frame is established, the more accurate it is. A leading researcher, Claus Henssge, who had worked hard to establish a formula based on a wide variety of variables, concluded that only if a body is found within twenty-four to forty-eight hours after death can time-since-death estimates be reliable.

Historically, time-since-death postmortem interval (PMI) estimations have been based on a variety of changes following death, because these changes were observed to proceed in a predictable order. None are wholly reliable, since all are affected by diverse internal and external factors, but taken together, some pathologists believe they provide a reasonable estimate (though this has also been disputed).

The early anatomists who dissected corpses gained a bit of support when the Emperor Charles V decreed in the 1500s that medical expertise be relied upon in all trials involving suspected murder or abortion. They were the ones who noticed how things like rigor mortis (state of muscle rigidity) or algor mortis (the body's cooling temperature) worked, and to the list they also added the progression of coloration changes known as livor mortis, or lividity (blood settling in the body at the lowest point of gravity).

In the late 1700s, French physician Pierre Nysten recorded the changes in rigor mortis from flaccid to stiff to flaccid and provided "Nysten's law," to the effect that the process begins in the face and neck and moves downward through the body. Even decapitation, he discovered, did not seem to change this.

In England, Dr. John Davey used thermometers to measure the diminishing body temperature of corpses to add a scientific time clock to that indicator.

The stage of digestion of a meal also came to be considered a significant factor, as did the level of potassium in a cadaver's eye.

However, as more data became available, the experienced pathologists grew less confident of the formula, and their time-since-death parameters became more generous. By the 1990s, even the potassium level readings appeared to have an indirect and unpredictable relationship to the PMI. Nevertheless, death investigators keep searching for something that will remain accurate despite different conditions.

The concept of degree days, for example, involves measuring the climatic temperature along with the rate of decomposition over the course of a specific number of days, with the temperature's effects on decomposition being recorded at various points. Adding up the measurements over a specific period of time can make the analysis of decomposition in one area of the world comparable to another, whether it's Siberia, Knoxville, or Peru. Roughly put, ten days of ten degrees has a similar effect on a body as two days of fifty degrees. Through a chemical analysis of body fluids in the soil from beneath a decomposing corpse, for example, while taking into account the surrounding temperature and weather, scientists can estimate how many degree days the found body has accumulated in that spot. Thus, they can better determine time since death.

Pathologists in Scotland have tested microprobe electronic thermometers thrust into various organs and monitored via computers that compare the temperature readings with standard cooling curves produced in cadaver experiments. Japanese pathologists have looked into light-absorption meters that measure lividity, and scientists in many countries keep watch on changes in eye chemistry to see if some other reliable decomposition by-product might be found there. A few are experimenting with electrical conductivity through dead tissue at various stages, and some concentrate on the changing activity of identifiable microbes such as aerobic and anaerobic bacteria.

As various death investigators teamed up with entomologists, it became clear that time-of-death estimates could better be found via those things that the corpse attracted than from factors within the corpse itself. Forensic entomology became a formally recognized discipline in the U.S. during the 1980s, although insect analysis first came into a Western court case in 1850 in France. A mummified infant was discovered between the walls of a building undergoing renovation, pointing the finger of accusation at a young couple who resided there. Yet other couples had lived there before them, so Dr. Marcel Bergeret constructed a time line based on the insect activity evident in the body. He established via logic and a naturalist's study that the infant had been placed between the walls two years earlier—before the current couple had moved in.

This case inspired widespread interest among pathologists, notably Edmond Perrier Mégnin in France, who regularly visited morgues and cemeteries, and eventually recorded eight distinct stages of necrophilous insect infestation. He wrote a book on forensic entomology, published in 1894, which identified the insects that assisted in PMI estimates over the course of three years, should a corpse out in the open last that long: egg-laying blowflies, beetles, mites, moths, and flies that liked fermented protein. The progression was different for buried corpses, and Mégnin warned that the results might differ in other lands and climates. Much work still needed to be done.

"We do not estimate the postmortem interval using insects," says Dr. M. Lee Goff, chair of the forensic science department at Chaminade University in Honolulu. "What we estimate is the period of insect activity on the body." In other words, the insects may not get to it right away if it is carefully wrapped or boxed, or if weather conditions delay infestation. Once flies do lay their eggs, the biological clock begins. By looking at the most mature species present on the body when it is found, entomologists work backward to determine how long it took the flies, under those conditions, to get to that stage. That becomes the minimum time since death.

During the 1970s, a fortuitous incident occurred that brought forensic entomology together with forensic anthropology in a way that inspired an entirely unique development.

4

Dr. William Bass III, forensic anthropologist, is the founder of the Anthropology Research Facility at the University of Tennessee at Knoxville, also known as the Body Farm. Here, researchers lay out corpses to study in many different conditions, and much of their work has been devoted to refining the time lines for necrophilous insect activity. There is no other place like it in the world, so how did it come into existence?

Bass began his professional work for the Smithsonian Institution in Washington, D.C., cataloguing the bones of Native Americans. He also taught at the University of Kansas, and while there, a case was brought to his attention that planted the initial seeds for the idea of the Body Farm. Since he was a forensic consultant to the Kansas Bureau of Investigation, which looked into crimes involving livestock, he was asked about a cattle-rustling case. One agent wanted to know if Bass could tell from the skeletal remains of a cow just when it had died. Bass was stymied. He could find no information on the subject, so he suggested an experiment that involved killing a cow and studying it. No one took him up on that, but he realized that if professionals in this field were to learn about decomposition rates, they'd have to find a way to study them quite rigorously in various actual conditions, under scientific controls. The idea remained theoretical . . . for the moment.

Moving to Tennessee in 1971 to teach at the University of Tennessee at Knoxville and consult with that state's law enforcement agencies, Bass realized that the denser population in the area made it likely that bodies would be found fairly quickly—before they had skeletonized. Often, he was faced with consulting on corpses covered in maggots. Once again, however, he found mostly anecdotal literature.

Bass wanted to replace guesswork with science, but it wasn't until the late seventies that he set the wheels in motion for the Facility. One day, he was asked to estimate the age of a skeleton dug up on property that had belonged to the descendents of William Shy, who had been a colonel in the Confederate Army during the Civil War. Bass said that the remains were those of a white male between the ages of twenty-four and twenty-eight, and that the man had been dead about a year. Bass soon discovered from the age of the material in the clothing, and its fashion, that he was far afield on the time of death. The corpse turned out to be that of Shy himself, and he had been dead and buried since 1864—some 113 years.

Bass realized that someone had to start a serious study of this subject, so he asked the university to give him a small plot of land for the research and he acquired the unclaimed cadavers of several homeless men. They received numbers like WM 52 8/86 on orange tags to identify their cases. As they lay out, exposed to the elements, buried, or placed in water, they provided a plethora of information about what happens to decomposing bodies under different conditions. As the research progressed and the researchers expanded in number and specialization, the Body Farm became a center for training and consultation in difficult cases—including cold cases. *Cold Case Files* developed one of these, called "The Baiting Game."

On a fall afternoon in 1992, some hunters reported a furniture dumping that exuded a terrible odor. Henry County Detective Ronnie Minter located a couch, and beneath it he spotted a human head. The dead man was wrapped in a sheet and was badly decomposed. There was no identification, so the first layer of skin from John Doe's hand, the epidermal glove, was removed and sent to the latent print unit.

The print specialist slipped the epidermal glove onto his own hand in order to stabilize it and roll a print from the right thumb. The resulting print was entered into the Automated Fingerprint Identification System, which produced a hit: The deceased was thirty-five-year-old Jerry McLendon, a sailor from Virginia Beach, Virginia.

Now the investigators needed to link him with his killer.

During autopsy, the pathologist found evidence of death by asphyxiation, and the toxicology report indicated high levels of alprazolam, or Xanax, a tranquilizer. So he had apparently been drugged and then suffocated.

The detectives went to McLendon's apartment, 250 miles away from the body dump site, and found signs of a struggle in the bedroom. A pillowcase, the design of which matched the sheet wrapped around the victim, was stained with what appeared to be bodily fluids.

A check on McLendon's ATM account showed activity over the past three days, and photographs captured the images of a man identified as David Deshazo and his fiancée, Roxanna Latham, withdrawing money. Detectives also discovered that they had moved to Henry County, just two miles from where the body had been found.

The circumstances were incriminating, but while these two clearly had robbed the victim, nothing definitely tied them to the murder. With no other suspects, the investigation went cold.

Yet there was too much circumstantial evidence to just give up, so after a few years the investigators turned to Dr. Bass. He agreed to analyze the McLendon crime scene.

He began by studying photos of the body when found and assessing the body's rate of decay, given the conditions. Bass managed to narrowed McLendon's estimated time of death to no later than September 27, 1992, but that was not as precise as the investigators needed, since McLendon had disappeared nearly a week before that. So Bass looked more closely at what the bugs indicated.

As it decays, the corpse emits odorous chemicals such as cadaverine and putrescine, which flies can smell from several miles away. They can find a corpse within minutes of death to lay their eggs, making the corpse attractive to other species. As different chemicals emerge with the postmortem changes, other insects such as carrion beetles are attracted, along with predators and parasites of the flies and beetles. Ants will consume the fly eggs and beetles will eat the newly hatched maggots. Wasps may lay eggs among the maggots, or eat them. One type of blowfly can feed on either body tissue or maggots. Finally, spiders use the body as a habitat to prey on other insects, and moths may decimate any clothing left on the corpse. Maggots, if they survive the predators, consume the flesh for some two weeks or so before leaving it, and they will make trails as they do so.

Insects can also yield information about a number of other things, from whether the corpse has been moved to whether the person had taken drugs or been poisoned (entomotoxicology). The insects go through stages of development and yield clues through what they have ingested from the body, all of which can assist detectives in their analysis.

In McLendon's case, there had been a maggot infestation, and Bass knew from his research that flies were only active in temperatures over fifty-two degrees. From the autopsy photos, he measured the maggot size. Then he studied the climatology reports from the middle weeks of September 1992 for the area in which the victim had been found and used all these factors to pinpoint the time since death more precisely. He announced that the victim had likely died between September 21 and September 22. That was as close as he could get to establishing the PMI.

In the meantime, the detectives had worked on the suspect couple. All relationships go through phases and this one was in bad shape—something cold case detectives count on. It was time to try to turn one person against the other. If a clearer picture could be gained about the time when McLendon had been killed, it could be compared with the scientific analysis.

Roxanna told detectives that Deshazo had been jealous of McLendon. He had spoken of murder, and on September 22 she had found him holding a pillow over McLendon's face. Fearing for her own life, she reluctantly helped to loot McLendon's ATM and dump his body in Henry County.

Roxanna agreed to call her ex-fiancé in a phone sting, but he provided details that she had not offered, and detectives realized that she might be more culpable than she had admitted. Deshazo claimed he had watched Roxanna empty her prescription bottle of Xanax into simmering spaghetti sauce. She had then poured the poisoned sauce onto a plate of pasta and fed it to Jerry McLendon.

That was good enough to make two arrests, and armed with the information from Bass's analysis, David Deshazo was convicted of murder one, while Roxanna Latham was found guilty of murder in the second degree.

5

To solve some cold cases, people who were buried may have to be disinterred to be examined again. We saw this with Chris Steiner in the case that opened this chapter. Let's examine this procedure more closely in "Through the Eyes of a Child."

From prison, George Morgan began to research his family genealogy, and in the process he received the death certificate for his sister, Michelle Morgan. To his surprise, it was dated 1976, which he knew was a full fifteen years after she had actually died. He could not understand how such a mistake had been made, but then he saw that the certificate stated that she had died from pneumonia. That, too, was not true. He had seen her murdered, so he corresponded with Deputy Coroner Bob Shay, who decided to investigate the death— though it had occurred thirty-five years earlier.

George Morgan claimed that when he was eight years old, he had watched his father's new wife, Mary, drown, stomp, and beat his sister to death. That was quite a charge, and it meant that a murderer had gone free. In order to pursue the case, the authorities needed some proof.

The investigators went to the military base where Morgan's family had lived and searched for an autopsy record. Just as Morgan recalled, Michelle had been only four years old when she died, and according to the report, she had sustained massive trauma to the chest. Records showed that she had been to the hospital twenty times, once staying there for a month. Among her injuries before the age of four had been a broken nose, multiple injuries to her chest and back, burns on her skin, and a broken arm. The detectives tracked down the pathologist and he recalled the case. Apparently the local prosecutor had reviewed the matter but had not pursued it. The investigators were now at a dead end, so they decided to exhume Michelle's body to determine the cause and mechanism of her death. Once the coffin was opened, the condition of her remains, even this many years later, told a story of terrible and continuous abuse to the point of death.

This evidence substantiated what Morgan had claimed about his stepmother, Mary Morgan.

They tracked her down and found her in West Columbia, Texas. She refused to acknowledge what they were telling her, but when they left, she made preparations to flee. She was arrested and eventually pleaded guilty to involuntary manslaughter. What surprised the investigators was that four of Morgan's children stood by her, despite the fact that she had confessed and that, collectively, they had taken 150 trips to the hospital before the age of five.

Thanks to a reinvestigation that went all the way to a little girl's grave, this woman was sentenced to five years in prison.

Historic exhumations have been performed for a variety of reasons:

▪ Sometimes it's done to set history straight, such as when Professor James Starrs exhumed remains from the grave marked Jesse James to use mtDNA analysis to indicate that the infamous outlaw had indeed died when reported and been buried in that grave.

▪ An exhumation of seventeen German soldiers from a mass grave in southwest France in 2003 revealed a secret kept by a village for nearly sixty years. These men had been prisoners of war, executed in revenge for an atrocity committed by Germans routing out French Resistance fighters. They were finally removed from their ignoble grave and laid to rest in a military cemetery.

▪ Abraham Lincoln, whose remains had been moved seventeen times since his original burial and his coffin opened five times, was exhumed in 1901 to move him to a more permanent grave to prevent thieves from ever disturbing him.

▪ Recently, a team of scientists was formed to exhume some fifty members of the Medici family, who were powerful merchants in Italy during the Renaissance, to study the lifestyle of the rich and famous in that time and place.

An exhumation differs from an excavation in that exhumations involve disinterring known bodies from a specific grave, usually in a cemetery. Excavations involve carefully removing soil with tools such as trowels and brushes from a discovered grave in which the condition of the remains, and usually the identity of the person, are unknown and must be recorded. Exhumations focus on the remains in a coffin, while excavations may also encompass an area surrounding the grave, as well as focusing on possible trace evidence. Each stage is photographed and soil samples are collected for later screening and analysis.

Exhumations in regular cemeteries generally take place before the cemetery officially opens, to avoid interfering with business. A backhoe is used to remove the dirt, and if there is a cemetery vault or liner, it must be broken open to get to the casket. (Several decades ago, as it became clear that deteriorating caskets made graves sag, many cemeteries required the use of a sturdy vault surrounding the casket to prevent the earth from settling onto the bodies.) Straps lift the casket out and it is then removed to a place where it will be opened.

If an autopsy was done before burial, the body will be examined to compare it to that report, to check for what might have been overlooked—or possibly what might have been fabricated. Sometimes it's discovered that someone was placed into a grave meant for someone else. At any rate, the point of an exhumation in a cold case is to find information on or inside the body that can enlighten investigators about aspects of the crime that they cannot acquire in any other manner.

Dr. Michael Baden, former medical examiner for New York City for more than two decades, described in his book *Dead Reckoning* how an exhumation helped to solve a case three decades old. Civil rights leader Medgar Evers was shot and killed in 1963 in Jackson, Mississippi. Investigators recovered a rifle and traced it to Bryon De La Beckwith, but two trials had ended in indecision with hung juries. With no other suspects or leads, the case went cold.

During the early 1990s, the case was reopened, and while the rifle that had killed Evers was located, the bullet was not. Baden explained that a re-autopsy could trace the path of the bullet trajectory to establish cause of death. So the team exhumed Evers from a plot in Arlington National Cemetery and transported the remains to Albany, New York.

With an X-ray, Baden was able to locate bullet fragments where the bullet had struck a rib before exiting the body. He provided enough information from the autopsy as to cause and manner of death for investigators to extradite De La Beckwith for trial. The man had believed that he'd gotten away with a serious crime, but he was wrong. He was convicted of murder and given a life sentence.

It's not just victims who get exhumed. Thirty-seven years after the rape/murder of a young mother in El Cajon, California, DNA was extracted from the semen sample removed from her and stored. The key suspect at the time was a Catholic priest, but he had since died. Police had another suspect as well, whom they would have to track down, so they decided first to exhume the priest to get a DNA sample from his tissues. By this means, he was eliminated, which put investigators on the trail of the still-living suspect, who proved to be a match and who was convicted in 2003.

Ultimately, an exhumation can produce remains that will speak from the grave to solve cases and bring killers to justice.

Italian financier Roberto Calvi, sixty-two, was found hanging from Blackfriars Bridge in London in June 1982. There were bricks in his pockets, along with approximately $15,000 in cash. Just days before, the Vatican-based bank of which he had been president had collapsed under massive debt. Calvi was linked with both organized crime and the Vatican. He was also a member of an influential but unauthorized and illegal Masonic lodge, whose clandestine rules included death to betrayers by being weighed down with stones and drowned. One inquest concluded that he had committed suicide, but his family insisted he had been murdered. A second inquest left the question open.

An informant indicated that the Mafia had killed Calvi to silence him about their money laundering and to punish him for losing their money. They had staged it, he said, to implicate the Masonic group.

Calvi's remains were exhumed in 1998 for a renewed investigation, coordinated between England and Italy, with the intent of applying the most up-to-date methods of forensic science. The panel of forensic experts who examined him failed to find the injuries to Calvi's neck normally associated with death by hanging. Their conclusion was that Calvi had likely been strung up from underneath the bridge, which he could not do himself. Thus, he had been murdered. That finding has led the investigation in a completely new direction.

From bodies to bones, the forensic analysis of skeletal remains requires a different kind of scientific specialty.

TWO

Skulls and Bones

1

On December 8, 1999, in Chicago, Illinois, <u>Larry Vincent</u> started to dig in his yard to make a garden. He hit something that felt strange and soon pulled out a plastic bag. When he gave it a tentative nudge with his shovel, he was shocked to see a small skull roll out. He called the police, who realized that a child had been buried there. A home-made dress, sweater, and pajama top buried with the skeletal remains indicated that they were likely those of a girl. For an analysis, police turned to Dr. Clyde C. Snow, one of the leading minds in the field of forensic anthropology.

It was Snow who had suggested the use of a computer for mass disasters during the examination of the mangled and burned remains of 273 people from the 1979 crash of Flight 191 near Chicago. He told his ideas to a computer specialist, who developed a groundbreaking program. Having the necessary information organized and available on a fast-retrieval device eased enormously the process of identifying so many remains. Around the same time, Snow also assisted in identifying the twenty-nine victims of serial killer John Wayne Gacy that were buried beneath his house in Des Plaines, Illinois, and in the 1985 investigation of the remains identified as those of Nazi death angel Josef Mengele.

Working with discovered bones, as Snow did, usually involves a standard procedure:

The bones are brought to the lab in a box or body bag, along with soil samples from the grave, and the anthropologist X-rays them for readings on bone formation centers and for comparison against medical records, if located. Then he or she systematically lays them out in an order that approximates a human skeleton lying on its back. In the case of the girl in the garden, the skeleton was complete (not pulled apart by animals), so it was easier to work with. In disarticulated (unjoined) remains, anthropologists use allometry, or the ability to estimate height from long bones and their association with other body parts.

Starting with the skull (cranium, facial bones, and hyoid), the anthropologist lays it on an ostiometric board for measurement, followed by the cervical vertebrae, the vertebral column, the sternum, and the ribs on either side. He then places the shoulders and arms: the scapula, clavicles, humeri, and ulnae. Next come the carpals, metacarpals, and phalanges—wrist bones, hands, and fingers. Finally, he lays out the pelvis and lower extremities—the long bones (femur), kneecaps (patella), lower leg (tibia and fibula), feet (tarsals), and toes (metatarsals and phalanges). Keeping in mind that the loss of muscle will lengthen the body, due to the relaxation of parts that were tense or tight in life, he can now measure for height.

He sees what kind of odor the bones put out, whether there was much cartilage left, and whether there is any dampness or grease. Then he can move on to a more sophisticated analysis.

Developing a biological profile relies on statistical descriptions from different populations and assumes that most people will fit within those parameters. The preferred means for determining sex is an examination of the size of the pelvic bone (being wider in females), but in children, this is difficult, since the bones have not fully

matured. A smooth brow ridge and smaller bones in general also tend
to indicate a female.

The fracture lines between the plates of the skull indicate predictable stages of growth before uniting at maturity, and the stages of
tooth development are consistent with specific ages. All this helps
determine the age at which the person died.

Once the basics are done, the anthropologist can examine injuries
to the bone that are not the result of burial or corrosion. He or she
may have to go to the original burial site for a full analysis, as well as
look at photos and notes of the recovery if the anthropologist was not
physically a witness to it.

Stains on the bones from surrounding dirt and rotting plants can
indicate how long the remains have been in the ground. In the case in
"Little Girl Lost," Dr. Snow estimated that the child had been buried
for at least ten years, and possibly longer, and he determined that
while alive her life had been difficult. Among the injuries suffered
were several broken ribs and a fractured lower jaw. Since she could
not have chewed food with that injury, she had probably also experienced severe malnutrition, with the consequent deterioration of the
bones. Then the killer had apparently ended the child's life by squeez-
ing her very hard. Snow noted a series of scratch marks along the rib
bones themselves, which he believed had been left by the killer's fingernails—going right through the skin and leaving small cuts.

His report to the police would include a full set of measurements,
analysis of the X-rays, a biological profile, a note of individualizing
characteristics found in the bone, and the type of trauma he observed
(as well as whether it might have occurred before or after death). He
would also describe his reference population and his level of certainty
regarding his findings.

On December 9, Detectives Jellen and Baiocchi set out to identify
the child. They reexamined the sweater, dress, and pajamas. On the
pajama top, a run number identified where it had been made. They
sent it to the FBI and were put into contact with the manufacturer,
who told them that due to the design, they could tell that this pajama
top had been produced only during 1968. This helped the detectives

to narrow the child's time of death to the late sixties or early seventies—putting her in the ground for possibly thirty years.

They looked for neighbors from that period who might know something. After interviewing almost one hundred people, they found a woman, Vera Rodriguez, forty-four, who had lived next door to the home during that time. She recalled the constant sound of a little girl crying and remembered that the girl had two brothers. Their parents' names had been Tom and Joan.

The detectives went to the Chicago Board of Education's records vault and were confronted with an overwhelming task: They had to search through more than fifty thousand index cards, with no set order, that spanned a century of enrollment. It was Jellen who found the breakthrough card: It listed Scott Blake, whose father was Tom Blake and mother was Joan Miller.

Detective Jellen found Scott Blake, but he had no memory of a sister. He tried hard and eventually came up with a vague recollection of his parents arguing about someone named Holly. But he could not relate anything about her.

Now the detectives had a name, but they first had to confirm that the girl had even existed. They searched records and found a birth certificate for a Holly Lee Blake, born March 2, 1962, to Joan Miller and Tom Blake.

The next day Detective Jellen told Scott Blake that he had indeed had a sister, and Blake believed that because his mother had been cold and intense, cowing his father, she may have been the person who killed Holly. Blake provided an address.

By the time the detectives found Joan Miller, sixty-six, she was on her last legs. On March 18, 2000, they visited her in an ICU at a medical center. She admitted that she had killed Holly but did not say why, or offer reasons why her daughter suffered while her sons did not. Five days later, Joan Miller died, but the case had closed with an identity for the dead child and a proper burial.

2

Like many other forensic sciences, anthropology crossed into the legal arena in the nineteenth century, developing the field of criminal anthropology, or the proof of criminality via body measurements. In fact modern criminology stems from Italian psychiatrist Cesare Lombroso, who proposed that some types of people are closer to primitive ancestors than others. He utilized the work of anthropologist Pierre-Paul Broca to create this "new science," which relied on facial measurements and anomalies of the skull, face, and body to determine who was or was not a criminal type. He believed there was a "born criminal" who was irresistibly compelled toward a life of crime; that this criminal was an atavistic being—a throwback to earlier hedonistic races; and that certain physical traits signaled those who belonged to this distinct species. Others could become criminals through weak natures or "vicious training." The born criminal had peculiar sensory responses, a diminished sensibility to pain, no sense of right and wrong, and no remorse.

This theory remained a strong force in the field of criminology for many years, especially in the U.S. The idea that criminal genetic patterns are outwardly manifested influenced film, novels, and real-life investigations, giving rise to the idea that a "monstrous" criminal can easily be spotted, and probably influencing longer prison terms for those convicts who looked "dangerous."

Yet much as Lombroso hailed his ideas as "scientific," they were in fact racist and based in erroneous assumptions. During the twentieth century, anthropologists stopped relying on physical appearance to assess moral nature and leaned toward a study of the physical and cultural differences among races. The information they gained became useful in criminal investigations in quite a different manner.

In 1932, the FBI set up the first government crime lab in Washington, D.C., and about five years later the agents discovered that there were bone analysis experts nearby at the Smithsonian Institution. It was clear that they were qualified to consult on the skeletal remains of victims that might otherwise go unidentified, so over the years a team was formed. As the demands grew, and many states asked for assistance from university-affiliated anthropologists, these experts honed their methods for detecting past injuries, noting indicators of illness or occupation, and providing information about the PMI. In 1972, the Physical Anthropology Section of the American Academy of Forensic Sciences was established.

According to the American Board of Forensic Anthropology, "Forensic anthropology is the application of the science of physical anthropology to the legal process. The identification of skeletal, badly decomposed, or otherwise unidentified human remains is important for both legal and humanitarian reasons."

Forensic anthropologists work on bones the police bring to them, as well as go out into the field to examine skeletal remains lying in the open or to coordinate an archaeological dig. Careful excavation and accurate mapping of discovered or buried remains can assist in trace evidence collection. If flesh remains on the bones and there's no critical reason to retain it, the anthropologist may X-ray the remains and then boil off the flesh. They may help to interpret outdoor death scenes (taphonomy), provide an interpretation of bone damage, lead a team in the recovery of the remains, and assist in getting remains identified via a biological profile. They may also offer information about the postmortem interval and the death event. While they serve primarily as consultants, they could be needed to testify in court as experts. In any event, they work as part of a forensic team.

Cher Elder had been missing since March 31, 1993. A suspect was identified in Tom Luther, a man who was seen with her at a casino in Central City, Colorado, before she went missing, but no evidence linked him to foul play. A girlfriend reported that around the time of Cher's disappearance he'd had battered hands, but on its own that information meant nothing. Nevertheless, he was a convicted sex offender who had nearly killed a woman after a brutal rape, and he was a suspect in other homicides.

An informant told police that Cher had been killed and buried off Interstate 70, near a stone marker. Investigators pinpointed Luther's presence in the town of Empire, but that was as close as they could come in a canyon area comprised of fifteen miles of rough terrain. So they called in NecroSearch.

The team relied on probes to find loose soil, equipment that indicated magnetic disturbances in the ground, a low-flying radio-controlled plane to take photographs that might indicate the presence of a gravesite, and a cadaver dog. They even used Forward Looking Infrared (FLIR) cameras that detect via shades of gray the minute differences in temperatures among objects. The differences are projected onto a computer monitor, outlining objects according to temperature gradations.

Yet they had no success. Months passed with many man-hours invested, but they seemed no closer to their goal. The case grew colder.

In 1995, a tip narrowed the search to a rocky area, but snow hindered anyone from going out. Then another informant indicated an area that Luther had pointed out to him where he had buried a girl under some rocks. Using a hand auger, investigators drilled a hole into the ground, but the earth seemed undisturbed, so they left.

A month later, they returned and drilled deeper. Sniffing for decomposition odors, they believed they had something. They drilled deeper still and came upon adipocere, a soaplike substance made from body fat. The NecroSearch team set up a grid for excavation. After two days of painstaking archaeological work by an anthropologist, they located the skeletal remains of Cher Elder. A botanist helped determine the age of the grave from plant roots at the site, and bullet fragments were found in the skull that matched a gun once owned by Tom Luther.

A jury convicted him of second-degree murder.

Forensic anthropologists generally work with forensic pathologists, odontologists, and homicide investigators to point out evidence of foul play and assist with estimates of the time of death. Piecing the identity puzzle together can require the coordination of different disciplines, as happened in the following case.

In 1961 in Wales, cave explorers came across a set of skeletal remains at Caswell Bay. When laid out, the bones constituted a complete skeleton that had been sawn through in two places: the thighs and the upper arms and spine. The size of the pelvis indicated the skeleton of a female, and she had been about five foot four. Her teeth suggested an age over twenty, but skull bones indicated she had not yet reached thirty. Some jewelry had been found with the remains, along with a hair clip and a deteriorated sack in which the remains had been wrapped. A wedding ring was dated 1918. That gave detectives some leads for investigation.

Newspaper files revealed the disappearance of a chorus girl named Mamie Stuart in 1920. George Shotten, already married, had married her as well in 1918. When she disappeared, she was twenty-six, and had been the right height to be this victim. Shotten was suspected in her disappearance, but nothing could be proven except that he was a bigamist. When the victim's identity was finally determined by matching the anthropological characteristics, teeth, and personal items traced by detectives to the missing woman, it was discovered that her probable killer had died some three years earlier. But at least she had been identified and moved to a more appropriate grave.

Many of the determinations in forensic anthropology derive from the area of osteology, or the study of bones (although as we saw in the previous chapter, some forensic anthropologists may also specialize in entomology and its relationship to body decomposition). It's important to first distinguish between animal and human bones, when only fragments are found, because many of their characteristics can be similar. There are certain indicators that set them apart, as well as reference collections for comparisons in complex cases. (The skeletons of the decomposing research subjects at the Body Farm are preserved for one such collection.)

The fully mature adult human body has 206 bones. The skeleton weighs about twelve pounds for the average male and ten for females. Aside from sex, height, and age, anthropologists can identify such things from a set of skeletal remains as race, previous trauma, body type, and possible cause of death if it involved poison, knife wounds, blunt force, or bullet holes. The *Cold Case Files* episode called "The Mark of Cain" is a case in point.

In 1994, in Mims, Florida, Jim McCutcheon gave James Drysdale, a convicted murderer, a job. One day McCutcheon disappeared and Drysdale told others that he had been arrested on a U.S. Customs warrant. Detective Scott Armstrong found no such warrant or arrest on file, but he did learn that Drysdale had asked around for a notary to sign papers granting him power of attorney for McCutcheon's checking account. Then he learned that Drysdale had disappeared.

The case went cold until 1998, when Detective Gary Harrell learned that Drysdale had resurfaced and made a Social Security claim. The authorities found him in Tennessee and took him back to Florida. They learned that he'd become religious, so they used that to urge him to clear his conscience and confess to killing McCutcheon. He did so, telling them that he had shot the man in the head with a .22-caliber rifle and buried him in the orange groves.

The forensic team started to dig and unearthed a skull. Inside the eye socket they found a Scolaro buckle, a device implanted during a type of eye surgery that McCutcheon had undergone. Detectives knew he had a tooth missing from near the front of the top plate of his dentures, and that plate was recovered. Yet the skull showed no evidence of a bullet hole.

Anthropology provided the answer. A greenish stain was noted on the back of the skull, which indicated contamination by a foreign object. Radiography revealed radio-opaque material in the skull, which turned out to be copper from a bullet. That helped investigators to determine that McCutcheon had been shot in the neck, not in the head.

On September 15, 1998, James Drysdale was sentenced to life.

As a staff member of the Body Farm team, Dr. Richard Jantz has developed ForDisc (forensic discrimination software), based on measurements and information from a vast collection of human skeletons. Using this continually updated database, ForDisc can estimate from a skeleton of unknown identity the gender, race, and stature of the person. This software can also be utilized by international tribunals for war crime and human rights investigations, such as the one into which forensic anthropologist Douglas Owsley was invited.

As documented in *No Bone Unturned*, in 1985, two American citizens, a writer and a freelance journalist, disappeared in war-torn Guatemala. Nicholas Blake and Griffith Davis had not been heard from in over two weeks, and it was feared that they had ventured into an area so perilous that the American Embassy would not send staff to search for them.

The families of the missing men searched for information for seven years, until they learned about the charred remains of two men who had spent the night in a small Guatemalan village and were shot by the local civil patrol. When their remains, dumped outside the village, had turned to bone, villagers were ordered to crush and burn them. But there were still fragments. The families paid a ransom to have the remains returned. Once they were back on U.S. soil, they had to be analyzed to affirm their identity.

Owsley received them at the Smithsonian in two crates, mixed with clay and soil, and went to work. Most of what he found was gray ash, but as he screened the dirt he picked out some tiny charred bone fragments and teeth. He asked for the missing men's medical records, including X-rays, and picked out those fragments that might make an identification possible. He needed a piece that was particular to an individual, and he located two bones that went together to form a partial right frontal sinus with an irregular line running through it.

Blake had X-rays from an earlier accident, but his head X-ray did not bear the telltale individualizing groove in the sinus bone. Then Owsley received records for Davis, and there on his head X-ray was a match to the bone fragments. But Owsley needed more. From the different bone colorations and from duplication of some bones, he felt certain the remains were of two people, and he knew they were both males, but he hoped for a more complete unit of bone, such as another piece of the skull for which he already had two bones. He was certain if they found the original cremation site, they would acquire more fragments.

That meant a trip to Guatemala, where he found teeth, glasses, a jawbone fragment, and the third bone he needed from the Davis sinus cavity. He was able to say with reasonable certainty that they now had the remains of the two missing Americans. The families at last had closure.

Owsley also had another cold case that involved burning, but in this incident, the bodies of the victims were intact. Burned remains are a subspecialty in forensic anthropology, because such experts are called on by insurance companies or other investigators to determine if the body of a well-insured person found in a burned car or house is indeed the victim named on the policy. Not only might they uncover insurance fraud, but possibly murder as well.

Dr. Bill Bass and his colleagues at the Body Farm have made painstaking efforts to learn what happens to flesh and bone during a fire. From their research building bonfires, they have documented how fire shrivels muscles as water evaporates, and how the stronger muscles bring fingers, arms, and legs into a flexed position—the "pugilistic posture" or boxer's stance. If that posture is not evident on a body at a fire scene, then suspicions are raised as to whether the person actually died in the fire.

Then there's an issue of the difference between what occurs in a normal house fire and one that is begun by accelerant-based arson. Typically, arson fires are more intense. Taking this into account, the researchers at the Body Farm burned body parts in hotter flames, and yet still found that the boxer's stance held true. In short, the changes a body undergoes in a fire will have characteristic patterns.

"Your arms and legs burn off first," Bass has explained. "Then the fluids inside the skull make the skull expand and disintegrate, and the last part to go is the pelvic area."

Burning bones can also bring out their distinct color, such that family members burned together in one place can be sorted into the right skeletal groups. And burned bones can still retain antemortem wounds.

A case that developed in Trumbull County, Ohio, in 1978, when a trailer went up in flames was depicted in the *Cold Case Files* episode "The Burning Secret." Donald Morris and sons Christopher and Eddie were trapped inside the trailer, while Judy Morris ran for help. A neighbor rescued Eddie, but the others died. Firefighters removed both bodies, which were badly charred. Fifteen feet north of the trailer lay a man's severed human ear, cut in the shape of a D. No one knew what to make of it, so it was thrown away.

When the deaths were declared accidental, no autopsy was performed. Yet the undertaker who prepared the bodies for burial mentioned to relatives that Donald Morris appeared to have cuts on his body.

The police investigated the trailer for signs of arson and found them. An arson squad confirmed that the fire had been started in three separate places and they came upon a book detailing occult rituals. In it was a ritual for cutting off an ear as an act of revenge. The surviving spouse, Judy Morris, had claimed to practice witchcraft. The investigators now wondered if those "accidental deaths" may have been murder.

Detectives petitioned for an exhumation to look for violence to the bodies but were denied, so they did no further investigation and the case went cold.

It was reopened fifteen years later, in 1993, when Detective Dan D'Anunzio remembered that Eddie, age nine at the time, had survived the fire and might offer some leads. No one had questioned him and his fear of his mother back then had kept him quiet. When D'Anunzio approached him fifteen years later, he related how he had seen his mother stab his father in the back, offering solid cause for an exhumation.

The remains were shipped to Dr. Douglas Owsley, who observed sharply defined cuts on the backside of Donald Morris's right ribs. The number ten right rib had been cut clean through in two separate places. He determined that these distinctive cuts could only have been made by the blade of a sharp knife. He also discovered seven additional cuts and ruled out the firemen's pike poles as the possible source. At trial, he demonstrated that these implements were too dull to have made the cuts he found on the bones.

In 1993, the jury found Judith Morris Delgross guilty on two counts of aggravated murder, and Donald Morris and his son are now a permanent part of the Smithsonian's teaching collection.

3

Identification of skeletal remains may be made with one or more techniques that rely on artistic facial approximation. One approach uses the skull itself, another relies on a cast of it, and yet another a digital image. In the first two, soft tissue is added as clay, based on a formula that anthropologists have devised for tissue density in different races, while in the third, the soft tissues are added digitally.

Using the skull or replica, small holes are made in it for thin wooden or vinyl pegs to be inserted to indicate skin depth. Then modeling clay fills in the muscles and features around the nose, mouth, cheeks, and eyes, and a thin layer of plastic or clay goes over the skull. Facial features are molded to capture the person's basic look, and a wig and artificial eyes are added, along with makeup.

Another technique is to set the skull on a turntable and use computer tomography. As the skull turns, information derived from it is scanned into a computer with a laser beam and mirrors, and assembled into a digital image of the skull based on input data from other faces with similar measurements and racial origins. Then, scans of digital images of tissue and skin are "wrapped" onto the skull image to form a face and warped to match the skull's topography. Then eyes, facial coloring, and hairstyles are added, based on estimations that consider such things as the subject's clothing, facial dimensions, and the time frame in which he or she was alive. The image is three-dimensional and can be rotated for a sideways angle.

Usually a photograph or drawing is produced from the approximation, so it can be published on a poster or in the newspaper. The accuracy of these sculptures depends on how closely the features of the person resembled features commonly associated with his or her identified ancestry, and whether or not he or she may have been overweight, worn glasses, had facial hair, or had a hairstyle quite different from the typical style at the estimated time of death.

The dismembered and beheaded remains of a woman were found in Bara-boo, Wisconsin, in 1999, but her face had been stripped of skin, so it was difficult to identify her by the typical means. There were also no matches with missing persons reports. When the police faced the need to deflesh the woman's skull for an anthropologist to make a clay model, they real-ized that this procedure could destroy valuable evidence, so they decided against it and the case came to a halt.

In 2000, police consulted with experts at the Milwaukee School of Engineering's Rapid Protoyping Center to try a new technique that prom-ised to develop a three-dimensional model of the skull without damaging the original. In about thirty hours of processing, these technicians did CT scans of the head, using thousands of thin layers of paper to assist a forensic artist in making a three-dimensional clay sculpture without removing the remaining soft tissue.

They showed the replica to Dr. Emily Craig, an expert in clay recon-struction. To her, it looked like a topographical map of the skull. She glued erasers onto the prototype at strategic points and connected them with clay to build up the face. Then she added eyes and a hairstyle. From this technicians took four photographs with slightly different looks (with glasses, a turban, long hair and short) and then created posters and dis-tributed them around the country. Within two months, the former sister-in-law of the victim identified her as Mwevano Kupaza and implicated Peter Kupaza, who was subsequently convicted of the crime.

It's controversial as to who actually made the first successful facial reconstruction, but it's often credited to the German anatomist W. His, who published the results of his studies in 1895. He had acquired a skull reputed to be that of the late composer Johann Sebastian Bach, and from it, he sculpted what turned out to be a good likeness.

To find out the general depth of the skin and muscles over the skull, His had plunged oiled needles into the faces of corpses and then attached a cork to each of the needles so that once the needle hit bone, the cork rested at the skin's surface. He then pulled the needles out, measured them, and made drawings based on the measurements. That way he managed to compose a depth map, which would later aid generations of anthropologists in making portraits from skulls.

In 1916, for forensic purposes, a sculpture was made by a police anatomist from a skeleton recovered in Brooklyn. He placed the skull on some rolled newspaper, put some fake eyes into the sockets, and covered the bones with plastic. A sculptor added sufficient details and this resulted in the identification of a missing woman.

It was in Russia, however, where the technique of forensic sculpture was more fully developed. Mikhail Gerasimov, a museum archaeologist, experimented with the skulls in his care. By 1935, he was adept at forming a skull into a face, and four years later, he helped to solve a murder.

Perhaps the most famous facial sculpture was the one that artist Frank Bender made of the missing John List. In 1971 in New Jersey, List had murdered his wife, three children, and aged mother, and then fled the state. Detectives failed again and again to find productive leads and the case went cold. On occasion, the FBI would revive it with age-progressed photographs published in nationwide tabloids, but it was the sculpture that Bender did that finally made someone sit up and take notice. For a television show that catches fugitives, he created a three-dimensional face based on a number of factors that helped him to imagine List's likely appearance in 1989—almost two decades after the murders. When this program aired, a former neighbor of "Bob Clark" in Colorado called. She sent detectives to List's new address, and through fingerprints, Clark was identified as List. Despite his initial protests, he was charged with the five cold-blooded murders, tried, and convicted.

4

Teeth last longer than bones, generally speaking. They can even endure the heat of a fire, and provide perhaps the fastest means for identifying a John or Jane Doe, as long as there are records available against which to compare them. From teeth, an odontologist or anthropologist can approximate age range, especially in young people, due to distinct developmental stages. (Permanent front teeth come in during the fifth or sixth year, while the last teeth to emerge are the third molars, generally coming in during late adolescence.) After that, the way the teeth have worn and other indicators assist in age determination, although the range of estimation increases.

Dental work, chips, missing teeth, teeth that grow in crooked, and gaps between teeth make an individual's teeth unique. As dentists take X-rays and keep notes on a patient's problems and on their own work, it becomes fairly easy to use teeth comparisons as a guide to the identity of an unknown deceased. When Lee Harvey Oswald, the assassin of President John F. Kennedy, was exhumed from his grave in 1981 to prove that he had in fact been killed and buried there, his teeth were compared to dental records from his stint in the military. Those who specialize in this procedure are known as odontologists.

Among the earliest cases where forensic odontology became an issue in the courtroom was the trial of John Webster in Boston in 1850 for the murder of George Parkman. In this case, both physicians and dentists were used as expert witnesses, and there were several unusual allowances, including three medical experts who testified on both sides.

Among Boston's wealthy Brahmins in 1849 was George Parkman, near sixty. On Friday, November 23, he went out to collect his rents and never returned. He was last seen around one-thirty that afternoon at Harvard Medical College, where he had gone to call on Professor John Webster, who had allegedly double-crossed him in a business deal. Parkman sought repayment on a loan, and Webster later claimed that he'd paid it and Parkman had left, but no one saw him exit the building. The place was searched, but nothing was found to incriminate Webster.

His uncharacteristic behavior during the subsequent week and his strange activity in the lab alerted the janitor, Ephraim Littlefield. He decided to drill through a wall into the pit for Webster's privy—the only place in the building that had not been searched. When he broke through, he saw human remains: a pelvis, a dismembered thigh, and the lower part of a leg.

In short order, Webster was arrested and the lab searched again. In a tea chest, they discovered a human torso, hollowed out to accommodate the other dismembered thigh. In the furnace lay charred bone fragments, including a jawbone with artificial teeth. A sink bore fresh nicks and there were acid stains on the floor.

It was still difficult to determine the identity of the victim, in part because Parkman had had no unique marks on his body aside from a great deal of hair—he was said to be a hirsute man. As well, the inquest jury pointed out that the two thighs found were different sizes, although the coroner explained that one had been exposed to fire and the other was waterlogged from the privy, so they could still be from the same person.

The inquest and grand juries both ruled that John Webster should be tried for the murder of George Parkman. Pliney Merrick, a former judge, and Edward Sohier defended Webster when the trial began on March 19, 1850, with Judge Lemuel Shaw presiding.

Attorney General John Clifford described how he believed Parkman had been killed, his skull fractured, and his various parts cut off and burned or dumped into a toilet. Dr. Jeffries Wyman, an anatomist, drew a life-size skeleton showing which parts of the body had been recovered and how they fit a frame the size of Parkman's. He said that in the furnace he had found bones from the head, neck, face, and feet, and he used actual bone fragments to demonstrate how they fit together.

Drs. Winslow Lewis and George Gay both helped to clarify the medical issues involved with the corpse, and how it differed from those used in dissection. Lewis, who was a former student of the defendant's, used Wyman's anatomy drawing to describe pieces of the body. He said that there was an opening in the thorax region that might be a stab wound, but on cross-examination he admitted that he could not be certain.

The defense attorneys tried to cast doubt on the idea that anyone could definitively identify these remains as those of George Parkman. They also sought to establish that the so-called "stab wound" was simply a cut that had been inflicted postmortem, during a routine dissection. They wondered, if this stabbing had killed a man, where was all the blood?

By the third day, it was clear that the prosecution was relying heavily on scientific medical testimony. First, Dr. Oliver Wendell Holmes, Dean of the Medical College, took the stand and said that someone with knowledge of human anatomy and dissection had done the dismembering. He also explained that a wound between the ribs would not necessarily produce a lot of blood, and that the remains were "not dissimilar" to Parkman's build—a careful sort of statement that would set a tradition followed even to the present day.

Then Dr. Nathan Keep, Parkman's dentist, discussed the fact that the jawbone found in the furnace, with the false teeth, was in fact that of George Parkman. He recognized his own handiwork from three years earlier, and while the gold fillings had melted, there were "peculiar angles and points" that he knew well. He had made a wax mold of the man's protruding jaw and filled it with plaster, and this he used to demonstrate how it matched the pieces of jawbone found in the furnace. Then he placed the loose teeth found in the furnace into his exhibit.

For the defense, Dr. Willard Morton, another dentist, said that nothing about the jawbone found in the furnace confirmed individual identification. George Parkman had a protruding jaw, yes, but many other people did, too. Morton produced a few false teeth of his own making, which fit nicely into Keep's mold.

In rebuttal, three more dentists testified that an artist knows his own work.

While this case marks a first for dental testimony, which presumably improved over the years, it's also notable for certain questionable procedures. Three of the doctors who had testified about medical facts for the prosecution also came in for the defense. Dr. Holmes talked about who the leading authorities were on quantity of blood in a human body (not himself) and said that there was no way to tell with certainty whether a human bone had been broken before being burned. The other two had little of substance to add.

It was assumed that since their expertise relied on objective knowledge and was therefore "neutral," it would not matter for which side they spoke. Whereas the esteemed presence of these men had given substance to the prosecution's side, they undermined that impression by seeming to appear on Webster's behalf.

Faced with the difficulty of having no body, the judge instructed the jury members that all they needed to make a judgment was a reasonable certainty. It was an interpretation that many thought swung the vote against John Webster.

On the same evening that they went to deliberate, the jury had a verdict: guilty. Webster was sentenced to be hanged. While he then admitted that he had murdered Parkman but had done so in self-defense, the sentence stood and he was hanged on August 30.

More recently, another case, featured on *Cold Case Files* in "One Night on the Bayou," identified the victim strictly from the jaw.

On September 1, 1994, in a bayou in New Orleans, Louisiana, alligators got into a tug-of-war over an old sail. The alligators ripped away at it, exposing a body, and they proceeded to gnaw at the limbs. What was left of the body floated to shore and was brought to the coroner's office in Orleans parish. It was clear that the male victim's hands had been tied behind his back and in hog-tie fashion to the ankles. The gators had ravaged the corpse from just under the chin all the way down to the left side of the chest, but the right side of the body was still intact, showing a stab wound. There was no identification on the body, but the gators had spared most of the victim's jaw. That made it possible for odontologists to chart the teeth and make a match to the dental records of fifty-eight-year-old Lester Hansen, a convicted child molester.

Thinking this murder might have been an act of revenge, detectives quickly focused on one parent, Rickey Alford, whose child was thought to have been a victim. Then Alford disappeared. A year later, he resurfaced and was convicted of another murder, which told New Orleans detectives that he was capable of killing.

Nevertheless, with no clear leads, the Lester Hansen case went cold.

Then when convicted thief Benjamin Scardino was caught trying to steal a bike, he offered information about the murder, implicating three men: his brother Raymond Scardino, his cousin Aristide Landry, and Rickey Alford. Cold case detective Dwight Deal went to the Massachusetts prison where Alford was being held and heard a different story. Alford admitted to being present during the incident but said that the other two had been an equal part of it. Together they beat Hansen, tied him up with his hands behind his back, and sat him in a chair for a mock interrogation about the alleged molestation of Alford's son. Raymond Scardino had Hansen by the hair and used a knife to cut his throat. Hansen fell onto the ground and, realizing the severity of his wound, allegedly decided to confess. Alford then rolled him onto his back, took the knife, and stuck it in him.

So Alford implicated Scardino and Landry as accomplices and they were indicted for murder, but then he offered a second confession that contradicted the first one. He took complete responsibility for the actual killing, saying he did it in a fit of rage. Alford pleaded guilty to murder and was sentenced to fifteen years in a Louisiana state prison. Scardino and Landry each pleaded guilty to the lesser charge of manslaughter, were given credit for time already served, and set free.

If not for the jawbone and teeth that helped to make the victim's identification, the crime might never have been solved.

Forensic scientists are turning increasingly to computers to assist in their investigations. Before moving on to other identifiers, let's see how computers are being used in many facets of cold case analysis.

THREE

Forensic Informatics

1

In Kansas City, Missouri, Christine Elkins, thirty-two, the mother of two boys, had a serious problem. She had become a drug addict, which had her running drugs for her supplier. She was caught, and while she was under arrest, investigators pressured her to turn on her boss, drug lord Tony Emery. She agreed, but word got to him about her deal, and he offered her money not to participate. He did not really trust her, however, and she realized he might kill her.

One day in August 1990, she dropped off her sons at the home of a friend and told him that if she did not return to look for her at the morgue. She left in her two-door Olds Cutlass. When Elkins missed her court date and Emery's, detectives feared she was dead.

Eventually a call came from Greeley, Colorado, with information from an informant regarding a homicide in Missouri. The man reported a murder committed by three men: Tony Emery, his cousin "Tug," and their friend Bobby Miller. The victim, a woman, had been beaten with a blackjack, rolled into a rug, and placed in a car,

which was then sunk in a rock quarry. But searches of quarries failed
to turn up Elkins or her car.

In time, detectives learned that she had been pushed into the Missouri River, not a quarry. But that had been six years earlier, and since
that time the river had flooded. The body and any evidence might easily have washed away in the strong currents.

Investigators called Naval Criminal Investigations (NCIS) to
request the use of a magnetometer, which measures changes in the
intensity of magnetic fields of ferrous metals below ground or in
water. Removing and replacing soil, for example, can change the
magnetic orientation of the dirt particles in relation to the Earth's
magnetic field, which a magnetometer would register. The larger the
object, the greater the depth at which it could be detected. The magnetometer consists of a console, which is strapped to the chest, and a
long pole with sensor coils attached. The readings are plotted on
paper as the geophysicist walks around with the equipment the way
one might carry a metal detector. This scientist knows how to read
the intensity levels and spot anomalies—recordings that appear
abnormal.

The investigators were referred to NecroSearch, the civilian team
in Colorado. NecroSearch member Clark Davenport presented the
case to his group, and they agreed it could be tough to find a car in a
large river. Those members attending the presentation asked about
the conditions of the alleged crime in terms of weather, lighting, and
characteristics of the vehicle. They also wanted to know about the
river's behavior, both during typical conditions and during the flood.
After feeling satisfied that they might be of some use, a NecroSearch
team made up of Davenport and geophysicist Al Bieber arrived in
Missouri to scour the Missouri River. Bieber knew how to use a magnetometer that could be attached to a boat and he had an underwater
video camera.

The team learned that the river was about twenty to thirty feet
deep in the target area, but that the water flow was swift. They also
found out everything they could about the Cutlass's weight and composition. Then they collected their equipment: a magnetometer, a

Global Positioning System, and nonmagnetic boats. The Coast Guard and Missouri State Water Patrol offered support for diving.

Finally, using magnetic anomalies, they pinpointed seven potential locations for a submerged car. However, the magnetometer failed them, so Bieber used a gradiometer. While not as accurate, this device could also measure changes in magnetic fields. After two long days, the NecroSearch team relied on the GPS to plot an underwater map.

Then divers went in, using weights and cables to prevent the current from sweeping them away. They had no success at first, but at the second anomaly site, Dennis Randle put his hand out in the darkness and felt a car bumper. The vehicle was a two-door, the style they were seeking. Randle removed the license plate and surfaced with it. The number matched the one for Christine's car. The team then brought up the car and opened the trunk. After removing debris from around a roll of carpet padding, they cut it away to reveal skeletal remains. X-rays from an earlier injury confirmed Christine's identity. Her skull had been shattered from a blow from behind, and with the help of informants, Emery was charged with her murder. A jury found him guilty in less than an hour and he was sentenced to life.

2

Informatics is the application of computer and statistical techniques to the management of information, and forensic informatics is specific to legal procedure and investigation. That informational organization can work for both criminals and law enforcement, and can apply to anything from electronic scanning equipment, to video image enhancement, to the development of vast databases for research and crime-solving. The Internet has made some crimes easier to commit, but it has also provided police with new ways to detect and solve a crime and collect evidence, as seen in *Cold Case Files* "A Map to Murder."

In St. Louis, Missouri, in 2001, police linked six cases of murdered prostitutes with DNA extracted from semen and they entered the profile into a database known as CODIS (Combined DNA Information System). No matches were found.

Then Bill Smith, a reporter for the *St. Louis Post Dispatch,* wrote stories about the victims and received a letter in response. The writer provided a map to "Victim number 17," which led to skeletal remains. Detectives then looked at the computer-generated map to learn as much as they could about it. The sender had removed the borders that would identify the map's origin, so investigators enlisted the Illinois State Police Cyber Crime Unit. Mark McAmish recognized the map as one from the Expedia.com Web site. Now he had a track to follow.

He contacted Expedia for computer logs with the IP addresses of computers that had visited the Web site. They provided a list of IP addresses of computers that had recently accessed maps. On it was an address just outside St. Louis, for Maury Travis. A background check revealed that he was a convicted felon, so detectives went to his home with a search warrant and found evidence of possible torture and murder.

They showed Travis photographs of the victims and he denied knowing them. But then he asked to see the "murdered" girls again. They had not mentioned that the women were dead. He broke down, cursing the Internet, and said he would lead them to another victim dump site, but then asked to be taken to jail. There he requested a can of soda, from which the detectives extracted a sample of his saliva for DNA analysis. It matched semen from the victims. They also got a match from tread marks that were found on one of the victim's legs to Travis's car. Eventually they linked him to twelve unsolved homicides, but then he committed suicide in jail.

Informatics involves the many processes of gathering, storing, classifying, manipulating, and retrieving forensic information. It also includes developing methods for searching databases quickly. Computer operating systems use virtual memory for retrieval and speed, which means that some information exists in fragile form, which may be erased or overwritten when a computer is switched on. (Savvy digital criminals may booby-trap their machines to destroy files if certain steps are not followed.) Computer specialists in law enforcement rely on equipment that can duplicate whatever is on a computer's hard drive without having to turn the computer on. Thus they can work on encrypted data without the risk of destroying it. In terms of evidence gathering, the role of the computer as a repository and organizer of information is both valuable and tricky.

The major dangers include loss of information and its potential alteration. It must be handled well to be admissible in court, with the gathering method invulnerable to challenge. The tools used cannot affect the data during collection, must be able to collect everything necessary, must be accepted by the forensic informatics community, and must produce replicable results. With chain of custody issues that demand an unbroken record from original evidence to whatever is presented in court, investigators will have to prove that the evidence to which they testify is an accurate representation of what was on the computer.

Information is now a digital asset, translated into machines and networks and guarded by software systems, passwords, and database access. The cyber world connects to the real world via a vast and complicated network of simulations. Thanks to the relentless development of computer technology, forensic science and investigation have become more sophisticated. The contents of large card files that once took up precious space have now been fed into computerized databases for easier access, and even the storage capacity in computers has significantly increased in size. Crime scene processing has become information-heavy, and that has amplified the demand for high-speed organization.

The first use of a computer in processing a crime occurred in 1964, in the case of the Boston Strangler. The task force, or Strangler Bureau, was faced with the imposing task of collecting, organizing, and assimilating over thirty-seven thousand documents from the various police jurisdictions involved in the case, which totaled over 800,000 pieces of paper. A Concord-based company, hearing of their plight, donated a computer to help keep track of it all.

Twenty years later, in 1985, in response to a plea for an efficient way to organize information, the FBI's National Center for the Analysis of Violent Crime had their VICAP system up and running to provide a national database for linking several crime scenes together, identifying missing persons who were homicide victims, and linking victims to offenders.

Computer crime tends to take the form of hacking into protected systems and sabotaging records, pirating software or trade secrets, planting viruses, stealing identities, altering records, disseminating child pornography, fraud, stalking, extortion, forgery, and illegal transactions. Initially, computer savvy criminals were many leaps ahead of law enforcement, who did not suspect just how facile the computer was for criminal enterprise, but laws were passed and detectives gained expertise, and soon devised their own ways to use the computer to catch these criminals.

In 2000, an e-mail labeled "I love you" went out to millions of people. When they opened it, a virus invaded their address books and replicated itself by sending out the same message to everyone listed there. Multiple computers crashed or experienced difficulties, including those at businesses. It was an expensive prank and a serious crime. Investigators looked for a way to trace it and found a key word that had been in a previous Internet virus. They tracked that one to a former computer student in the Philippines. In his apartment, police found discs that implicated him. Since there were no laws there regarding such activities, he was not arrested, but the case did inspire legislation to ensure that the next such malicious hacker would face serious legal consequences.

The entry of computer-savvy law enforcement into the cat-and-mouse game of criminal investigation increased the stakes. Criminals who view themselves as geniuses delight in outwitting even the best protections and heightening the sense of danger. The new generation of computer intruders seem attracted to the high of beating the system and eluding law enforcement. While they're aware that deleting a file merely changes its name, sophisticated users encrypt their files and protect them with passwords, or leave instructions for the destruction of evidence should an intruder enter their computers.

While hackers sending viruses are one breed of cyber criminal, there are others who feed compulsive addictions that harm others—pedophilia and child pornography. A man convicted of performing an indecent act with a child in 2003 had found a way to take pictures with an Internet camera of his own daughter undressing. She discovered it and told her mother and the police. A search of his home turned up nothing, but there was a large encrypted file on his computer. He refused to provide the password, so for nineteen weeks a police computer specialist cycled through various combinations until he found the password. Inside the file were nearly nine hundred illegal images and video footage from child pornography sites. The man pleaded guilty to some of the charges and received six years in prison.

Other pedophiles use chat rooms to pose as teenage boys or girls to lure children to meet them. The police have responded by entering the chat rooms and posing as children to lure the criminals to meet *them*. Many police departments assign such officers to full-time computer policing, often with a focus on child predators, and numerous arrests have been made. In fact, the largest international pedophile ring, known as the Wonderland Club, was cracked by police from twelve counties in a coordinated effort. Over a period of two years, 107 people were arrested and many were convicted of having pornographic images in their possession. One committed suicide.

In 2003, police from Britain, Australia, and North America launched a crackdown on the extensive international Internet trade for child pornography, calling it Operation Pin. They set up fake Web sites promising images and leading visitors through the site directly to law enforcement. Repeat offender data goes into an Interpol database and provides information for cyber dragnets. In one such bust, the names of more than seven thousand collectors of child pornography were acquired.

Law enforcement agencies can form their own high-tech crime centers or consult with such organizations as the High-Tech Crime Consortium, which provides education and training in detecting and analyzing cyber-world crime. These consultants have backgrounds in computers, forensic investigation, criminology, intelligence analysis, and behavioral psychology. Some companies offer instruction in retrieving electronic evidence.

3

For more than two decades, Richard Banister had been on the run as a fugitive, jumping bail in 1973 for drug smuggling in Albuquerque, New Mexico. He assumed a new identity in Crested Butte, Colorado, under the alias Richard Neil Murdock. However, he had not just made up this name; he had stolen another man's bank, credit, and asset records. With these, he had made substantial purchases, which caused havoc for the real Richard Murdock, as recounted in the *Cold Case Files* episode "Life on the Run."

Once notified of this identity theft, the U.S. Marshals tracked down the fugitive, but he had already taken off. Three years went by before they learned about a man named Grafton Moller in Taos, New Mexico, who was using Banister's social security number. They found him in a thrift store and he admitted that he was Richard Banister. He'd lived as someone else all those years, and the people whose identities he'd assumed had suffered.

With identity theft, a person's computerized information can be wiped out in seconds and transferred to someone else, while the unsuspecting victim can be granted an entirely new identity—including one saddled with debt or a criminal record, as was the case with the character Angela Bennett in the movie *The Net*. The perpetrator may access bank statements, mortgage records, and tax filings, and the victim may not realize what has happened for months—certainly providing time for the criminal to get away and leave no traces.

Identity theft is a fast-rising crime that depends on the pervasive availability in the computer age of people's personal information, from bank accounts, to social security numbers, to home addresses gained via computerized databases. There's also an old-fashioned method of simply going through people's trash to retrieve credit card statements or stealing bills from mailboxes. These thieves may also buy information from or sell it to others.

In 1992, Trans Union Corporation, a credit bureau, recorded less than three thousand inquires a month regarding identity theft. Five years later, there were more than forty-three thousand each month. A Federal Trade Commission identity theft hotline reported a fourfold increase in complaints between the end of 1999 and the spring of 2001, and Image Data, a protection service, put out a report that found that one out of every five Americans had been or was related to someone who had been a victim.

Once thieves access a little information, they can use it to get more. They may call a credit card company with an unsuspecting person's number and change the address, then run up bills and leave before anyone can catch them. Or they'll open a new account with someone else's information. They may take out mortgages and fail to pay them, or purchase cars or weapons. They may open a bank account and write bad checks. Their crimes are accomplished anonymously, with a devastating impact on the victim, who may spend years trying to rectify the situation and restore his or her credit status.

Crimes like this have a high probability of going cold, in part because the criminals can be difficult to catch and in part because institutions that become victims are reluctant to report it for fear of losing customers. Identity theft is a common way that terrorist groups targeting the U.S. have managed to get training, driver's licenses, bank accounts, and access to sensitive information.

An eight-month investigation in New York against eight Nigerians resulted in an indictment that leveled over two hundred charges of fraud and theft. The perpetrators had diverted victims' important mail to temporary addresses and within a month had everything they needed to steal assets and make other investments. They made millions in a very short period of time.

Anyone can be a victim, even a dead person. Investigating this crime takes a lot more effort than effecting it, and can cost the victim much more than he or she will ever recover.

4

Databases have been developed in many areas of forensic science, especially where comparisons are crucial. The best-known and oldest database is for fingerprints. Fingerprints were once stored on cards and an examiner might take weeks to make a single comparison. Now fingerprints are digitally stored on AFIS (Automated Fingerprint Identification System) in each state and at the FBI, and operators can make the same comparison in a matter of hours, even minutes. The system works with the images of fingerprints acquired from a person or a surface and scanned into the computer. The print features are extracted from the unique pattern and stored as specific formulas or algorithms. Individual and grouped prints then become available for comparison with a fingerprint lifted from a crime scene or a corpse.

Handwriting, DNA, tire impressions, cartridge cases, drugs, footwear, carpet fibers, and paint chips have gone the same route. They even have a database for bare feet and another for ear prints. Often, several databases are used together to solve a crime.

On March 29, 1974, in Phoenix, Arizona, Dale Sechrist, the owner of a Travel Lodge motel, was shot with a .22-caliber gun during a robbery. He had managed to shoot the robber before he died.

Detectives acquired ten fingerprints from the scene and were faced with the task of comparing them against prints they had on cards in their files. At that time, this process was done by hand, and it took approximately eight hours to compare a single print against one hundred print cards. No match was found on any of the prints from the scene, so the case went cold.

Twenty-two years passed before Detective Ed Reynolds from the

Phoenix Police Department coordinated a search with Anne Wamsley of the FBI's AFIS database. She determined that only one print had a sufficient number of identification points to be run through the system. In a matter of minutes, she compared it to more than 10 million sets of prints. Those prints that were closest were offered by the computer, and a match came up, linking the crime scene to Joseph Gillum. He had been sixteen at the time and had lived close to the Travel Lodge. He also had a criminal record and a booking photo, which revealed a scar on his face—possibly from a bullet. When questioned, he acknowledged being at the crime scene and fingered his partner in crime, John Riley, for the shooting.

Riley was also a good candidate, with convictions on his record and the right type of handgun, a .22. But now the task lay in locating him. That, too, involved a database. Detective Reynolds used a Web site called Faces of the Nation, a tracking system that accesses public records. Riley was located in Tacoma, Washington, where he was the pastor of a church. Upon being questioned, he admitted that he was part of the robbery scheme and that he had shot the clerk.

Similar success to fingerprint comparisons often occurs with the next well-known database, CODIS, for DNA. Cold cases have been solved, people have been exonerated, and crimes have been linked with offenders from biological samples found at scenes. The database itself is limited to the DNA codes of whatever population the law in a given country allows to be collected, such as known sex offenders. Yet even with that limitation, many offenders can be identified.

In St. Louis, Missouri, by 1998, the police had thirty rapes to investigate in fourteen years, all of which had been matched up via the same DNA. The police and press called this unknown offender the Southside Rapist. While the DNA made it possible to link the victims, it offered no clues if a suspect was not in the database.

Over a period of six years, investigators made more than six hundred comparisons without getting a hit. However, each day, there were more additions to the database, and along with that came hope that one day the perpetrator would be identified. They also began to realize that more than half of the sex offenders studied had also committed property crimes, such as burglary and home invasion, which indicated that many who invaded a home might have the intent to rape as well. That gave the police an idea.

They had some leads on area burglars, including a license plate number that they had tracked to a man named Dennis Rabbitt. They found him and persuaded him to offer his DNA and fingerprints, and these turned out to be a match to the rapist's profile. But while they were in the process of analyzing the information, they had to let Rabbitt go, and he skipped town.

The following year, he turned up in Albuquerque, New Mexico, with a fifteen-year-old girl. Under questioning, he admitted that he had raped the women in St. Louis because of a recurring dream he had of a headless succubus coming to him at night to have sex with him. His desire to discover her identity had driven him to violence. He turned out to be one of the most prolific known serial rapists in history.

Rights to privacy often clash with the public's demand for safety, so while a crime spree such as a serial killing might inspire a call for a DNA dragnet, calmer times favor individual rights—and that can hinder solving crimes, which occurred on *Cold Case Files* in "Killer in the County."

Around Wichita Falls, Texas, in the mid-1980s, three young women were brutally raped and murdered, but without a way to link them or find suspects, the cases all went cold for five years. As DNA analysis became available, two of the three were linked to the same perpetrator via semen.

Investigator John Little made circumstantial connections among all three victims, and a convicted killer on parole, Faryion Wardip, had confessed to killing one of the women and had mentioned knowing another. Because he was not a convicted sex offender, his DNA was not in CODIS, so Little went to where Wardip worked, found a cup from which he had drunk, used it to collect DNA via saliva, and matched his DNA to two of the victims. When Wardip learned that the police had his DNA, he confessed to killing all three victims and added a fourth. Found guilty, he was sentenced to die by lethal injection.

Databases also exist for:

* *Handwriting analysis*. A subject's handwriting is digitized with a scanner and the strokes, slants, letter heights, and distances between lines and words are then analyzed, usually by one of two standardized systems.

* *Paint chips*. The formula for paint used by car manufacturers differs, so a paint chip from a crime scene can be analyzed for its composition and compared against these databases for automobile identification.

* *Tool marks*. The entries into this database come from tools the police have picked up at crime scenes that appear to have been used to gain entrance or in some other criminal activity. A three-dimensional image can be developed and compared to an earlier crime, which may link it to the same person or team.

* *Cartridge cases*. The parts and mechanisms in firearms that come into contact with a cartridge leave distinct marks when the gun is fired. Irregularities in the barrel also leave an impression, as do the lands and grooves. These marks are computerized as images and can be compared against a test-fired bullet or within the database to link crimes. Drugfire and IBIS (Integrated Ballistics Information System) have been the typical databases used for making such comparisons, but IBIS is standard in the U.S. Other countries use other systems.

* *Soles of shoes*. If a clear shoeprint impression is left at a crime scene, a large database of footwear on the market can be useful to determine what brand and model the person was wearing—especially for those shoes whose soles are patterned.

As valuable as databases are, there can still be problems.

On August 27, 1992, in Los Angeles, California, Jeri Elster was attacked and raped in her home. She learned that her case would become a priority for DNA testing only if a strong suspect could be developed. Fingerprints from her home were run through the state fingerprint database, but there was no match.

Jeri Elster's case went cold.

But she did not give up.

On July 27, 1999, almost seven years later, the offender databank registered a hit from her rape to Reginald Miller. But then it was discovered that the California statute of limitations for rape was six years, meaning investigators had run out of time. Thanks to the database, Elster knew who had most likely attacked her but she could not see him brought to justice.

5

On February 23, 1991, in Dane County, Wisconsin, the badly beaten and partially decomposed body of an adolescent female was found under snow, as described in *Cold Case Files* "The Boy and the Monster." There was blunt force trauma all over her body. Her missing hands were severed at the wrist, and five days later a hunter found them with the fingertips removed. That was an indication that the person who killed and mutilated her knew her and knew something about criminal investigation.

Photos of Jane Doe, taken in the morgue, were downloaded into a computer and enhanced to make her look more like she had in life. This image was placed on a poster and distributed across the country.

Four months later a woman in Illinois spotted the poster and reported that she had seen that girl with a pimp from Milwaukee named Joseph White. The girl was from a group home in Decatur, Illinois. Police took the image to the home and people there identified Doris Ann McLeod. She had been abused and had run away. The police suspected that her pimp had beaten her to death. They learned his address and called on him. Doris's personal items were found in his apartment, but the evidence was merely circumstantial.

Then a three-year-old boy named Joe approached the officers and they asked if he knew the victim. He looked at the enhanced image and identified her as "Dee." He had seen her "hanging" and had seen "the monster" bite her fingers. He showed the officers where.

They searched a basement and behind a panel found a blueprint for the secret workings of one of the largest and most violent gangs in the country. Written into this document was the punishment for breaking the rules, an ordeal that closely echoed Doris's autopsy report. Now the case against White was more than circumstantial.

The jury returned a verdict against Joseph White of guilty of first-degree murder and Doris's name was put on her gravestone.

Since photography was invented in 1836, it has been a valuable tool for documenting and sharing visual information. Law enforcement has relied on photographs in many ways, from mug shots to crime scene photos to suspect images, and more recently as the basis for identifications involving age progression and other computer-generated alterations of missing people and fugitives. The forensic artist has become a facial identification specialist.

The identification of a subject from one photo to another requires a skillful observer and interpreter. The comparison process is not considered a science and it has its limitations, yet positive comparisons can nevertheless assist in the identification of someone long missing. In that regard, computerized enhancement and manipulation can be most helpful.

For example, comparisons of images of poor quality, such as those available from in-store video cameras, can be digitally enhanced by an "imaging specialist." Then the artist can make a drawing from the enhanced image to use as a basis of comparison, or if it's good enough on its own, the enhanced image can be compared on a point-by-point basis to a suspect photo.

Computers can also assist with alternate looks. If one photo of a suspect includes a hat, beard, or glasses, these can be added via computer to another photo of that person to aid in the comparison. If someone has been a fugitive for a long time, and his or her current appearance is unknown, the computer can generate a variety of looks.

In her book *Forensic Art and Illustration*, Karen T. Taylor, a forensic artist who has taught courses at the FBI Academy at Quantico, provides guidelines. First, she says, it's important to gather as many photos as possible to assist in the comparison, and second, the imaging specialist must use the best-quality photos available. If the face is at an angle, the specialist will know that the facial shape or some of the features may be distorted. To guard against mistakes in perception, Taylor suggests that the identification process should "consider the base of the nose in relation to the ears." It may also help to turn photos upside down to view the features with greater objectivity. She points out that faces do not age backward, so if one photo appears younger than the one to which it is being compared, either cosmetic surgery has been performed or it was taken at an earlier time.

Many photo comparisons rely on knowledge of the natural aging process, and another type of computer alteration technique can further educate the identification specialist: age-progressing an outdated photograph. This process was first used during the 1980s for missing children, to assist in retaining their essential features despite the changes produced by growth. It is also used for adults who have been missing for long periods of time, including fugitives on the run.

It's important to incorporate as much information as possible about the subjects under scrutiny. Their lifestyle factors (such as smoking and exercise), racial ancestry, degree of exposure to the sun, known medical conditions, and other types of information can affect how their faces age. If available, it's best to have photographs of family members—especially older siblings or parents—for inherited aging patterns.

Once those calculations are made, an important consideration for deciding on a computer program for facial alteration is the quality of the tools offered for image modification. A program should allow for fluid movement and the adjustment of features in all directions, and for change in coloration and scale. Some systems incorporate "draw" or "paint" functions, where the artist can use a stylus on a pad to capture subtle nuances in small increments. It's almost like drawing.

People tend to believe, based on television shows, that computers can miraculously perform transformations on a photograph from one age to another, but these changes actually result from the skill of an experienced and knowledgeable user. The critical task is to maintain the "look" of the person, particularly in the area of the eyes. Also, most people tend to maintain a certain recognizable manner of expression throughout their lives. One advantage of using computer-generated alterations from photographs is that the baseline expression remains the same throughout the alteration process.

Then there are certain visual decisions to consider, such as color and angle. If the only available photograph is black-and-white, it's wiser to work within that schema than to speculate about color—unless color information is available from verbal descriptions and something like hair color is a distinctive trait. If the face is angled away from the camera, then only certain types of manipulations are possible.

In a cold case, the production of an altered image that looks usable can give new life to an investigation and can generate sufficient interest to result in closure. Thanks to computer enhancement and alteration, fugitives have been caught, unknown bodies have been identified, and crimes have been solved.

Even before databases were developed, the science of identifying criminals was seeking some means for linking crime scenes to perpetrators via individualizing traits, and they found one that proved to be rather handy.

FOUR

The Science of Identification

1

In January 1974 in Phoenix, Arizona, police responded to a call about an abandoned pickup truck, a story told in the *Cold Case Files* episode "Signature of a Killer." Inside the cab, they found blood. The vehicle was registered to twenty-year-old Taylor Courtney, who lived nearby. When the police went to his home, they found Courtney lying facedown on the floor. They turned him over and discovered that his genitals had been removed and were missing.

They surmised that Courtney had been shot in the truck and then dragged to the house, where his body was mutilated. Technicians lifted several sets of prints, some of them bloody. Two suspects were identified, but while both said they had been with the victim, they claimed to have alibis. These could not be corroborated, and they appeared to have undisclosed knowledge about the crime scene. One of them, who was nervous during an interview, said that the other was married to a woman with whom the victim allegedly had a relationship. Yet this information failed to identify the killer, and without better leads, the case went cold.

It was two decades before Detective Ed Reynolds revisited the case and found the unidentified prints in the file. Only two had a sufficient number of points of identification to run through AFIS, but two were better than none, so he entered them to compare against the database for the entire state of Arizona. On October 11, 1995, Reynolds got a hit from a left index fingerprint found on the screen door to Courtney's apartment. It was not one of the bloody prints, but it matched Larry Gibson, a man with a criminal record who had gone to high school with the victim. Gibson denied being in Courtney's apartment or killing him.

Reynolds located Elana Bennett, Gibson's ex-wife, and she admitted that Gibson was intensely jealous and had believed she was involved with Courtney. She had not known what he had done until one day when he handed her a package. She said that it contained the parts missing from Courtney. Afraid, she had kept quiet.

On December 3, 1998, Larry Gibson stood trial for the murder of Taylor Courtney, and was convicted.

Yet in 2002, he won an appeal based on the fact that the trial court had applied the wrong test in precluding evidence that the original suspects may have been involved. They had seen the victim shortly before he was murdered, had offered false alibis, had knowledge of the crime scene, and had shown suspicious behavior afterward. The trial court had decided that nothing the defendant offered had "an inherent tendency" to connect the others to the crime.

The appeals court, however, indicated that the evidence should have been admitted if it was "relevant" and if its probative value was not substantially outweighed by risk of prejudice or confusion. The case was remanded for a new trial, which is pending.

Despite that development, Gibson had denied being where his fingerprint placed him, so the physical evidence will still be an issue for him in court.

2

Dactyloscopy, a subcategory of lophoscopy, is the study of finger-prints. The smooth, hairless surfaces of the body—inner surfaces of hands and soles of feet—are covered with raised ridges known as fric-tion or papillary ridges. Those from the fingers are known to be unique to each person and can therefore serve for identification purposes when the sweat glands discharge perspiration to leave an impression. These ridges form in the inner layers of the dermis in the developing fetus and remain the same throughout life. The characteristics that make a fin-gerprint unique are called minutiae or points of identification.

Several ancient societies recognized the individualizing value of the ridged patterns of fingerprints. The earliest datable prints were left in Egypt about four thousand years ago. Other cultures, such as China, used prints to authenticate a person's work. In the third cen-tury B.C., finger- or thumbprints showed up on official documents for business or court dealings. In the first century A.D., a Roman attorney proved that a palm print was used to frame someone for murder. Yet no written record makes it clear that fingerprints were regarded as a way to individualize people.

Centuries passed before scientists began to see the value of using fingerprints for criminal investigations. By 1798, several researchers had taken an interest in the formations of human skin, and J. C. Mayor of Germany suggested that the ridge patterns on the tips of human fingers might be unique. By 1823, Professor Johannes Purk-inje had classified nine basic fingerprint patterns. Twenty-five years later, William Herschel recognized the individuality of fingerprints and used them for contracts. He also fingerprinted prisoners in jails.

By 1880, Scottish physician Henry Faulds had discovered that the perspiration from the fingerprints could be made visible with powders, and he used a fingerprint at a crime scene to both eliminate a suspect and implicate the true perpetrator. Along with his groundbreaking work, other researchers discovered the significant fact that finger-prints were unchanging over time—and would even heal back to the same pattern after superficial injuries. He suggested that "finger-marks" left on objects at a crime scene might lead to the offender's identification.

Yet before prints became a principal part of crime scene investigation, a movement arose in France to identify criminals—especially those who repeated their crimes—from a set of standardized body measurements. During the early 1880s, Alphonse Bertillon, a file clerk for the French police, devised this system, which he called anthropometry but which others in Europe referred to as *bertillonage*. As criminals came in, Bertillon carefully took eleven to fourteen separate measurements, from the length of the foot to the length of the left middle finger to the width of the jaw, to classify them as small, medium, or large, and recorded the measurements on cards placed in one of 243 categories. He believed that no two people would have precisely the same measurements. While this method quickly became popular throughout Europe and was introduced in the U.S. in 1887, certain problems arose, notably that not all who were taking the measurements were as careful as Bertillon, and the time it took to do this right proved to be quite cumbersome.

Eventually, fingerprinting eclipsed anthropometry. Getting a set of prints proved to be much easier than taking all these measurements. Nevertheless, it required several sensational trials before fingerprinting was acknowledged by the courts as credible evidence.

In 1892, Sir Francis Galton published the first book about fingerprints and their forensic utility. He proposed that prints bore three primary features and from them he could devise sixty thousand classes. He had some trouble and it took a number of years, but he eventually inspired others to devise a classification system based on five types that provided a basis for the system in use today.

The first modern trial in which a fingerprint was used as evidence was in Argentina. Juan Vucetich, a police officer, devised a fingerprint classification system and in 1892 opened the first fingerprint bureau, in Buenos Aires. Within two months, he used what he knew in the courtroom. Francisca Rojas claimed that a man named Velasquez had murdered her two children in their beds. A search of the crime scene turned up several

bloody fingerprints. But they did not match the accused man. Instead, they matched the mother. When confronted, she confessed and was sentenced to life in prison.

Independent of the developments in Argentina, and unaware of them, Sir Edward Henry started his own fingerprint classification system in India, which he published in 1900. Then he became assistant commissioner of police at New Scotland Yard, where he established the Fingerprint Office. In 1902, the first British conviction based on fingerprints was obtained, and Henry's ten-print system influenced those that were put into use around the world.

Henry separated fingerprints into five basic patterns: plain arches, tented arches, radial loops, ulnar loops, and whorls. Each could be translated into codes. Thus, prints were filed via numeric values and could easily be retrieved for comparison. It shortened the time involved in looking up prints. However, the system was limited, because it required the prints of all ten fingers for an identification, and crime scenes often turned up only a few—even just one. Single-print systems were developed years later.

Fingerprint evidence got a big boost in 1903 in the U.S. when two convicts with the same name—Will West—similar appearance, and very similar anthropometry measurements were found in Fort Leavenworth Penitentiary in Kansas. Since their fingerprints clearly distinguished them, this case brought fingerprinting into its own as the leading tool for identification. Anthropometry clearly could make a mistake. Fingerprinting had not yet been shown to do so. Yet the system needed a sensational court case to really make its mark.

The year was 1905. It was 8:30 A.M. in Deptford, England. A young man entered Chapman's Oil and Colour Shop on High Street to report for work. Oddly, no one seemed to be around, which aroused his suspicions. Then he found Thomas Farrow, his boss, lying dead in a bloody heap under a chair. Farrow's wife had been attacked as well and was dying upstairs.

An empty cash box revealed the motive as robbery. Chief Inspector

Frederick Fox and Assistant Commissioner Melville Macnaghten from Scotland Yard's Criminal Investigation Department took over the case.

They figured that Farrow had been deceived into opening the door while still half-asleep. Then he'd been hit. He came to, went after the robbers, and was hit again. The robbers had then gone up to the bedroom, hit Mrs. Farrow, located the cash box, and fled with the goods. They had cut stockings for masks but left them at the scene.

Macnaghten considered using the case to bring notice to fingerprinting, which had only been used once before in a burglary case. He used his handkerchief to pick up the cash box, on which he had spotted a clear impression on the underside of its inner metal tray.

Detective Inspector Charles Collins was in charge of the fingerprint division of the CID. The print on the cash-box tray appeared to have been left by a thumb. There was already a print file for housebreakers, so Collins compared these to the unknown offender's, but there was no match. Yet the prints also did not match the victims or investigators.

From witness reports, the CID had developed strong suspects in Alfred Stratton and his brother, Albert, but the witnesses could not identify them with certainty. Collins used the thumbprint to get a match to the elder brother.

Much now hung in the balance. If the print was barred from court, that would set the technology back considerably. If it was admitted and actually contributed to a conviction, it would become a legal precedent and an incredible coup for the joining of science and crime scene investigation. Objective techniques could one day supplant the more subjective eyewitness testimony. It wasn't just the British public who watched this trial closely; law enforcement departments the world over who were using or considering using fingerprint evidence for criminal investigations were interested as well. However, they faced an important question: Would any jury vote to hang a man based only on one print?

To make matters more difficult, the renowned fingerprint specialist from Scotland, Henry Faulds, became a vocal detractor. He believed that one needed all ten prints to make a definitive identification.

Nevertheless, Scotland Yard proceeded.

At first, the trial did not go well. Each prosecution witness was vigorously cross-examined, yet on the other hand the brothers had masks in their possession similar to those found at the crime scene, had tried to persuade someone to give them an alibi, had more money after the murder than before, and had changed their appearance after reading an account of the crime.

Finally, the fingerprint experts were called. Everything rested on this evidence. When Collins showed the jury with enlarged photographs how the thumbprint from the scene matched the elder Stratton on eleven points of comparison, it was impressive. He also told them that he'd been working for more than four years with files that numbered over ninety thousand prints. The defense had an expert who pointed out the dissimilarities, but when the prosecution produced a letter written by this expert to the effect that he would offer testimony to the highest bidder, he was dismissed.

It took the jury two hours to side with the fingerprint interpretation. Both men were convicted of the murders and hanged.

3

In 1910, based on a print left in wet paint in a murder case, an appeals court in the U.S. declared that fingerprint technology had a scientific basis (although it was still more than a decade before the courts would set up guidelines for the admissibility of scientific evidence).

In 1912, French criminalist Edmond Locard presented a different kind of identification system for fingerprints. He called it poroscopy, because it was based on the number and shape of the numerous pores found next to the ridges of a fingerprint, through which the finger sweated to produce the print. This approach did not catch on.

Congress eventually established a national depository of fingerprint records at the FBI in 1924, which took custody of over 800,000 fingerprint files from various prisons. Since 1972, fingerprints have been retrievable via computer. State and local agencies built up automated fingerprint identification systems (AFIS), and in the 1980s the FBI opened the National Crime Information Center (NCIC), which expedited the exchange of information among law enforcement agencies. Each day this centralized agency receives over thirty-four thousand fingerprint images to add to the database. They introduced a standard system of fingerprint classification (FPC), so that information could be uniformly transmitted from one AFIS to another. Each image has corresponding demographic data.

The computer scans and digitally encodes prints into a geometric pattern, a unique mathematical algorithm based on characteristics and relationships among print features and formations. Palm prints are divided into segments to allow for easier searching capability. In less than a second, the computer can compare a set of ten prints against a half million (although getting actual matches can take longer). At the end of the process, it comes up with a list of prints that closely match the original. Then the technicians make the final determination, which involves a point-by-point visual comparison.

Modern systems offer gray-scale images of varying levels to provide examiners with the maximum detail. Some computerized images are coming under scrutiny and may yield to three-dimensionally scanned prints, such as those done by Livescan, but the databases would have to be redone since these prints "read" differently.

The results don't always come with the click of a button, as one might see on television shows. Sometimes it takes a lot of persistence, and that's where the cold case detectives or technicians shine.

On August 2, 1991, in Dallas, Texas, a man entered the apartment of Felicia Prechtl when her son and brother were gone, bound her with duct tape, assaulted her, and then shot her in the head.

Pat Genovese, a crime scene technician, collected a roll of duct tape from the floor and found a half-smudged fingerprint on it. He processed this through AFIS, placing what he guessed was the center of the print (the core) and the axis (used to orient the print vertically) on the finger-

print. He knew that if he missed the core, the system would not pick it up. He had no hits, so he tried again and still got nothing. But he was not about to give up. He kept the print—the only lead—close by and over a period of five years kept running it through the system. In 1996, he finally established the name of a suspect: Karl Eugene Chamberlain. The suspect print had more than twenty points of identification that matched Chamberlain's, so the Dallas Cold Case Squad took over.

They learned that Chamberlain had been arrested a month after the murder and convicted of robbery, and that he had lived in the same apartment complex as Felicia Prechtl. When police questioned him, he offered a confession—he had been intoxicated at the time and had seen that she was alone, so he'd gotten some duct tape and a rifle and gone into her place. A jury sentenced him to death by lethal injection.

So how does it work?

Identification via fingerprints relies on the detection of the patterns of minutiae (or Galton's details) on a print and a comparison of their relative positions on a reference print. Examiners compare where the ridges start and end, where they split, and where and how they join, as well as where dots and other structures are positioned. The purpose may be to identify a suspect at a crime scene, to identify an unknown body, or to eliminate someone from consideration as a suspect. Fingerprints taken properly can last a long time and solve cases many decades old.

For example, as described in the *Cold Case Files* episode called "Family Secret," on November 28, 1958, the police were called to the scene of a murder and found Officer Charles Bernoskie, one of their own, in a pool of blood. They surmised that he'd come across a robbery in progress at the Miller Cadillac Agency in New Jersey and had been shot. Inside the shop, among the items that had been moved was a can of Prestone antifreeze. Dusting for prints produced several. Employee prints were eliminated, one by one, until police felt sure that one unidentified print was from the perpetrator. Now they just needed a suspect.

Neighbors described two young white males running from the place. Hundreds of suspects were questioned, and their prints compared, but none proved to be part of the team police were after. Investigators worked hard on the case for three years, but finally had to give up and move on.

In 1999, over forty years later, they got a break. A man named Robert Zarinsky had written to a postal inspector from prison, where he was serving time for murder, alleging that he had been the victim of identity theft. Indeed, a checking account had been opened in his name with a false driver's license and Social Security card.

It turned out that the thief, Peter Sapsa, was married to Zarinsky's sister, and she agreed to cooperate. In the process, she solved the long-unsolved murder of Charles Bernoskie. Her brother and a friend, Teddy Schiffer, had come home announcing that they had shot a cop. She indicated that their mother had sworn the family to secrecy.

The police located Schiffer and compared his fingerprints to the lone usable print lifted from the Prestone can. It was a match. To minimize his culpability, he agreed to a plea deal in which he would testify against Zarinsky, who he said had been the officer's killer.

However, with only Schiffer's fingerprint at the scene and no physical evidence against him, Zarinsky was found not guilty. Yet the case was considered solved, as Schiffer had pleaded guilty to first-degree murder in exchange for a fifteen-year sentence and Zarinsky was already there for other crimes.

4

Fingerprint patterns are divided into four primary groups, with multiple subgroups. Different examiners have different divisions and even different names for some of the types, but the FBI recognizes nine basic patterns, derived from the following:

- *Arch.* A ridge that runs across the fingertip and curves up in the middle, with tented arches showing a spiked effect. It has no backward turn, is generally missing a small triangle called the delta, and is the least common pattern.

- *Whorl.* An oval formation, often making a spiral or circular pattern around a central point. If a pattern contains two or more deltas, it will probably be a whorl.

- *Loops.* These show a stronger curve than arches, and the ridges exit and enter the print from the same side, folding back on themselves. Radial loops run in the direction of the forearm bone known as the radius, whereas ulnar loops run in a direction toward the ulna bone. They constitute between 60 and 70 percent of the patterns encountered.

- *Composites.* Combinations of the other patterns within the same print, and "accidentals" are freak patterns or patterns that do not conform to conventional types.

Once the basic pattern is established, examiners can concentrate on the finer points. There are several basic ridge characteristics: the ending (dead end with no connection), the bifurcation (forked ridge), and the island (enclosed ridges) or dot (isolated point), and these may form composites such as double bifurcations, ridge crossings, or bridges. These are used as the basis for points of comparison, and some areas of the print yield more points in a given space than others (the center versus the tip, for example). A minimum of twelve identical points of identification are generally required to establish that a print of unknown origin matches a reference or suspect print. The fingerprint examiner maps out the best comparison points, but is faced with problems from latent print collection such as variations in pressure, partial prints, and smudged prints.

Widower John McManus, fifty-six, was lonely and looking for company. He sometimes picked up men in the Center City area of Philadelphia and took them to his home in Cheltenham Township. One night in 1988, he made a grave mistake. He picked up a man posing as a hustler who actually meant to rob him, and that was the last night anyone saw McManus alive. He was murdered in his home, viciously stabbed thirty-four times, and his car was missing. There were no obvious suspects, but once the scene was processed, bloody

fingerprints were found on a vacuum cleaner. They were photographed and preserved.

Then, following a massive snowstorm, McManus's car was
located a few days later parked and empty on a street in Philadelphia.
Yet it was suspiciously clean, and it soon became clear that whoever
had taken the car had wiped it free of evidence, including fingerprints.

The case was investigated for several years, and the vacuum
cleaner fingerprints were submitted several times to the FBI, but
investigators received no response. With no other leads, the case took
a backseat to more immediate demands.

Then in 1998, Detective Mike Santarelli, who had been a patrol
officer when the crime occurred, took this case off the shelf to evaluate its potential to be solved. He noticed that the fingerprints had
been photographed and wondered why there had been no arrest.
With the AFIS systems in place, he thought it would be an easy case,
so he gave it top priority. Yet it was not as easy as he had hoped.

Santarelli worked with Detective Richard Peffall from the Montgomery County Detective Bureau, and when they attended a seminar
on violent crimes one day, they learned something about AFIS they
had not realized. At the seminar, agents from the FBI's Behavioral
Analysis Unit invited participants to present older cases.

"Rich and I presented the case," Santarelli recalls, "and among
the panel members from the FBI was a fingerprint guy. He looked at
the one-to-one photo of the latent prints and said, 'They should have
made an identification from this. There's enough detail in the prints.'"

Then a state trooper from Pennsylvania who investigated homicides approached Peffall and Santarelli after the presentation to
inform them that he'd once had a similar case. He had learned then
that the various state AFIS systems do not communicate with one
another. He suggested that they send a copy of the one-to-one photographs to the AFIS terminals around the country.

"So we had copies of the fingerprint made for all fifty states," says
Santarelli, "and Richard had the secretary type letters to them all."

To their surprise, many terminal operators returned the print,
indicating that the prints were "not of AFIS quality." In other words,

if there wasn't much surface or the print wasn't clear, it would take extra work to put it through the system. Yet within a month, they received notification from New York that they had a hit. Their print was a match to George Lutek, a man from the Kensington section of Philadelphia who had been arrested there. Clearly, they should have had a hit right there in their own state. They were grateful that the AFIS operator in New York had put in the extra effort to work with the print they had.

They went to Records and Identification in Philadelphia to pull Lutek's original inked card and had one of their better examiners acknowledge the match.

"Once we had an identification through the fingerprints," Santarelli recalls, "we had to build the rest of the case. We couldn't use just that in court."

They happened to have bumped up against a surprise pretrial ruling by Judge Louis Pollak, a senior federal judge in the Eastern District Court of Pennsylvania, who had entertained a motion to evaluate fingerprint evidence against U.S. Supreme Court standards set in 1993. The Supreme Court case was *Daubert v. Merrell Dow Pharmaceuticals*, and the resulting standards had given judges guidelines to bar junk science from the courtroom. In short, when scientific testimony is presented, judges must determine if the stated theory is testable, its potential error rate is known, it's been peer-reviewed, and it's relevant to the case.

A long history of admissibility of expert testimony from fingerprint examiners did not impress Judge Pollak, nor did the fact that experts check one another. He found that the standard technique used for fingerprint examination failed *Daubert* on three points, notably that the error rate had not been quantified, the "peers" were not scientists, and the millions of prints on record had never been analyzed for possible duplication.

Pollak's ruling focused on whether latent prints, which are generally partial, could be accurately matched to inked prints, which are complete. In a forty-nine-page opinion, he discussed the lack of scientific standards that controlled the technique. He would still allow experts to show how comparisons were made, he said, and even to say that no two people have the same print, but not that a specific latent print was made by a specific person. This was a blow to prosecutors.

Discussions in the courtroom considered the impact Pollak's decision might have on the future of forensic testimony—even in technical areas like ballistics and handwriting comparisons. DAs worried about making stronger cases, especially when all they had were fingerprint comparisons, and in such cases they urged detectives to get more corroborating evidence.

"So now we were concerned about how Judge Pollak's ruling would affect the case," says Santarelli, "and altogether it took us three years. We read through all the statements of all the people that were known associates of the victim, and interviews with Lutek's associates and relatives—six thousand pages of reports. We started rounding up Lutek's associates and relatives, and they had a lot to tell us about his exploits in Center City. We learned that he and his cronies would routinely roll homosexual men for money. They hung out in Center City, made conversation with them, and then beat them up to steal from them."

One part of the case that had been in the back of Santarelli's mind was that the victim's car had ended up under I-95 off Front Street, not an area that the initial investigation revealed that the victim would frequent. "I wondered why it was there, and as we were going through the defendant's family's statements, we learned that Lutek's sister had lived within half a block from where the car was parked."

On September 12, 2001, they arrested Lutek for murder.

Prosecutor Kevin Steele spent many hours in preparation for the trial, particularly with regard to the fingerprint issue. He anticipated that Pollak's controversial ruling could become a significant factor. As the trial date approached, Santarelli learned that the defense had hired a fingerprint expert in light of Pollak's ruling and probably in anticipation of fighting the best piece of evidence they had, but even that expert conceded in his confidential report that the print matched the defendant.

Half an hour before the trial started, Lutek pleaded guilty. Since he had intended merely to rob the victim and not to kill him, his crime was considered murder in the third degree, and he received fourteen and a half years in prison.

A footnote to this case was that Judge Pollak reversed his own opinion and fingerprints were back in favor with the courts.

5

Fingers leave readable impressions from sweat mixed with amino acids, by touching something that clings to the skin, or by pressing the finger into a moldable substance like soft wax. Touching any surface transfers the perspiration and leaves a detailed impression. Sometimes it's only a partial impression, but that can be sufficient to provide a lead. One can leave visible prints (also called patent), such as those made in ink or blood; latent prints, which are largely invisible except under certain procedures or lighting conditions; or plastic prints, left in soft surfaces.

The latent print must be made visible, and the quality of the print will depend on the type of material on which it was left. At first, prints were developed on nonporous surfaces using a soft brush with fine, gray-black dusting powder, and this is still practiced today. It works best with fresh prints, before the oils dry. The excess powder is blown off, leaving a clear impression from the powder that adheres. The print can then be photographed, lifted with a tape, or placed onto a card for preservation.

On December 23, 1988, in Griffin, Georgia, Beverly Eller, thirty-six, was murdered in her home. A crime scene analysis, detailed on *Cold Case Files* in "The Fingerprint File," indicated that Ms. Eller had been stabbed in the back bedroom and had run from her attacker, but had died at the front door.

Charles Moss, a latent fingerprint examiner, looked for items that might yield evidence. He spotted a beer bottle in the bedroom and a Pepsi bottle in the trash can. Dusting them, he found no obvious prints, but he took the items to the lab to analyze for latent prints that might be resistant to traditional print powders. Under a fuming hood, a one-hundred-watt bulb heated Superglue so that its vapors could coat the surface under analysis. The next phase involved dusting the print with powder and a fiberglass brush to enhance what the vapors brought out.

Moss lifted three prints. He put the images into AFIS but found no match. With no other physical evidence and no leads, the case went cold. Yet on a daily basis for seven years Moss entered the print into the system.

"As latent print examiners," he said, "we live to make identification. Any time we can get a match in a case means that possibly we have solved a crime."

Finally he got a hit. The name was Walter LeParker Leonard, and ironically his print came up because he had applied for a job with the Georgia Department of Corrections. Based on the fingerprint evidence and a collection of circumstances that placed Leonard near the crime scene, a jury convicted him of the murder and sentenced him to life in prison.

Ways to detect and lift good prints are improving all the time. The more irregular or absorbent the surface, the more difficult it is to lift a good print, although advances have been made. It was once impossible to lift prints off plastic bags or human skin, but now there are ways to do it, as we see in the *Cold Case Files* episode "Mommy Rules."

In 1984 in California, the bound and burned body of a teenage girl was found amid some plastic bags and diapers. Her features were too far gone to identify her. Her body was autopsied, but no prints could be lifted from her burned hands. She also had no dental work. A wound on her back indicated that someone had poked a knife into her, but it did not appear to be the cause of death. A drawing made from her face elicited no responses. All police managed to get from this case were latent fingerprints from the bags.

A year later in Nevada, a box turned up containing a nude female corpse wrapped in bed linens. She had been tied up before being killed and her front teeth were broken. The box had once been used for popcorn cups. Again, the potential leads went nowhere and this case, too, went cold.

Nine years later, Terry Knorr linked the cases to her abusive mother, claiming that her mother had murdered her older sisters, Suesan and Sheila. Knorr had called the television show *America's Most Wanted* to find out what to do. She told police that she had seen her mother shoot Suesan and take the bullet out with a kitchen knife (which accounted for the back wound in the autopsy findings). When Suesan became ill, Mrs. Knorr forced her sons, Robert and William, to help burn her alive. Sheila had been kept in a closet without food or water until she was nearly dead. Knorr's brothers placed her body in a box and dumped her in a lake.

The tale was unthinkable, but it corroborated the evidence police had. They returned to the latent prints lifted from the bag at the first crime scene and ran them against the Knorr family members. A match was made with Terry's brother Robert. Terry's brother William had worked at a movie theater and she said that he had taken a box from there—consistent with what they had found. Terry also indicated that her mother had knocked out Sheila's front teeth. Once they had this information, investigators traced the box to the theater where William had worked. He also admitted under interrogation how he and his brother were forced to be involved.

In 1995, Mrs. Knorr was charged with both murders. In exchange for an agreement to spare her sons from prosecution, she pleaded guilty and got twenty-five years to life.

In November 2003, an article in an Australia-based science journal indicated that chemical sprays had been developed that would allow technicians to lift fingerprints from surfaces as rough as bricks and rocks or as slick as vinyl. Since traditional powders obliterate 10 percent of fingerprints, generally need a smooth surface, and don't always pick up older prints, this new technology could be a significant improvement. The spray contains iodine-benzoflavone or ruthenium tetroxide as an alternative to dry powders, and can treat large areas much faster than powders can. It does not replace the powder, which still works best on many surfaces, but it expands the type and quantity of surface that can be analyzed. On the downside, these sprays require the use of protective equipment while lifting a print, and special equipment for cleaning the crime scene afterward.

Other methods have been developed for surfaces like paper and cardboard. Prints can also be developed with chemicals like iodine, ninhydrin, and silver nitrate. And along have come digital imaging, vacuum metal deposition, dye stains, and the aforementioned Superglue fuming, as well as many other methods. Colored powders were developed to contrast with surface colors, and some powders or dyes glow under alternative light sources.

Since print comparisons are a matter of interpretation, mistakes can certainly be made, so experts work with many cases to hone their abilities. Before comparing them, the print technician must first make sure that prints are taken of everyone who was or who might have been at the scene, including dead bodies. To take a print from a person, an ink roller is run over the fingertips and the tips are then pressed against a card. The fingertip may also be scanned with special equipment. The fingers are numbered one through ten, starting with the right thumb. The left thumb is number six. Then they get coded according to their patterns, including any missing or scarred fingers.

6

Prints must often be lifted from dead bodies for which there is no identification. And there can be problems. The epidermis of the skin may be missing, loose, mummified, or coarsened. If it's merely loose, as it will be during certain stages of decomposition, the fingerprint can be cut off and examined on slides. If the skin is badly wrinkled, water or paraffin can be injected to make the surface firm, or a finger inserted into it to provide a firm surface.

If it's mummified or decomposed into a dehydrated state, the skin may be too hard to work with. Some methods of hydrating the skin have been effective (injection with water or glycerin), but the investigator may actually have to read the print from the finger rather than roll it onto a print card. In some cases, the print can be photographed or cast with dental casting material. If they're too stiff or deteriorated to deal with otherwise, it's also possible to cut the fingers off at one of the middle joints and soften the skin with hand lotion or fabric softener.

When the body is in a state of rigor, the joints may need to be massaged or bent back to loosen them for taking the prints. If the fingers are rigidly bent toward the palm, it's sometimes necessary to cut some tendons to bend the hand backward as far as possible. Then the fingers may be braced together with a device called a spoon so that the tips can be inked and pressed against thin fingerprint cards.

One way to take prints without using ink is with Livescan. The finger is inserted into a machine that has a sensor pad that scans it as a digital image that can be sent to an AFIS database. However, not all morgues and hospitals have access to this.

In 1991, in Newport Beach, California, Tammy Scriven reported her best friend, Denise Huber, missing. With investigators unable to locate her or even say what might have happened, the case went cold. It would be three years before some clues surfaced.

Police learned about a stolen truck at the home of John Famalaro in Yavapai County, Arizona. On July 13, 1994, they went to Famalaro's home and found a freezer inside the truck that contained a plastic bag. Inside was a frozen, handcuffed female body. The Ryder truck and its makeshift morgue were sent to the Maricopa County Lab, while John Famalaro was arrested.

In his home, detectives found a revolver, sledgehammer, and shotgun. Under the bed lay a pair of handcuffs and two knives. In the garage detectives found a box containing a hammer and nail puller, both speckled with blood. Other boxes held items once belonging to a woman. They also found a woman's wallet with cards and identification for Denise Huber.

As the body thawed, it began to fall apart. Using a hair dryer, technician Mike Winney hastened the thawing. Then he tried lifting a fingerprint from the paper-thin skin. He held the corpse's finger tightly, rolled it across an inkpad, and managed to extract a lift. The print was then compared to the fingerprint stamp on Denise's driver's license. The deceased was Denise Huber. Blunt force trauma to the skull had caused her death. She had suffered thirty-seven separate blows from a hammer and nail puller.

Since Denise was from California, the death could have occurred there—especially with evidence from a receipt that the freezer had been purchased in California. Arizona police called California authorities, and from the receipt found in Famalaro's home that indicated a freezer delivery to a specific address, they located a storage facility that seemed the likely site for the murder. Using a blood-detection chemical, luminol, investigators found evidence of human blood in one area. DNA testing confirmed it to be Denise Huber's.

On June 18, 1997, John Famalaro was convicted of murder.

Even more impressive than fingerprints at times are clues that could be easily overlooked but can make all the difference as to whether or not a case is solved. They're called trace evidence, and there are times when they really are just a trace.

FIVE

Microscopic Clues

1

In the "Soft Kill" episode of *Cold Case Files,* the story was told of Sophia Silva, who was kidnapped from her front yard in September 1996. After five weeks of no word on her whereabouts, the sixteen-year-old Virginia girl turned up dead. Based on fiber evidence, police arrested a suspect.

Fiber analysis involves determining first whether a fiber is natural or synthetic, or some combination of the two. Every type of fiber has characteristics specific to it and each fiber has imperfections that consist of twists and bends that can only be seen under a microscope. Cotton, for example, is twisted, and linens are more tubular. The more unique the fiber, the more useful it is as evidence. Under a microscope, the examiner measures the precise diameter, color, and other characteristics of the material. The examiner might also shine a beam of infrared light on the sample to get the absorption spectrum, or polarized light to find refractive indices. Chromatography can separate dye compounds into specific chemicals, and comparisons can be made from a specific fiber of something like a carpet to a manufacturer's product.

Seven months later in the same area, a pair of sisters, Katie and Kristin Lisk, disappeared from their home, and within five days, they also turned up dead. Based on the similar modus operandi, the police believed the cases were related, but the Silva suspect could not have killed the Lisk girls because he had been locked up. So either he was innocent or the cases were in fact unrelated.

Detectives on the Silva case asked the FBI to reexamine the fiber evidence. They did so and stated that the original analysis was in error. Thus, the indictments against the suspect were dropped.

The FBI lab had also linked the fibers from Silva to fibers found on the Lisk sisters. Since there was no suspect, profilers relied on information about the victims and behavioral clues from the crime scenes to offer an analysis: The killer was a white male, age thirty or older, and likely to be charming rather than forceful. Yet the few leads investigators had went nowhere and both cases went cold.

Then on June 24, 2002, in Columbia, South Carolina, a teenage girl reported that she had been raped and she provided an address where the crime had occurred. The apartment was rented to thirty-eight-year-old Richard Evonitz, a convicted sex offender. His background information placed him in Virginia, close to the unsolved Silva and Lisk crimes.

Members of the Silva-Lisk task force joined South Carolina detectives to search Evonitz's apartment. While one team collected fiber evidence, a second team searched his green Ford Taurus, which was the same car he had owned at the time of the murders. A technician dusted for fingerprints inside the truck, and a set of child's prints came up on the inside of the lid. They were matched to twelve-year-old Katie Lisk.

The FBI issued a warrant for Evonitz's arrest, but he fled in his car. When he ran over steel quills that punctured his tires and forced him against a curb, he came to a stop, and then used a gun to commit suicide.

2

Locard's Exchange Principle holds that "Objects or surfaces which come into contact always exchange trace evidence. Every contact leaves a trace." In other words, when someone commits a crime, that person leaves something behind at the crime scene and also takes something from the crime scene with him or her. Invisible debris clings to us as we move about in the world, and reveals our encounters. This, then, can become trace evidence in a crime.

What's the story behind this principle? We can look to Edmond Locard in Lyons, France, not only for the basis of this principle but also for one of the first cases in which a scientific analysis of trace evidence solved a homicide case. Inspired by the tales of Sherlock Holmes and mentored by Alexandre Lacassagne, Locard sought to hone his skills of observation and to create a place like Holmes's cluttered rooms wherein he could collect together the tools of crime detection. He bought reference books, microscopes, and measuring devices, and gathered ideas from the best minds at the time in forensic techniques. He called this "police science." It went beyond interrogation, undercover information gathering, and clever ruses. Instead, it relied on scientific reasoning and the analysis of physical evidence, and he believed that someone could not commit a crime with intensity without leaving traces of his or her presence. It might be a fingerprint, it might be soil from shoes, it might be a shed hair. He once said, "To write the history of identification is to write the history of criminology."

Few people took him seriously, yet he persisted, and in 1911, he got a break. Counterfeit coins were being used around town to buy goods, and the police thought they knew the identities of the culprits, but they couldn't find a way to nab them. Locard was assigned to help with the case.

Three suspects were arrested and brought in, and Locard asked if he would be allowed to examine their clothing. No one understood why he wanted to proceed in this manner, but he was granted permission.

Using a pair of tweezers, he went over one man's clothing to remove specks of dust from around the pants pocket area. He then turned his attention to the shirtsleeves, brushing dust off them onto clean sheets of white paper. He took these samples away to examine under a microscope. Under magnification, it was evident that the dust contained characteristics that allowed Locard to learn about its origin. Specifically, he was looking for minute traces of metal, and he found them. Chemical tests applied to the dust grains affirmed what he saw, and the proportions of metal that were in the dust matched those in the counterfeit coins.

It only remained to find the same traces of metal on the clothing of the other two suspects, which he promptly did. That kind of evidence pressured the men to confess, which provided Locard with the publicity he needed for his method of sleuthing and the scientific identification of suspects. With his trained eye, he looked for clues that the police generally failed to see. Like Sherlock Holmes and Eugene Vidocq, he was a detective, but one with a purely scientific orientation. It wasn't mere reasoning that solved the case for him, but solid physical evidence—even if it was only in tiny amounts.

In fact, dust is one of the key mediums for finding such evidence, and among criminalists today, there are special vacuums for collecting fine debris at a crime scene. In dust can be found items like pollen or dirt from a foreign place, paint chips, fragments of glass, hair, and even skin cells. Yet only the most alert observer will see them. Most police officers during Locard's time did not use microscopes, so they were clearly missing a whole realm of potential evidence.

With lenses, the microscope enables the human eye to observe enhanced or enlarged images of very small objects. Some can enhance surfaces and some can see right through an object or specimen.

Ancient Romans had magnifying glasses, but the earliest microscopes—tubes with lenses—were dubbed "flea glasses" because they allowed people to see images of things as tiny as fleas. In 1590 Dutch spectacle makers Zaccharias and Hans Janssen invented the forerunner of the compound microscope, which relies on a combination of lenses to produce an image larger than that yielded by a magnifying glass. Two decades later, Galileo improved it with a focusing device and more finely ground lenses to produce even higher magnification power.

Anton van Leeuwenhoek, considered the real father of microscopy, figured out curvatures that increased the magnification power of a lens and made numerous biological discoveries. The stereoscopic microscope added a double eyepiece and prisms that provided three-dimensional images. In the 1920s, the comparison microscope improved the process of comparing two objects at once, and during the next decade the electron microscope used beams from fast-moving electrons that were absorbed or scattered to form an image on an electron-sensitive plate. This enabled scientists to see much smaller objects than was possible with a light microscope.

The microscope was among the first scientific tools to be used in a murder case. In America, a 1912 Massachusetts-based murder was solved with the microscopic analysis of threads on a coat from which a button had come loose and fallen at a crime scene.

We've seen how something from the crime scene stays with the offender. Now for the second part: the perpetrator leaving something behind. Locard had gained a reputation, so he got another tough case to crack. Emile Gourbin, a bank clerk, was a suspect in the murder of his girlfriend. However, he had an alibi. At the estimated time of the murder, he'd been with friends, he said, playing cards, and his friends affirmed this. The police were stumped about how to get around his story and prove that he was the killer.

Locard examined the victim and noticed scratches on her neck. He went to where Gourbin was being kept in a holding cell and scraped under his fingernails. Under the microscope, he found in this debris tiny flakes of skin. That's not very conclusive, since it could have come from the suspect, and it would not pass as good evidence today without a DNA match, but there was something more. Locard noticed some color on the skin, as if something had been applied to it.

He tested it and found the ingredients common to cosmetics. When he tested the face powder that had belonged to the victim, not only was it consistent with the fingernail scrapings, but it also turned out that the makeup had been made especially for her. It was unique!

The evidence was impressive—even to Gourbin. He finally confessed and admitted to how he had turned the clock back at his friends' house to have an alibi, and Locard had another victory for affirming the crime lab. He received more staff and more funding. With greater resources, he went on to prove the value of dust and fibers for revealing what people have brushed against in their daily worlds.

Locard went on to classify many different types of dust through long hours of microscopic examination and to set forth the principles of handling trace evidence:

- Never turn pockets inside out to look inside, but remove them at the seam and go through them carefully with tweezers.

- Collect all dust particles on clean paper.

- Use magnets to separate out the metal fragments.

- Remove dust from shoes in layers.

- Keep layers separate from one another on clean paper.

No matter how much someone tries to clean up a crime scene, something is generally left behind. It may not always be detected, but it's difficult to take any kind of violent action without shedding something. This principle became the motivating factor in the development of forensic science.

Trace evidence, though often insufficient on its own to make a case, may corroborate other evidence or even prompt a confession. Because trace evidence can be any number of things, from a paint chip to a piece of glass to plant debris, there are numerous different methods used for analysis. For some objects, databases are available for comparisons. The main point is that some apparently foreign object or piece of material is present at a crime scene, and tracing its origin can assist in an arrest and conviction. Similarly, finding some trace from the victim or crime scene on a suspect can have a strong impact on a case.

Three prostitutes had been tortured and murdered with a hammer in Delaware, each one with wounds worse than the last, and on each battered body were traces of blue carpet fiber. There were no clear leads and the case appeared to be going nowhere, so an undercover female officer began to watch the area. One evening, she spotted a blue van, so she strolled over. She noticed that this van had blue carpets, so as she talked with the driver, she ran her fingernails over the carpeting on the inside of the door. When she stepped back, she had fiber specimens for trace comparison. They were found to be consistent with the fibers on the bodies and they identified the driver, Steve Pennell, as the offender. With this evidence, he was arrested and convicted.

3

One of the tiny clues that can be picked up from a crime scene is hair. People shed hair all the time, so the presence of hair at a scene does not automatically link someone to it as the offender, but a single hair can make the difference between a case being solved and going cold.

On December 15, 1994, Joann Katrinak and her fifteen-week-old baby disappeared from their home in Catasauqua, Pennsylvania. The next morning, Joann's husband, Andrew, called the police to say he had found her abandoned car. He was an immediate suspect, but the police could not find the bodies. With no other leads, the case went cold.

It took the thawing of snow to reveal the whereabouts of Katrinak. She and the baby were both found in a wooded area. The forensic pathologist determined that Joann had been beaten and shot in the face, while the baby had died from exposure. Now that they had a clear case of murder, the police returned to the car and the crime scene to search for evidence. In Joann's car they picked up six eight-inch-long blond hairs. They found similar hairs at the crime scene. These strands had been forcibly pulled from someone's scalp and their roots showed that dark hair had been dyed blond.

It began to appear that Joann's killer had been female. Detectives looked into women whom Joann had known, as well as into her husband's past relationships, to try to determine a link through a motive—especially for killing the baby too. They zeroed in on a viable suspect: Five years earlier, a woman named Patricia Rorrer, who now lived in North Carolina, had been involved with Andrew. Under questioning, he admitted that she had recently tried to contact him, but Joann had answered the phone and told her to leave them alone.

Detectives traveled to North Carolina to meet with the suspect, whose hair was black. Rorrer denied that she had made such a call. They had a DNA analysis done on the hair follicles of the found strands and it was consistent with Rorrer's. Then they found a photograph that had been taken of Rorrer close to the time of the murder, which showed her with dyed blond hair. Despite her denials, she was convicted of murder and sent to prison for life.

Among the first cases in which hair was analyzed was the 1889 murder of a court bailiff in Paris, France, named Gouffé. He turned up missing, and while a body that resembled him was found three weeks later downriver at La Tour de Millery near Lyons, it was in such bad shape that the examiner determined that it could not be Gouffé. Among the marks of identification used was the fact that Gouffé had chestnut brown hair, but this mangled corpse had black hair.

The corpse was buried and Gouffé remained among the missing. But one detective, Chief Goron of the French detective agency known as the Sûreté, could not let the matter rest. Even after the pathologist had described the man's hair and beard as black, he still believed that the circumstances indicated that the corpse was the missing man. When he determined that parts of a broken trunk that had been found downriver had been shipped from Paris on the very day that Gouffé disappeared, he felt so certain that he petitioned for an exhumation and another pathologist's eye.

Alexandre Lacassagne, chair of forensic medicine at the University of Lyons, performed the re-autopsy of the four-month-old corpse. He washed the dead man's hair and beard and thereby discovered that the "black" hair was actually chestnut brown. Under a microscope, he compared the hair taken from Gouffé's hairbrush with selected hairs from the corpse. He also analyzed their chemical composition for the presence of hair dyes. The thickness of the hairs from the brush corresponded exactly with the thickness of the hairs from the corpse, so this evidence, along with anthropological measurements, finally confirmed that the murdered man was Gouffé.

Once the police had his identity, they acquired leads to his associates and were able to track down his killers, a pair of grifters seen with him who had robbed and strangled him before stuffing him into a chest that had eventually ended up in the river.

Since 1889, hair analysis has improved, but the basic approach remains the same: microscopic and chemical comparisons. A clear match can be crucial evidence, and sometimes a single strand of hair will do the job, as occurred in *Cold Case Files* "Terror in Telluride."

In August of 1990, Eva Shoen, a forty-four-year-old mother of two, was shot to death in her home in Telluride, Colorado. She was married to U-Haul entrepreneur Sam Shoen, who was absent that night. He wondered if this had been some revenge shooting from someone in the family who disputed his handling of the corporation.

Clues discovered in the bedroom included bloodstains and a .25-caliber shell casing. A microscopic examination of the bullet that had killed Eva showed two separate grooves from a design flaw in the barrel. That pointed to only one .25-caliber gun on the market, a Lorcin.

However, with no suspects, the case went cold.

In April of 1993, *Unsolved Mysteries* aired the case. Detectives received a phone call from Kelly Lemons in Farmington, New Mexico, who believed that his brother-in-law, ex-con Frank Marquis, had committed the murder.

At the time Eva Shoen was killed, Marquis's time card showed he had not been at work, and he had also not shown up the next day. In fact, he had gone to Telluride with another employee, Jeff Beale, for a jazz festival. Sheriff Masters tracked down Jeff Beale, who claimed that Marquis had borrowed a handgun from another employee, Jarred Ward. Ward was found and said that he had given Marquis the gun, a Lorcin .25-caliber automatic, the same type used to kill Eva Shoen. He turned it over to the police.

But upon examining the weapon, they found that lines had been gouged into the rifling of the bore, rendering the gun worthless for comparison purposes.

Beale's report of Marquis's strange behavior, however, on the ride back from Telluride kept detectives alert. Marquis had thrown clothing out the window, claiming he didn't need it anymore. While it might have been the clothes he wore when he killed Eva Shoen, the chances of finding it now seemed remote. Nevertheless, Investigator Jim Prendergast cruised the New Mexico highways with Beale as his guide. They covered more than three hundred miles and made a few unproductive stops. Then they found a mound of dirt pushed there by the highway department, and in it they discovered articles of clothing. They bagged them and sent them to the crime lab.

On one shirt, a painstaking technician found a single hair. Under the microscope, its length and medulla were found to be consistent with hairs from Eva Shoen.

On October 28 that year, Marquis confessed. He described Eva's death as a simple burglary gone wrong. Marquis pleaded guilty to manslaughter and was sentenced to twenty-four years.

*   *   *

Like fibers, hair specimens are viewed in forensic research as a "class characteristic." A single hair strand may have enough similar properties compared with a known sample to be "consistent with" the sample; it can't be said definitively to be a perfect match. While hair samples can be used to exclude a suspect, they can only be considered as contributing evidence for a conviction.

In homicide cases, hair is picked up at the scene and is generally collected from several different parts of the body, including several areas of the scalp. Because different hairs on the same person can show many variations, the larger the sample for analysis, the better. If the hair strand has a follicle, or skin piece, it can be analyzed for DNA as well.

Hair analysis can indicate whether the source is human or animal, and also whether the source is a member of a particular race. It can determine if the hair has been dyed, cut in a certain way, or pulled out, and where on the body it was located. In some cases, evidence of poisoning shows up in the hair.

A hair shaft has three forensically relevant layers: the cuticle, the cortex, and the medulla. The cuticle has overlapping external scales. Within it, the cortex is comprised of spindle-shaped cells that contain the color pigment, and the way the pigment is distributed helps to identify hairs from particular individuals. The center of the shaft is the medulla.

Hairs from different parts of the body have distinctly different shapes. Eyelashes are quite different from beard whiskers and head hair has a different shape from pubic or armpit hair.

In the 1950s, a technique called neutron activation analysis became a valuable forensic tool, in which a sample such as hair is bombarded with neutrons while inside the core of a nuclear reactor. The neutrons collide with the components of the trace elements in the sample and make them emit gamma radiation of a characteristic energy level. The scientist can thus measure every constituent part of the sample. In a single hair, more than a dozen different elements can be identified, measured, and used for comparison.

4

On February 26, 1985 in Prince William County, Virginia, Enrique Elizarbe was found bleeding from the head in a warehouse building. A fellow worker, Ronald Wheeler, reported it. As the ambulance team carried him off, Elizarbe managed to indicate that a coworker had hit him.

Under questioning, Wheeler stated that he opened the back door and saw Elizarbe covered in blood. He retrieved a piece of cardboard and put Elizarbe on it. According to Wheeler, Elizarbe did not stay put, but sat down on a stacking crate while Wheeler ran to get help.

Elizarbe died the next day. An autopsy concluded that the cause of death was blunt force trauma. Detectives Bob Zinn and Dave Watson examined the minute creases of each fracture in Elizarbe's skull and discovered a tiny green particle. They hoped it might be transfer from the murder weapon.

In the warehouse, the investigative team discovered blood spots, as well as a twenty-inch crowbar painted green, with traces of human blood on its surface. Outside, detectives found footprints in the mud, bloodstains inside a green trash can, and a piece of blood-soaked cardboard. Patterns indicated that the cardboard had been inside the warehouse when it was splattered with blood. Also, a blood trail was found across the floor and out the back door.

This evidence contradicted Wheeler's tale and turned him into a suspect. Yet because he could not be clearly linked, the case went cold. It stayed that way for fifteen years.

During a cold case examination, Eileen Davis, trace evidence examiner for the Virginia State Crime Lab, put the paint evidence inside a scanning electron microscope, which can magnify up to 100,000 times and provide information about a compound's elemental composition. She concluded that the chip from the skull matched the paint on the crowbar, placing Elizarbe inside the warehouse when he was attacked.

Particles generally flake off of a painted surface, or scrape off because of contact with something. In this case, impact with the skull had caused a paint chip to get embedded in the bone fracture. Once paint is found at a crime scene, its chemical composition must be analyzed. Sometimes its shape can be matched against a surface where a chip is missing, but not in this case. Since police had the suspect murder weapon, they had only to determine that the paint chip was the same in composition as the paint on the weapon. (If paint is from a car, databases include a range of colors and compositions used by the larger manufacturers.) A microspectrophotometer, which electronically measures energy wavelengths of absorbed and emitted light, can indicate via composition analysis, whether two paint samples of a similar color came from the same source.

There was other evidence as well. Andy Johnson, impression expert, compared Wheeler's boot against the photograph of the footprint found outside the warehouse, concluding from the size and from the mark left by a nail embedded in the sole that Wheeler had been outside. Analyst Carol Palmer swabbed the boots with chemical re-agents and found a positive reading for blood, indicating that the boots had been wiped clean before Wheeler had reported the crime.

Wheeler was arrested and tried. On January 2001, he was sentenced to life imprisonment.

5

Nature contains a wealth of clues, from seeds to pollen to different types of soil that may cling to shoes or clothing. Soil must be analyzed under a microscope to determine its type, particle shape, and color. Its pH level may also be measured, as well as how much plant decomposition it contains. Dust and dirt inside a home can be analyzed for its distinct room-associated composition (bathroom versus kitchen, for example). Seeds found in dirt can help to pinpoint location as well as the season in which someone may have died.

In the 1960 kidnap and murder case of ~~eight-year~~-old Graeme Thorne in
Australia, seeds from a rare type of cypress found in pink mortar on the
body told investigators that the body had been moved from the murder
site. A cypress tree found in the garden of a house built with the same kind
of pink mortar pointed the police in the right direction. Inside the house
was a tassel from a rug that had belonged to the boy's family. Further evidence, including hair analysis from a dog, built a solid case against
Stephen Bradley, who was convicted and sentenced to life imprisonment.

Palynology is the study of palynomorphs, or pollen data, trapped
in or found on materials associated with a crime. Many forensic
botanists criticized the investigation into the double murder of Nicole
Brown and Ronald Goldman in Los Angeles, because the plant life in
the yard had made it possible to look for pollen on the murderer's
clothing or in his vehicle—yet no one had thought to do so. Because
of its predictable production and dispersal rates in specific regions,
pollen can help to link a suspect to the scene of a crime.

From soil and debris in the wheel wells of the abandoned car of
a missing couple, scientists found pollen from a horse chestnut tree,
which was rare in England. They looked at maps and told police
where such trees might grow in locations where fishermen, like the
missing couple, might park their cars. Investigators were able to
locate the bodies near where leaves and nuts had fallen from a
horse chestnut tree. It wasn't long before they found evidence
against the couple's son, who was convicted and sentenced to life in
prison.

Pollen can be found in surprising places, and since we breathe it
in, pollen may even be found inside human remains.

In 1994 in Eastern Germany, construction workers turned up a pile of
bones in Magdeburg. Forensic anthropologists pieced together the
remains of thirty-two people, all of them young men. It was difficult to
establish how long they had been there, and the final estimation varied
from thirty-five to fifty years. Both the Gestapo and Soviet counterintelli-

gence had in turn dominated the area, and there had been some rebel-
lions. Reinhard Szibor from Magdeburg's local university had expertise in
plants, so he analyzed the pollen content of the soil where the bones had
been discovered, as well as inside the nasal cavities of the skulls. He managed to show that the pollen content matched the time of year when a pla-
toon of Soviet soldiers had been ordered to put down an uprising in 1953,
and had resisted. Then the soldiers had disappeared. Given the poor state
of the dental work of these remains, which was characteristic of conditions for the Soviet army, it seemed likely that the discovered pile of
bones was the result of a massacre of soldiers who had disobeyed orders.

Dust and soil particles generally yield something about their origins, whether from a concrete floor, bricks, cement, a beach, or a garden. They might offer leads about where someone lives or works, or
where they might have been, as they did in the *Cold Case Files*
episode "Final Fare."

In February of 1961 in Columbia, South Carolina, sixty-three-
year-old cabdriver John Orner picked up his fare at the Officer's Club
and drove off. Then he disappeared. His cab was found and there
were blood spots on the front seat. On the outside of the car, investigators noticed bits of mud stuck under the fender. Samples were collected and sent for analysis to the South Carolina Law Enforcement
Division (SLED). Under the microscope the mud was revealed to be a
coarse but fine grain of sand found in only one area of the state, the
Sand Hill Region.

Three days later, in Richland County, a team of police and volunteer cabdrivers found John Orner's body dumped in a ditch alongside
a country road. Orner lay facedown with a single gunshot wound to
the back of the head. Three bullet fragments were extracted. Ballistics
identified them as SMW Lubilow, copper-coded, lead ammunition
from a .32-caliber Harrington & Richardson revolver. Within days
they located the log from Capital Loan Company, a local pawnshop,
that indicated that the gun's buyer was Edward Freiburger, an army
private at Fort Jackson. From army records, it was learned that

Freiburger had been AWOL since the night Orner was killed. He was now a very good suspect.

On March 29 in Newport, Tennessee, a trooper found Freiburger with the gun. He explained that he had just purchased it in a pawn-shop in Knoxville. While ballistics did not eliminate Freiburger's gun, the small amount of shell fragments that were available for examination meant that investigators couldn't conclude that it was the murder weapon either.

With no other evidence, the case went cold, and remained that way for four decades—forty long years for the victim's grieving family.

Then, cold case investigators asked Ira Parnell to reexamine the evidence to see if a ballistics match might now be possible. Parnell found stored in an old cigar box the bullet fragments pulled from Orner's skull and two identical .32-caliber Harrington & Richardson pistols, one of which had been confiscated from Freiburger in 1961. Once again, however, examination of them was inconclusive.

Investigators then decided to find a specialist. John Cayton was a criminalist and tool mark examiner who ran a forensic lab near Kansas City. When he examined the bullet fragments found in the victim's skull, he noticed some blood and tissue on them. He soaked the fragments in a solution of warm water, saline, and soap. Then he used a sonic agitator to loosen any remaining bits of tissue. Now that he could examine the bullet fragments more closely, he was able to prove that they had been shot from Freiburger's gun.

Forty-one years after the incident, Edward Freiburger was found guilty of murdering cabdriver John Orner. Soil had shown them how to find the body and ballistics had concluded the case.

SIX

Ingested Evidence

1

Robert Curley, thirty-two, began to grow ill in August 1991, entering the hospital in Wilkes-Barre, Pennsylvania, for what would turn into a series of stays before he finally died in September. His doctors went through several diagnoses for his puzzling symptoms, which included his skin burning, numbness, weakness, repeated vomiting, and rapid hair loss. Just before he died, he became more agitated and aggressive and he was transferred to a hospital that could perform tests for heavy metal exposure. Sure enough, he had elevated levels of thallium in his system.

First discovered and named in England in 1861, this carcinogenic substance had been applied in limited doses for ringworm, sexually transmitted diseases, and gout. It was also used in rat poison but was eventually banned.

A search of Curley's work site at Wilkes University turned up five bottles of thallium salts in a stockroom of the chemistry lab, but none of his coworkers showed symptoms of inadvertent thallium exposure.

The levels measured in Curley at autopsy were so high it was determined that he'd been deliberately poisoned, and his death was ruled a homicide via severe hypoxic encephalopathy, secondary to thallium poisoning. His brain had swelled so much it had pushed down into the spinal cord.

Investigators searched the Curley home, where his wife of thirteen months lived with her daughter from a previous marriage. They found several thermoses that tested positive for thallium. Joann Curley said her husband took the thermoses to work. In addition, tests done on Joann and her daughter showed elevated levels of thallium, but not in such toxic proportions.

With no leads on suspects, however, the case went cold. Curley's widow sued the university for wrongful death. She had recently collected over $1 million from a car accident involving her first husband, and she had gained $297,000 in life insurance from Robert's demise. She looked suspicious to the police, but they had nothing to prove that she had killed her husband.

Several years later, authorities approached Dr. Frederic Rieders of National Medical Services in Willow Grove, a private toxicology lab, to do a more thorough analysis of the tissues. He wanted more samples, so Joann agreed to have her husband exhumed. Hair shafts were removed from various parts of Curley's body, along with toenails, fingernails, and skin samples.

Dr. Rieders conducted a segmental analysis on the hair shafts to devise a time line of thallium exposure and ingestion. The hair strands from Curley's head were sufficiently long to plot approximately 329 days of his life prior to his death. Thallium levels in the hair shafts at different times were recorded using atomic absorption spectrophotometry. That means Rieders's team used a chemical to break down each segment of hair into individual atoms and then excited the atoms to the point where they absorbed energy. Every substance has an individual, measurable absorption rate, and through this method, the quantity of the substance can be determined.

The results were surprising. While investigators had figured August 1991 as the initial exposure period, concentrations of thallium were measured over the course of nine months, with spikes and drops on a chart that suggested a systematic ingestion long before Curley had begun his job at the university. There was a massive spike just a few days before his death that suggested intentional poisoning. Hair from other parts of his body, as well as his toe- and fingernails, supported this data.

This time line was compared to events in Curley's life, which indicated that when he was away from home or in the hospital, his thallium levels dropped—except for the few days prior to his death. At that time, his family had brought in some food and his wife was alone with him.

The pressure was on Joann Curley, and in 1997 she confessed to having murdered her husband with rat poison in order to enrich herself with his life insurance payment. In a plea deal, she received a sentence of ten to twenty years in prison.

2

"All substances are poison," wrote Paracelsus in the sixteenth century, "there is none that is not a poison. The right dose differentiates a poison and a remedy."

In other words, any natural substance—even water—can be turned into a murder weapon, whether it acts swiftly or over a long period of time. This means that physicians sometimes believe that someone died of natural causes when in fact that person was murdered. For centuries, poison was a common murder weapon, but as methods for its detection improved, its use dropped off. While some estimates today indicate that poison is used in just one out of every hundred murders, medical people believe that's only because it can still go undetected—the percentage is probably higher. Some poisons show clear symptoms, while others just vanish into the body.

The study of poisons, going back about two centuries, is known as toxicology, and those cases of toxicity that have legal implications come under the auspices of forensic toxicology. This discipline applies to postmortem drug testing, workplace drug testing, and the investigation of prohibited drugs. It also covers the detection of foreign substances in the body, such as alcohol, industrial chemicals, illegal drugs, or drug overdoses. Sometimes it's just a matter of analyzing a blood sample, urine sample, or strand of hair. Other times it involves a full autopsy in which tissue is removed from various organs. Typically a person is tested for a suspected substance with a basic kit, such as a breathalyzer, and if that registers a positive result, a more sophisticated analysis may be required for proof in court or to make a cause-of-death determination.

Most cold cases that involve forensic toxicology also involve the aspect of death investigation. Toxicological analysis is important not just for investigating suspected foul play. It is equally important in making a determination between accidental death and suicide. For example, a poison common to suicide is carbon monoxide, and domestic medications are also widely used, whereas accidental deaths often result from overdoses of drugs such as opium, hyoscine, morphine, and heroin. Popular poisons for murder include aconitine, atropine, strychnine, thallium, antimony, arsenic, and cyanide.

The first person to suggest a chemical method for the detection of poisons was Dr. Hermann Boerhaave, in the early 1700s. He would place suspected substances over red-hot coals and test the resulting odors.

In the early stages of forensic toxicology arsenic was the poison of choice. It was known as the "poison of poisons" and since many heirs used it to gain wealth, it was also called the "inheritance powder." One such case involved the first murder trial to actually feature toxicological testimony from medical experts.

It occurred in England in 1751. Mary Blandy had married Captain William Cranstoun, a man of supposed wealth and position, but he turned out to be both poor and already married. Mary's father ordered him gone, but Mary was in love and she continued to meet with him secretly. He gave her a powder to use in gradual small doses on her father's food so that they might inherit his estate.

Mr. Blandy soon grew ill with gastric distress, which inspired a suspicious servant to examine what he was eating. She found the white powder and asked an apothecary to examine it. He wasn't certain of its nature, but the servant told the old man of her suspicions that Mary was using arsenic on him. Mary tried to destroy the powder, but the servant saved it. Nevertheless, Blandy still ate the food his daughter prepared and he soon died.

Cranstoun fled to Europe, but Mary was arrested and tried. Four doctors who had observed Blandy's internal organs at autopsy gave testimony about the substance that had killed him. They said that the preserved quality of these remains was suggestive of arsenic poisoning. One doctor had applied a hot iron to the powder that the servant had rescued and analyzed it by smell. The servant also told what she had observed, and Mary was convicted and hanged.

Fortunately, the state of "science" regarding poisoning made some advances beyond these rudimentary "tests."

One of the early improvements occurred when chemist Karl William Scheele in Sweden discovered arsine, a by-product of arsenic when mixed with chlorine water and put in contact with metallic zinc. Then in 1787, Johann D. Metzger discovered the "arsenic mirror." This was one of the first methods to detect the presence of arsenic in solutions. Metzger observed that when arsenious oxide was heated over charcoal, it formed a mirrorlike metallic deposit on a cold plate.

In 1806, Valentine Rose moved this understanding forward with a method for discovering arsenic in human organs by using nitric acid, potassium carbonate, and lime. He evaporated that mixture into powder and treated it with the coals to get the mirror. Around the same time, in 1813 in France, Mathieu Joseph Bonaventure Orfila, who came to be known as the "Father of Toxicology," published a *Treatise of General Toxicology*, which summed up everything known about poisons at the time. Orfila also refined Rose's method for greater accuracy.

For a criminal case in 1832, James Marsh tested the coffee of a supposed victim of poisoning, but was unable to explain clearly to the jury how he had found arsenic, so he decided to improve his methods. He treated suspected poisoned material with sulfuric acid and zinc in a closed bottle. From this bottle emerged a narrow tube through which arsine traveled and formed the expected mirror substance. His method, known as the Marsh Test, was sufficiently precise to test very small amounts of arsenic. It was also more easily demonstrated before a jury than earlier methods.

The case that established the use of this science in the courtroom was the prosecution in France in 1840 of Marie LaFarge for the murder of her husband, Charles.

Marie, twenty-four, was married by arrangement to the owner of a rat-infested forge, and was accused of poisoning her husband with arsenic. During the months preceding his death, she had purchased the toxic substance, allegedly to exterminate the rats. Her husband had become violently ill in a manner consistent with arsenic poisoning, and servants had witnessed Marie stirring white powder into his food. A local pharmacist tested the food and found the poison.

However, when the prosecution's expert chemists used the Marsh Test on the contents of LaFarge's stomach, they failed to find arsenic, so they requested that he be exhumed. The tests on his organs also proved negative. Yet food from the LaFarge household did test positive for arsenic.

Mathieu Orfila was asked to make further tests. He reperformed the Marsh Test on the same substances, proving with his discovery of arsenic in the body that it was not the method that was at fault but its bungling practitioners. Marie LaFarge was convicted.

3

Once poisons could be detected in human tissue, the next issue with metal-based poisons was determining how much was present in the body. It was no longer sufficient for the toxicologist to say that the amount of poison found was fatal, without having specific numbers to back up the statement, including knowledge of fatal levels of various substances. Courtroom procedures were becoming used to science and expecting more exact results.

In a murder case in 1911, Dr. William Willcox developed the first method for quantifying arsenic. Frederick Henry Seddon was arrested for poisoning Elizabeth Barrow to steal her assets. Scotland Yard authorized Willcox to make some tests. He ran hundreds of weight tests for arsenic and then used his method to figure out how much arsenic was in each of the poisoned woman's internal organs. He calculated the amount via body weight in milligrams, and his careful work stood up against vigorous challenge and contributed to a conviction. His method was eventually refined over the years to the point of being able to detect the presence of arsenic down to the microgram (one millionth of a gram) in both the human body and in soil.

A famous case that involved quantifying poison was that of the "Black Widow of Loudun."

Marie Besnard was accused of killing twelve people with arsenic, including her husband and her mother. The string of deaths stretched across two decades, from 1929 until 1949. Marie benefited in some manner from each of the murders, thus providing the prosecution with a motive. All of the bodies were exhumed to be tested and high levels of arsenic were found in each one. However, aside from the poison, the prosecution had only circumstantial evidence against Besnard.

When the case went to trial, the defense attacked the lab technique of the toxicologist, Dr. Georges Beroud, as careless. This caused sufficient doubt that a second investigation was requested from a group of four toxicologists. While this second investigation was being performed, the defense learned about a new theory that through anaerobic bacteria arsenic could enter the hair of a corpse from the ground. This meant that the prosecution's experts would now have to prove that the arsenic in the bodies had not been introduced after burial.

When complete, the second investigation also found significant levels of arsenic in the corpses. However, one of the toxicologists,

Griffon, had been careless in his determination of arsenic in hair. The procedure required that the hair be subjected to radioactivity for twenty-six and one-half hours. Griffon had only exposed it for fifteen hours, thus again calling the results into question.

A third investigation was performed by another group of toxicologists in a case that had now spanned some ten years, but when they could not disprove the defense's theory, Marie Besnard was acquitted on December 12, 1961, for lack of evidence against her.

As the detection of arsenic in the body became more refined, some famous older cases were scrutinized. It seemed irresistible to revisit history for a retroactive investigation, to see if anything more could be learned from seemingly unsolved cases. As long as such items as hair, bone, or tissue remained, it was possible to make a more definitive report than had been made with the more primitive means of the past.

A case in point was Napoleon, the French emperor, who died in May 1821. A man who had made his mark across Europe as a military genius, he was exiled to the island of St. Helena to live out his days as a captive of England. Some say he died there of stomach cancer or a liver disorder. Others insist there was a conspiracy to bring about his end with poison.

Napoleon was forty-seven and in good health when he arrived for his second term of exile after the 1815 defeat at the Battle of Waterloo, but he deteriorated quickly. His legs swelled up, and he suffered numerous aches and pains, and experienced headaches, diarrhea, and sleep disorders. It went on like this for about six years, with jaundice setting in, and during the weeks prior to his death he endured episodes of severe vomiting. He believed he was being poisoned.

During the early 1960s, a team made up of a dentist, an amateur toxicologist, and a Napoleona collector who had read the memoir of an eyewitness (Napoleon's valet) reviewed the former emperor's symptoms and noticed that they were consistent with those of gradual arsenic poisoning. In 1840, Napoleon's grave on the island had been opened and his remains moved to his current entombment in Paris. The preserved condition, reported at the time, of his unembalmed body after nineteen years in the grave also alerted the 1960s team. They obtained samples of Napoleon's hair which were reputed to have been removed on the day after he died, and applied a technique that was popular then called neutron activation analysis.

In this process, a specimen is placed in a nuclear reactor and irradiated with a stream of neutrons. It then becomes destabilized in terms of the ratio of protons to neutrons in the sample's atoms and becomes radioactive, emitting gamma rays of a characteristic radiation level. The rays are then examined in a spectrometer, and the treatment allows the scientist to measure even the sample's smallest constituent particles and identify the separate elements. If a person ingested arsenic, the procedure separates it into its component parts and makes it possible to measure how much was ingested over the course of just a few days.

The Napoleon investigators found what they believed was a higher than normal level of arsenic in the emperor's hair sample, as well as evidence of the gradual introduction of the arsenic over time.

Yet twenty years later, a hair sample taken from a staff officer present on the island with Napoleon and subjected to better technology found normal arsenic levels but elevated levels of antinomy. Mercury and antinomy have been found to complicate an analysis for arsenic, so the earlier results on Napoleon were now suspect.

Others jumped in with explanations about how arsenic could have been present in Napoleon without necessarily being administered by a murderer. Arsenic was commonly used in wallpaper, said one. Also, many medications at the time contained arsenic, as did hair ointments. But there are problems with these counterarguments, and the case of Napoleon has not yet been definitively resolved.

A lesser known example of retrospective historical toxicology involved Charles Francis Hall, who in 1871 was in charge of an expedition in search of the North Pole, supported by a congressional grant. Hall was experienced in arctic conditions, but he often had disputes with the crew's physician and chief scientist, Dr. Emil

Bessels. They arrived within five hundred miles of their goal and Hall decided they would winter in a harbor at Greenland. Bessels and another officer insisted that for safety they go father south. Hall stood firm.

Then on October 24, after drinking coffee, Hall became ill. Bessels gave him medications, but he only grew worse. Hall believed he was being poisoned and he wrote about this in his notes, but before anyone could do anything for him, he died on November 8. The crew buried him there in Greenland. An inquiry determined that Captain Hall had died from natural causes, but not everyone agreed, especially those who studied the case over the years.

It was nearly a century before two other scientists, suspicious of the circumstances of Hall's untimely death, decided to find out if he had been poisoned. Professor Chauncey C. Loomis of Dartmouth College and pathologist Dr. Franklin Paddock went to Greenland to exhume the remains. They found the right spot, but the body and coffin were frozen into the grave, so they performed an autopsy right there on the ground. Hall's corpse was remarkably well preserved, especially the internal organs. The scientists removed samples from strategic places, including strands of hair and fingernails. They also took samples from the soil surrounding the coffin. They then subjected all of this to neutron activation analysis. The soil, it turned out, contained a high percentage of arsenic, so if they did find arsenic in Hall, they would have to show that it was not from the soil.

In the patterns of growth in Hall's fingernail, they found evidence that he had received a large amount of arsenic during the last two weeks before his death. Since the nail had shown different levels of arsenic over the course of its growth patterns, that finding stood against the idea that arsenic had leached through the coffin into the body. Hall's hair samples displayed the same thing. Had the arsenic come from the soil, the distribution would have been more uniform. Given Hall's reported symptoms, his suspicions, and the results of the analysis with modern forensic technology, those involved in the investigation agreed that the chances were good that Hall had been murdered.

Yet even with the likelihood of murder, there was no telling the perpetrator's identity. Despite Bessels being the most obvious suspect, there was no evidence tying him to the crime.

4

Forensic toxicology is not just about the detection of chemical poison. Another major step forward in its history was the development during the nineteenth century of methods for detecting the presence of vegetable alkaloids, such as caffeine, quinine, morphine, strychnine, atropine, and opium. Plant alkaloids leave no demonstrable traces in the human body, thus requiring relatively complicated methods of extraction before an analysis can be performed. These poisons affect the victim's central nervous system. Even Orfila had no success and he thought that the isolation of alkaloids from human tissues might be altogether impossible.

Yet his student, Jean Servois Stas, had a different idea. In a murder trial in 1850, the male victim showed clear chemical burns in his mouth, tongue, and throat. Stas searched for three months for the agent, using ether as a solvent, which he then evaporated to isolate the drug, and he eventually managed to remove nicotine from the body tissues. Nicotine was, in fact, the murder weapon. The man's killer had extracted it from tobacco and force-fed it to the victim. With Stas's testimony, the killer was convicted.

Stas became the first person to develop a method to extract the material containing plant alkaloids from the organic material of the human body, and for many years thereafter, with some modifications, his method was the standard. Other toxicologists then developed qualitative tests with the Stas procedure to determine the presence of various alkaloids in the obtained extract.

A case in which this method played a significant role was the murder of the young French widow Madame de Pauw. Her alleged murderer was a homeopathic doctor, Couty de la Pommerais, who was her lover. Pommerais was in financial trouble at the time, and de Pauw had a large life insurance policy of which Pommerais was the beneficiary. One day, de Pauw mysteriously fell ill and died within hours. An anonymous note alerted the police to foul play.

The forensic pathologist, Professor Ambroise Tardieu, suspected from the victim's odd symptoms before she died—especially her racing heart—that Pommerais had used the paralyzing drug digitalin. In order to demonstrate the presence of digitalin in Madame de Pauw's body, Tardieu injected several frogs with the extract he had obtained using the Stas method, as well as with a standard solution of digitalin. The reactions from those frogs injected with the standard and those injected with the extract were exactly the same. This evidence held up in court, and on June 9, 1864, Pommerais was convicted of murder and executed.

Yet there was also a problem with these tests: false reactions. At times, an alkaloid might develop in the body after death that mimicked the reactions of the qualitative color tests used for the vegetable alkaloids. These substances are known as "cadaveric alkaloids." In order for the toxicologists to be certain that they were identifying a poison correctly, they needed a method that was specific only to that vegetable alkaloid, or they had to run a number of tests and obtain positive reactions to all of them. This discovery of cadaveric alkaloids created a need for new, more refined tests to be developed.

An important case that involved cadaveric alkaloids was the murder in the late 1800s of Annie Sutherland. She owned a saloon which Dr. Robert Buchanan frequented. Eventually Buchanan and Sutherland married; however, Buchanan was having financial troubles at the time. When Sutherland mysteriously died, he was heir to all of her assets, so investigators realized that he had a motive to kill her. Toxicologists determined that Sutherland had died of morphine poisoning, despite the fact that she did not display the determining characteristic of having narrowed pupils. It was soon discovered that Buchanan had put drops of atropine in her eyes to dilate them and foil the doctors. The toxicological evidence seemed overwhelming, but on the stand, Professor Victor Vaughn proved the existence of a cadaveric alkaloid that mimicked morphine in all of the known morphine qualitative tests. This cast a shadow of doubt on all of the toxicological evidence. In the end, based on his own self-incriminating testimony, Buchanan was still convicted in 1895, but the jury did not take the toxicological evidence into consideration.

This forensic fiasco inspired toxicologists to look for new methods of demonstrating the presence of alkaloids in the body—so a setback became a means for improvement. Dr. William Henry Willcox was the first to promote the idea of using the melting point and crystallization patterns of the alkaloid as an identifier. However, even this method had its problems, as some alkaloids proved to have similar melting points. Thus, melting points and crystallization could only be used in combination with other qualitative tests. More and better tests were developed, and by 1955, there were thirty tests for morphine alone.

Another problem for the toxicologist in the second quarter of the twentieth century was synthetic alkaloids, developed with the growth of pharmaceutical chemistry, which required entirely new methods of separation from the body extract and a different means of identification. One of the responses to this problem was from A. S. Curry. He proposed the use of column, or paper, chromatography as a means of separation based on molecular size or polarity. The method makes colorless alkaloids visible and easily separated onto filter paper.

This was a good thing, because with industrialization, poisons of all types for both suicide and murder were becoming available to millions in the form of cleansers, medicines, and pesticides, and their many variations were multiplying.

5

As featured on *Cold Case Files* in "The Perfect Murder," Dr. William Sybers did double duty as the medical examiner in Bay County, Florida. His wife, Kay, had been in good health and was only fifty-two when she suddenly died on May 30, 1991. Sybers concluded that she had died of a heart attack. He reported that she had complained early that morning of chest pains, and since she was overweight, no one questioned this. Sybers had used a syringe, he said, to draw some of her blood for testing her blood sugar level, but had been unsuccessful. Deciding to forgo the required autopsy, he sent his wife directly to a funeral home and had her embalmed and prepared for transport to Iowa for burial.

But Sybers's colleagues insisted that an autopsy be performed, so he yielded. This procedure was conducted on June 1, and during this time the Florida Department of Law Enforcement received a tip that Sybers had murdered his wife. Three investigators attended the autopsy. Agent Scott Sanderson saw the needle mark on Kay's right arm, so he had another pathologist remove part of the embalmed tissue for a toxicology analysis at the crime lab. Because of the embalming fluid, they were unable to get reliable results, and Sybers said he no longer had the syringe. The death was initially ruled natural but this was later changed to "undetermined causes."

Yet Agent Sanderson was not satisfied, so he checked around and heard rumors about an affair that Sybers was having with a female lab technician. Phone records supported that possibility, but with no other leads, the case eventually went cold. One of the Sybers's sons, Tim, distraught over his mother's death, killed himself in 1993.

The investigation continued, and in 1994 forensic scientists provided a list of poisons that one might use for undetectable murder. Dr. Frederic Rieders of National Medical Services in Pennsylvania explained that potassium chloride was a good choice for murder and was in fact the third and final drug utilized in executions by lethal injection. The substance was indigenous to the human body and so was undetectable in a routine autopsy. In normal human blood, iron exists in a ratio of one to one with potassium. That ratio, Rieders said, should not be affected by embalming fluid, which contained no potassium or iron. It followed that if potassium had been administered, the ratio of potassium to iron would go up. In one of the specimens removed from Kay before burial, the ratio was eight parts of potassium to one part of iron. This indicated that potassium had been introduced into her system.

Some fluid that had been extracted from Kay's heart, which was mixed with embalming fluid, was sent to Dr. Rieders, and he used the blood ratio analysis to determine that Kay had been poisoned by potassium. That finding warranted a request for an exhumation to test other bodily tissues for the same potassium levels, but the family fought it. A district court granted the state the right to do the exhumation, but the family appealed, and a higher court ruled that the science behind Rieders's ideas was controversial and as yet unproven, so the family's wishes in this matter were to be respected. Kay Sybers was not exhumed.

Yet in 1997, Florida authorities indicted Dr. Sybers, so the toxicological search continued.

Next on the list of possible poisons was succinlycholine, which also causes an increase in potassium. Because it quickly broke down in the body and was undetectable, it was thought to be the perfect murder weapon. It paralyzes the muscles, including the diaphragm, the muscle that helps a person to breathe. In other words, someone injected with it will be aware that he or she is dying but be unable to get help. Forensic toxicologist Kevin Ballard was asked to screen for the drug in Kay. What he discovered was a profile of succinlymoncholine, a by-product of succinlycholine and an indication that the poison was present in Kay Sybers's body. Yet if succinlycholine was so unstable, the logical question was how Ballard had managed to find it after the body had been embalmed and the organ sample had been on a shelf for eight years. Ballard stated that the decision to embalm Kay right after she died had been fortuitous. The embalming process had actually helped to preserve the succinlymoncholine.

This discovery occurred just as Dr. Sybers's murder trial was set to begin in 2001. The jury found him guilty of first-degree murder. He was given a sentence of twenty-five years, but following an appeal that granted him a new trial based on the fact that the testing in the first trial had not been verified, he pleaded guilty in 2003 to a lesser charge of manslaughter. He was sentenced to a hefty fine and the two years he had already served.

6

For both alcohol and drug detection, the most state-of-the-art analysis will involve spectrometry and often some form of chromatography. The real workhorse of a crime lab is the gas chromatograph with mass spectrometry (GC/MS). Most things encountered at a crime scene are complex mixtures, and with this method they can be separated into their purest components. Thin-layer chromatography is also used, where the sample is placed in a vertical gel film and then subjected to a liquid solvent that breaks it into its constituent parts. With this method, tests can be done directly on the material under analysis rather than having to go through the tedious process of extraction.

For gas chromatography, a small amount of the suspect substance or unknown material is dissolved in a solvent and then injected by needle into a hollow tube. A flow of inert gas (helium or nitrogen) propels the heated mixture through the coiled glass tube, where a highly sensitive, computerized detector identifies the separate elements at the other end. Since each element moves at its own speed, as it crosses the "finish" line it can be identified. The amount of pure substance in the mixture is measured as well, producing a chart that offers a composite profile (via travel time measured in minutes). Comparison, or control, substances are also put through the GC. This helps to identify suspicious substances, such as an accelerant on a piece of charred wood when compared against wood without accelerant. GC can be used to identify many things, from poisons to drugs to explosives. It's even used for blood alcohol evaluations.

Linked with the mass spectrometer, the GC separates the sample into its component parts and the MS bombards the sample with electrons produced by a heated cathode, breaking it into electrically charged fragments. These fragments pass through the spectrometer, accelerated by an electric field. A magnetic field deflects them onto a circular path, the radius of which varies according to the mass of the fragment. As the magnetic field is increased, a detector linked to a computer records the energy spectrums. The position of each fragment on the spectrum measures its mass, and its intensity indicates its proportion in the sample. This comes through as a printed readout.

From one type of signature to another—those made by implements, machines, or weapons require a different type of laboratory analysis.

SEVEN

Mechanical Signatures

1

On June 2, 1976, Dr. Stephen Scher went out with his friend, lawyer Martin Dillon from Montrose, Pennsylvania, to shoot clay pigeons. Only Scher returned, claiming that Dillon was dead. They'd been walking to get some cigarettes, he said, when Marty had spotted a porcupine, grabbed Scher's Winchester16-gauge pump-action shotgun, run off after the animal, and tripped about 250 feet away and fallen onto the shotgun, which had accidentally killed him. Scher had found him facedown, lying atop his gun. Upon turning him over, he'd seen a gaping chest wound. Dillon's shoelaces were undone, so Scher had surmised that he'd stepped on one. Scher was so overcome that he'd smashed the gun against a tree.

Photos of the scene showed Dillon with his pant legs pulled up—an odd happenstance for someone who'd been running. There was also a clay pigeon near his hand. Yet the two men had both been close to the DA, so the death was quickly declared accidental, without any investigation, and closed.

At least, it was closed for everyone except Marty's father, Lawrence Dillon, who firmly believed that his son had not died by any accidental shooting. He thought it was suspicious when two years following the incident, Scher married Dillon's widow, Pat—a woman with whom he'd worked and with whom he'd been rumored before the incident to be having an affair. As town mayor, Lawrence Dillon pressured for an investigation, but resistance was strong. Yet this "closed" case was in fact only a cold case, just awaiting a review.

Years later, in 1992, Lawrence Dillon's efforts paid off. He hired a private detective to look into the matter and review the evidence. It turned out that there was blood spatter on Scher's clothing, along with a piece of flesh pierced by fibers on his pants—evidence that he had been standing closer to Dillon than he'd admitted. Dr. Isadore Mihalakis, a coroner and forensic pathologist, agreed to reexamine the case.

He looked at the death scene photo and wondered about the pant legs hiked up and the lacings on the boots. How could Dillon have landed in such a way while running? And if his boots had been unlaced and he was running, why were they still snug against the ankle instead of loose? Dillon also held a clay pigeon in his left hand, as if he'd been in the process of picking it up rather than running after a porcupine. None of what Mihalakis saw in the photo added up to the story that Scher had told. He thought it would be important to measure Dillon's arms to be sure he could have even reached the trigger by accident, and that meant exhuming the body. In the process, they would have another look at the wound and try to determine whether it had in fact been a contact wound, as the original pathologist had concluded.

Dillon's remains were exhumed in 1995 and were well preserved. A measurement of his arms against the type of shotgun he had used indicated that he could have reached the trigger, but the gun muzzle had to have been very close to him. There was no blackening around the wound to indicate a close-range shot, but there were tiny pellet markings ("scalloping"), so the investigators decided to try to duplicate the wound's appearance by shooting a similar type of weapon into a pig carcass, wrapped in a cotton shirt identical to the one that Dillon had been wearing that fateful day. They also compared the condition of the shotgun cup to determine what it would look like when the pellets began to open up during velocity at various distances from the target. When the pig was shot close up, the cup did not resemble the cup that had been found near Dillon. Yet when shot from a few feet away, it did. There was speculation that Dillon might have dropped and reached for the gun, grabbing it by the muzzle, but if he had, he would have had residue up his arm, which was not found on his skin or clothing. And the blood spatter on his trousers would hardly have occurred if he had fallen onto the gun.

The investigators' conclusion was that the muzzle of the shotgun that had killed Martin Dillon had been at least three and a half feet away, not an inch or two. In addition, no twig or branch could have accidentally pulled the trigger as Dillon pulled the gun toward him by the muzzle (which in any event no experienced hunter was likely to have done). The angle of the wound also strongly suggested that he'd been shot from above.

To see how the gun might have landed when falling, investigators dressed police cadets in padded clothing and had them run on rubber mats with a rope tied to one of their ankles. Someone would jerk the rope, and each time a cadet fell, the gun landed muzzle down. At no time did the gun flip and point the muzzle at a cadet.

An FBI lab analyst said that the high-speed blood spatter on the boots Scher had worn would have been left from blood flying hard at closer range than the distance Scher had described. There were also no close-range powder burns on Dillon's shirt, and the fine mist of blood on his boots suggested that he'd been sitting or crouching when shot. Investigators also concluded that if he had dropped the gun, it would not have gone off by accident, and if he had shot himself, there would have been blowback blood inside the barrel, and there was not.

The death was declared a murder, staged to look like an accident, and Dr. Scher was brought to trial. The scenario presented by the wound and blood spatter evidence was that Dillon had been crouching with a pigeon in his hand, readying the machine, when Scher shot him. The size of the round, designed for hunting not skeet shooting, indicated premeditation.

Confronted with this evidence, Scher confessed that he had shot Dillon, but he said that it had been accidental as they argued and then fought over the gun. However, Dillon was wearing earplugs when found, so Scher had had a "conversation that led to an argument" with a man who couldn't hear him. His attorney claimed Scher's due process had been violated, because many witnesses from 1976 had died. He also pointed out that the chest wound that had been incised could not be found when the body was exhumed again in 1996 for the defense pathologists to make their own examination.

Yet in 1997, Dr. Scher was convicted of first-degree murder and sentenced to life in prison. However, two years later, he was released from prison in a decision that has implications for the legal resolution of many other cold cases. The Pennsylvania appeals court agreed that Scher had been denied due process, because of a twenty-year delay, faded memories, dead witnesses, and lost evidence. The attorney general argued that Scher himself had delayed the investigation by misleading the police about what had happened in 1976. The case was appealed to the Pennsylvania Supreme Court in 2000 to have the conviction reinstated, and in August 2002 they upheld the first-degree murder conviction.

Then in 2004, a Superior Court ordered a new trial for Dr. Scher, based on how the presiding judge had handled the dismissal of a distraught juror during the first day of deliberations. On April 6, 2004, the attorney general's office announced that they will appeal the Superior Court decision. As of this writing, the case is undecided.

2

Guns leave two types of signatures: marks on a target and marks on ammunition. The analysis of both have a long history in forensic science, with emphasis on wound analysis.

While the study of wounds and the study of projectiles were

brought together early in the twentieth century under the banner of forensic medicine, it was clear that forensic pathologists would develop the science of wound and pattern analysis, while ballistics experts would concentrate on the specific mechanical marks made by guns. Together, these forensic professionals would develop into a coordinated team.

Gun wound analysis by a pathologist evaluates both the external wounds (entrance and exit) as well as where a bullet traveled through a body (trajectory path), as seen in *Cold Case Files* "Til Death Do Us Part."

In 1978, in Copperas Cove, Texas, police responded to a report of shots fired at the home of Jack and Sharon Reeves. Jack said that his wife had shot herself. They found her lying naked on the bed with a shotgun between her legs, and listed the death as a suicide.

But when another wife—a mail-order bride—disappeared sixteen years later, detectives in Reeves's new county of residence decided to reexamine the death of Jack's first wife. They looked at old photos of the scene, felt skeptical of the gun's position after a suicide, and decided to exhume the body. Bits of the shotgun pellets that took Sharon's life remained lodged in her organs, enabling the medical examiner to trace a clear trajectory path. His findings established the exact angle of the shotgun used to kill Sharon Reeves.

Detectives recreated Sharon Reeves's alleged suicide to see if it was physically possible for the victim to have actually pulled the trigger, and they determined that it was not. On March 21, 1995, they issued a warrant for Jack Reeves's arrest.

Just as he was going to trial, the body of his missing second wife was pulled from a shallow grave. He was convicted in both murders.

Forensic medicine has long had to deal with the size and nature of bullet wounds, specifically to determine whether someone has been shot accidentally, intentionally, or by his own hand. Exit wounds had to be differentiated from entrance wounds, and distances had to be measured between the gun and the wound. Unburned particles of powder that move through the gun barrel toward a target person hit the skin and leave certain telltale effects, as do gases that penetrate the wound and lift the skin from underneath. Pathologists had these formulas nearly worked out when the advent of smokeless powder during World War I forced many changes in the analyses.

In 1926 in Scotland, Donald Merrett reported his mother's suicide, and although she had survived for a few days after the shot to her head and had affirmed to a friend that she had not shot herself but had been shot by her thieving son, no one in authority questioned her for details. Once she died, her testimony was lost. But the son's behavior afterward alerted officials to the possibility that Mrs. Merrett had been murdered. While a doctor had found that the entry wound and trajectory path of the bullet were consistent with suicide, other physicians were not convinced. Yet the case appeared to be closed. At least it was closed for all but those who believed there was something amiss.

This was among the first cases that turned many forensic specialists from the study of wounds to the study of guns. Harvey Littlejohn had seen five hundred cases of suicide by shooting, and his student, Sydney Smith, had published his book *Text-Book in Forensic Medicine* in 1925. In it, he stated that ballistics was a branch of forensic medicine, not something to be left in the hands of gunsmiths. He had done numerous experiments that measured shooting range and had observed how bullets enter skin under many different conditions. He advocated using a suspect weapon and its ammunition to make comparison shots under conditions as close as possible to the original crime. Each weapon, he said, produced a characteristic pattern.

Smith asked Littlejohn to get the pistol used in the Merrett murder, along with its cartridges, and urged him to make some comparison shots from various distances. He could then examine these in the context of the powder marks left on the skin. Littlejohn fired the pistol at white paper from several different carefully measured distances. He then washed the sheets of paper, in case the doctors attending Mrs. Merrett had done so with her, and found that with close-range fire some residue stubbornly remained.

Another doctor, John Glaister, was brought into the case, and he and Littlejohn repeated the experiments with skin taken from an amputated human leg. When the gun was shot at close range, no amount of wiping would remove the powder burns. It was clear evidence that the gun had not been held close to the victim's head, and thus the death was not suicide.

Yet a celebrity expert witness swayed the jury and Merrett was not convicted. Nevertheless, twenty-five years later, he confessed, vindicating the claim that comparison tests done with a suspect weapon were the best means for making such determinations.

3

Barrels of guns are machine-bored into a cylinder, and cutters incise grooves into the barrel in a spiral pattern to impart a spin to bullets that pass through. Under a microscope, the cutter's edges are jagged and get worn, so they leave individual marks on the weapons being made. Those marks would show up on bullets, made of softer metals, as they spun and twisted through the barrel on their way out. In a semiautomatic, for example, the firing pin leaves a distinctive dent in the firing caps, imperfections in the breech leave a mark on the cartridge, the ejector mechanism also hits the cartridge, and rifling grooves scratch the bullet.

Different manufacturers developed different types of rifling and different numbers of grooves and lands (the raised areas between the grooves). The number of spirals through the barrel, their angle, and the direction of the grooves' twist to the right or left are all factors that affect how a bullet may be marked. Because each time a bullet is fired, there is some slight wear on the inside of the barrel, bullets fired from the same gun will show closely similar striations. On bullets encased in cartridges, even more marks are made, helping investigators connect a bullet to a gun.

Firearms evidence identification via both the firearms themselves and the projectiles fired, which would become the field of forensic ballistics, was born in 1835 in England when the unique ridge on a bullet taken from a victim was linked with a bullet mold in the suspect's home. Confronted with the evidence, the suspect confessed.

At first, the ballistics experts were gunsmiths, who knew how weapons were made. They were able to testify about whether certain shots had been fired from certain weapons. In 1889, Professor Alexandre Lacassagne removed a bullet from a victim and observed seven clear streaks on it. He studied the markings to try to match them to the revolver found in the suspect's home. The suspect weapon was placed in a collection of similar revolvers and based solely on a study of the bullet, he picked the one that he believed had shot the bullet. He was correct. On this basis, the man was convicted. While it was a primitive method and may well have been in error, it was a start in the right direction for scientific ballistics testimony (which hopefully did not cost an innocent man his life).

The first time an expert proved in court that a specific gun was used for a murder was in America in 1902. Oliver Wendell Holmes conducted the trial. He had read a book about firearms identification, so he called a gunsmith to test fire the alleged murder weapon into a wad of cotton wool. He then used a magnifying lens to match marks on the bullet from the victim to the test-fired bullet, and these he showed to the jury.

Yet the "science" had to undergo much refinement before courts in general accepted it. No one had yet characterized the factors to be learned from the many gun barrels in existence.

In 1905 in Germany, Richard Kockel suggested that impressions be taken both of bullets used in crimes and of test missiles. To get what amounted to negatives of the entire surface area undistorted by curvature, he froze the area and rolled it in a mixture of softened zinc white and wax. The results were more precise than anyone had been able to achieve with photographs, but in another decade, researchers had turned away from bullet impressions and toward examinations of the distinctive marks left on cartridges by firing pins, breechblocks, extractors, and ejectors.

To develop the science of firearms comparison, the most important tool was the microscope. The earliest crude microscopes were invented in the 1600s, allowing a magnification of ten to twenty times, but images were still blurred. The invention of the compound microscope that relied on multiple lenses fused together improved the situation, as optics magnification and clarity increased exponentially. The science of ballistics itself inspired the invention of another device, the comparison microscope.

It was the year 1920. Charles E. Waite had an ambition. Concerned about the growing number of murders that occurred each day in America, and the percentage that went unsolved, he hoped to collect enough data to build a reliable means for determining from bullets the type of weapon used. He wanted to catalogue all weapons ever manufactured in terms of construction, date of manufacture, caliber, number, twist and proportion of the lands and grooves, and type of ammunition used. He visited one gun manufacturing firm after another and acquired their cooperation. It was a monumental task, but after three years, he had data on almost all of the types of guns manufactured in the U.S. since the 1850s. He saw that no type of gun was exactly identical to any other, and he was soon able to tell from which type of gun a bullet had been fired.

Then he learned that two-thirds of the guns in America came from Europe. He could either give up his ambition as hopeless or go and do in Europe what he had just done in America. Like anyone who is at least near the halfway point of a challenging goal, he decided to persist. At the end of his year in Europe, he had collected over fifteen hundred more models of firearms to test and catalogue.

To look at the peculiarities left during the manufacturing process, Waite needed a microscope. Optician Max Poser developed a device fitted with bullet holders and measuring scales. Waite looked for associates in this work and found John H. Fisher, who invented the helixometer, through which one could inspect inside a gun barrel, and a device for accurately measuring the lands and grooves; and Philip O. Gravelle, whose extensive work in microphotography and whose need for precise comparisons inspired the comparison microscope.

No matter how quick he might be, Gravelle did not trust his

memory to provide accurate results as he placed successive bullets under a microscope, so he combined two microscopes into a single unit to be able to closely observe two bullets side by side.

Into this Bureau of Forensic Ballistics came Calvin Goddard, whose work on identifying the weapons used in the 1929 St. Valentine's Day Massacre in Chicago would inspire the nation's first multi-investigation crime lab. He advised the FBI in 1932 when they set up theirs, and their first piece of equipment was the comparison microscope.

4

Firearms these days are of two basic types: handheld and shoulder, with many variations of each type. Handheld pistols include single-shot and multiple-shot models, such as revolvers and self-loading pistols. Shoulder firearms have long barrels and include rifles, machine repeaters, and smoothbore shotguns.

"Rifled" weapons (rifles and many handguns) fire single bullets, and the weapon may also eject shell casings. If no casings are found at the scene, it may indicate that the shooter used a revolver, which retains spent cartridges until manually reloaded. Smoothbore shotguns fire multiple pellets.

The caliber of a bullet is determined by the bore's diameter, expressed in hundredths of an inch or in millimeters. Bullets found at the scene (or in a victim) offer plenty of vital information, as depicted in the *Cold Case Files* episode "A Rose Among Thorns."

On Sept 21, 1981, in southwestern England, an intruder entered the home of Juliet Rowe and shot her in the back, head, and chest with a Colt .22-caliber weapon. Three shell casings were left behind.

Although crime scene investigators lifted 333 fingerprints from around the house and found ten that could not be linked to anyone who lived there, they had no suspect for comparison. Rifles and pistols were seized from people in the area and over ten thousand were test fired and compared against the shell casings found at the scene. They found no match.

Eight years later, widower Gerald Rowe was approached by a stranger who introduced himself as Keith Rose. He pressed Rowe for information about the murder, so Rowe left, but then six weeks later he saw that Rose had been arrested for the kidnapping and ransom of the son of a prominent businessman. Rowe called the police.

Cold case detectives reopened Juliet's case and ran Rose's prints against their ten unknowns. Three of them matched Rose. Rose provided a story about having been in the house for legitimate purposes, so detectives turned to the shell casings to look for more evidence. They realized that some of the bullets used were rare Remington Yellow Jacket rounds. Only a few thousand had been in circulation at the time of the murder. Yet a few months before, Rose had purchased two hundred rounds.

Investigators still needed the murder weapon. They learned that in 1981 Rose had owned four guns. Three had been test fired and eliminated during the initial investigation, but a Colt .22, which had been in pieces, was never tested. Superintendent Paul Sincock recovered that gun from a local gun shop where Rose had stored it and found that the pieces appeared to have been soaked in some corrosive material. They seemed untestable, but the magazine was still intact. Ballistics experts noted a strange mark on the casings recovered from the scene, so Sincock asked the FBI and the Colt Company for assistance. Their analysts found a flaw in the magazine and ejection mechanism that had made the unusual mark on the casings—before being ejected, the bullet had struck the lip of the magazine.

They placed the magazine into a working Colt .22, duplicating the suspect gun's flaw, and fired it on a test range. The test-fire marks were identical to those found on the shell casings collected at the crime scene. That flaw had created a unique "fingerprint" for the gun. Rose was convicted of murder.

* * *

Ballistics experts examine the different parts of a bullet: the bullet itself; the compartment containing the propellant (black or smokeless powder); the cartridge casing that wraps around all of this and is stamped with a manufacturer's mark and caliber; and the metal cap at the cartridge head, containing the primer.

When triggered, the gun's firing pin hits the cartridge at the primer, or explosive. That charge burns the gunpowder, which builds pressure and forces the bullet outward. At the same time, the cartridge moves backward against the weapon's breech, stamping an impression of the impact onto the cartridge head. In addition, the mechanisms that extract and eject the shell leave their own characteristic marks. Whatever scratches the cartridge picks up are essentially unique to that gun.

If a spent bullet is recovered, finding the point of impact is essential to tracing its trajectory path from the gun barrel. An investigator might achieve this with a series of strings or by sighting through the bullet holes. Calculations are then made for computerized reconstructions.

Matching an ejected casing to a gun may mean shooting the suspect gun (if recovered) in the lab's firing range. Then a comparison can be done between the casing from the scene and the one shot by the scientist. The firing range can also serve to measure the distance from the muzzle to the target to try to determine the distance in the crime, based on the size of the hole and the diameter of gunpowder residue. If the gun is close enough for the residue to hit something before being pulled downward by gravity, the residue leaves distinct patterns, with the size in diameter depending on distance from the target. Replicating the size of a burn by trying shots from different distances yields the actual distance measurement.

Since the test bullet must be recovered, the gun is fired either into a tank of water, cotton batting, or a box of thick gel. Then it's compared to the suspect bullet for the telltale microscopic scratches of the gun's fingerprint. This happened in the following case, from *Cold Case Files* "Vintage Murders."

After the execution-style rape-murder of Dawn Magyar in the early 1960s, Michigan State Police recovered three .22-caliber slugs and placed them on a comparison microscope. The ballistics expert determined that all had been fired from the same firearm. Investigators also got a DNA profile from semen, but had no suspect and no suspect gun.

A year later, a .22-caliber revolver was found in a river, inside of which were three spent shells, two Remington and one Winchester. The gun was traced to a pawnshop in Yuma, Arizona, and then to Robert Shaw, who had purchased it. A driver's license check was run in Michigan for all Robert Shaws that would have been old enough to purchase the gun at the time of the murder. There were twenty-nine, so detectives went to all twenty-nine addresses.

One of these people told detectives that he had been stationed in the army in Yuma, Arizona, from 1964 until 1966. The gun was purchased in 1965. He admitted that he had purchased a similar firearm from a pawnshop in Yuma, but he did not know where it was. However, he was not a DNA match. Yet he recalled a Jerald Wingeart, who might have taken it, and when police recovered that man's trash, the DNA from cigarette butts was a match to semen found in the victim.

Wingeart admitted to having sex with her, but said it was consensual. The semen samples indicated that the sexual contact had occurred at most six hours before Magyar's death. Wingeart was sentenced to a term of life in prison.

If the gun is not recovered, there's another approach. It's possible to tell something about the make of a gun from the type of cartridge case or bullet found. Smith & Wesson guns have five lands that twist to the right, for example, and the six lands and grooves in a Colt .32-caliber revolver twist to the left. Technicians examine how the lines of striation angle from the base to the nose of a bullet, and they add the number of marks around it. For microcomparisons, crime labs generally have a supply of bullet types on hand and access to a computer database.

On November 25, 1993, in Kingsley Lake, Florida, Greg Wood, thirty-five, was found dead, shot close to the head. His belt had been cut, and his two guns and wallet were missing. This was no hunting accident.

Five days earlier, there had been a similar incident in the Osceola National Forest, involving Don Hill, sixty-three. A task force was formed, but without physical evidence to work with, they had few options. The stolen guns were entered into a database for the National Crime Information Center, which tracks stolen weapons from around the country, but that produced no leads.

It was four years before something came up. In another county, records clerk Gloria Southern entered a pawnshop ticket for a magnum .357 into her computer, which linked to the NCIC. It turned up as stolen—Greg Wood's gun. A woman had pawned it, and her boyfriend, Larry Watts, had a record for drug offenses. This led investigators on a convoluted track of the gun changing hands several times and ending up with two brothers who were hunters, Paul and Mikel Tyler. They seemed like possible suspects, but they had an alibi. They admitted, however, that they had purchased the gun from their cousin, Jimmie Ray Beagle. When detectives found him, he confessed to the homicides, but then locked himself in a restroom and committed suicide.

Crime lab computers can be networked to statewide and nationwide databases (even international), similar to an AFIS system for fingerprints. One is called Drugfire, sponsored by the FBI. The Integrated Ballistics Information System, IBIS by Forensic Technology, also offers automated comparisons of evidence images.

Thus, when there's a shooting in one locale and the casing is recovered, its image can be recorded into a database. If the gun is recovered, it may be test fired and that spent casing used. To get a comparison on the way that gun's firing pin left an impression, the ejected casing is placed in a device with a video camera that links to a computer. An image is taken of the casing and run through the database to find the closest matches. These comparison images can be moved around on the screen to get better side-by-side views. Examiners eliminate all but the most likely candidates, which go to a microscope for a more precise comparison by an experienced expert. The computer doesn't do it all, but it does cut down on the amount of work.

At times a spent bullet is too damaged for comparison purposes, but clues from it may lead to evidence that helps to solve the case, sometimes in a surprising manner, as happed in the next cold case file.

In the spring of 1970, Doreen Morby, thirty-four, was raped and shot to death in her home in Ontario, Canada. Two weeks later, Helen Ferguson was similarly attacked. Twenty-two-caliber slugs were recovered from both victims and matched as originating from the barrel of the same gun. Semen collected at each crime scene revealed the killer's blood type, but there were no suspects or leads, so both cases went cold.

Then a quarter of a century later, Ronald Glen West was arrested, convicted, and sent to prison on five counts of armed robbery. His home was sold and the new owners began to renovate the basement. As they ripped out ceiling boards, they found a hidden envelope that contained two 1970 firearm permits for Ron West for a nine-shot .22-caliber pistol. They turned these over to the police, who recalled the twenty-five-year-old crimes and learned that West used to vacation near where Doreen Morby had lived. That heated the case right up.

With information from the permits, detectives contacted the Provincial Weapons Enforcement Unit and asked for their assistance in tracing the weapon's serial number. With that, they tracked it to its current owner, secured it, and shipped it to a lab in Toronto for analysis. Finn Nielsen had been with the lab for thirty years and had examined the very bullets that had killed the two women. He now test fired West's gun and each shot revealed a pattern of striation on the bullets that was unique to that weapon. However, the fragmented nature of the original slugs made any meaningful comparison difficult. They needed more evidence than just the bullets. Surprisingly, they still had the semen.

On March 26, 1999, Ron West submitted to a court order for a DNA test, which clearly implicated him in both rape-murder incidents. Thanks to a fortuitous discovery and the registration of a gun, thirty-one years after his crimes, Ron West pleaded guilty to two counts of murder.

In some cases, the police measure lead content to try to determine the manufacturer of a suspect bullet, possibly to see if it came from a box of bullets associated with the suspect. If the lab can make a match, experts claim that the two bullets are analytically indistinguishable—a strong statement. In other words, the lead content is so close between the two that the odds of this bullet having been in that box of bullets are astronomical. It seemed like an appropriate means of comparison until a recent study, funded by the FBI, challenged it.

Late in 2003, the National Academy of Sciences concluded that some of the FBI's assumptions about chemical composition and their techniques for matching bullets were too flawed to be admissible as evidence. The Bureau's chemists were urged to stop the practice known as data chaining, which involves matching the lead content from bullet A to B, and from B to C, to conclude that bullets A and C are a match. An Iowa State University study showed that just because two bullets have similar chemical compositions does not prove they have the same origin. That is, chemical composition is not a chemical fingerprint, so the statistical significance often cited in the past for the results of this procedure might have to be more conservatively described. "The leap from a match to equal origin is enormous," said one researcher at the facility, "and not justified given the available information about bullet lead evidence."

5

Firearms examiners are also often tool mark examiners. Ballistics and tool marks are usually analyzed in the same department of a crime lab, because some of the same instruments, such as the comparison microscope, are used to examine both items.

Tool marks are typed as compression tool marks (in soft material), sliding tool marks (showing striations), and cutting tool marks (a combination of the first two). The quality and retention of a tool mark impression is determined by the surface against which it is made. Soft metals are most retentive, as are many plastics and painted surfaces. Hard surfaces generally do not retain tool marks. A study in 1952 concluded that among five thousand chisels, no two made the same mark, indicating that even individual tools can have a distinct signature. That same can be said for a machine that produces an item, such as in the following case, from *Cold Case Files* "The Cuff Link."

In 1986 in Ingham County, Michigan, the body of thirty-six-year-old Jeanette Kirby was found with three stab wounds to her chest. She had been bound with police-style flex cuffs. Then a second body surfaced not far away and this victim was identified as Cynthia Miller. An ex-con implicated himself and another man in that murder, but each had an alibi for the day Jeanette Kirby was murdered, so they were not investigated for that crime. Soon the Kirby homicide went cold—and stayed that way until five years later, when the police made an interesting discovery.

David Draheim was convicted of an attempted kidnapping and rape. When he was arrested, police found flex cuffs inside his car. They soon learned that his roommate, Mark Greko, had once purchased an old police car. While installing a radio in the car, he found a plastic bag full of flex cuffs. He gave some to Draheim, and those that he had kept for himself proved to be identical in brand and manufacture to those found on Jeanette Kirby. However, thousands of such cuffs had been produced and sold in the United States. That meant that someone had to take a closer look.

The idea with tool mark analysis is that, whether a handheld tool or a machine made the mark, certain parts wear down through use, and edges acquire nicks and microscopic ridges known as striae that individualize the impressions the tool edge leaves. The more pronounced an imperfection, the better for analysis. A questioned tool mark, such as that placed on these plastic cuffs during their manufacture, is compared to the machine or tool that is suspected of having made it. However, as a tool continues to be used, it wears down further and can become less valuable for evidence examination.

Scott Marier, a forensic tool mark examiner for the State of Michigan, got the job of trying to make a match in the Kirby case. He focused on the small metal tabs on the cuffs that were used as a locking mechanism and the small scratches found on each tab—tool marks created when the tab was machine cut at the processing plant. The match told Marier that the tabs were cut in the same plant by the same machine.

In January of 2001, investigator Pete Ackerly visited the manufacturing plant of Thomas and Betts. With the help of plant officials, he identified the actual machine that had cut the tabs used in the two cuffs. But the question was how many cuffs could the blade cut before it began to wear down and its pattern of striation changed? Ackerly took one sample, which consisted of five flex cuffs, and then looked at every hundredth sample made, going through the first one thousand. After that he took a sample of five after every one thousand samples, until he had gone through a total production run of thirty-two to thirty-four thousand.

Marier put them under a microscope and noted the rate of change in the markings over the course of the machine's run. During the examination, he found that there were significant changes in markings between one and one thousand samples. That meant he could determine when the cuffs associated with Draheim (from his roommate's bag) and the cuffs from Jeanette Kirby had been cut. It turned out that they had been cut by the same machine within a thousand samples of each other. That discovery narrowed the odds considerably.

In April of 2001, David Draheim was finally charged with murder in the death of Jeanette Kirby, and his past use of flex cuffs in another crime contributed to the evidence against him. The verdict was guilty of murder in the second degree.

*   *   *

In other uses of tool mark comparison, tools used to pry open a door or window, break a lock, or carve something at a crime scene can be similarly analyzed, but the added feature is that something from the scene itself may now be present on the tool and can be matched back to the scene.

Crime scene investigators look for such marks whenever there is a break-in or other type of fresh damage. They will photograph the marks for computer enhancement and for their location in the crime scene, as well as document them on a map. To get these marks back to the lab, they may have to saw off part of a door or window. It's also possible to use a resin to make a cast of the mark, which will provide a clear impression.

If making a comparison via testing might damage the suspect tool, examiners will use an identical tool first to make sure they have the right kind. While they will not acquire the tool's unique signature this way, they can at least narrow down the range of tools they want to examine. Test marks are generally made using the same surface, and the marks (generally made against soft metal surfaces) must duplicate as much as possible the original mark. Comparison with similar tools helps to distinguish class characteristics shared by other such tools and unique characteristics that help to leave that tool's special "fingerprint."

In deciding whether or not they have a match, examiners look for points of similarity, and the more they find, the more weight that evidence has in the case.

Guns and tools leave the distinct signature of machines. But there are other types of impressions that also require expertise in evaluation and comparison.

EIGHT

Reading Impressions

1

In 1969, Amado Hermicello, forty-six, was found dead in an alley in San Jose, his wallet missing, his skull fractured, and his face bruised. On his forehead was a small abrasion, but no one could determine what had made it. The crime was written off as a robbery, but the family refused to accept that. They suspected Jack Burns, the bartender at the Derby, but when witnesses would not speak out, the case went cold and stayed that way for twenty-seven years.

Then one day in 1996, Hermicello's daughter, Lisa Chairez, read in a newspaper that the San Jose Police Department was forming a Cold Case Investigative Unit, so she contacted them and talked with Detective Will Manion. He agreed to reexamine the case. He looked at the old photos and noticed the unusual abrasion. That didn't appear to be the work of a mugger. Then he looked carefully at crime scene photos, as well as photos from inside the Derby. Looking specifically for something that could have made such a mark, he spotted a Miller Lite beer sign on a wall just inside the Derby's front door.

A raised pattern along the bottom of this sign seemed to match the abrasion on the victim's forehead. The detectives returned to former witnesses to ask some pointed questions. One man finally confirmed what the family had suspected, that the bartender had gotten rough with the victim, and that it had not been a random mugging. He'd been killed accidentally and the witnesses had covered for the offender. Jack Burns died before investigators could confront him.

Making the comparison between a weapon and a wound, such as in this cold case file, is called pattern injury recognition, and this specialization involves not only a strong working knowledge of the injuries certain weapons make, but also the ability to notice injuries that are the result of some unusual implement. Most murders are fairly straightforward, committed with guns, knives, or by asphyxiation, but when a blunt instrument is involved, it can leave bruises that provide a way to individualize the attack and lead to the attacker. However, unless the weapon is found, there may be no way to make the match, since the ability to recognize patterns relies on having a number of similar samples, and that is not usually the case with a unique imprint. Nevertheless, keeping in mind the bruise patterns can help to solve a cold case, even years later. That's what happened in the *Cold Case Files* episode "Murder on the Menu."

On December 15, 1978, in Stearns County, Minnesota, a woman and three of her children were slaughtered. The children were shot to death with a shotgun, but the mother was hit as well with a blunt instrument. There was one survivor. Eleven-year-old Billy Huling, who had played dead when the killer came into his room, ran from the home for his life. When the crime was discovered, investigators searched the house and found nothing but shell casings. The weapon used to batter Alice Huling could not be found and her bruises were too unusual to explain.

A few days later, in a neighboring county, a deputy ran a check on the car of a man who was harassing a waitress at the Clear Water Plaza Truck Stop. The license check indicated that the car had been stolen. The man inside, Joe Ture, was arrested for auto theft. Among the items found inside the car were handwritten lists that included names of women, many of them waitresses. There was also a ski mask, a twenty-seven-inch metal bar wrapped in black patterned vinyl, and a toy Hot Wheels Bat Mobile. No links were developed between Ture and the Huling murders at that point, although one of the Huling victims had been a waitress.

Eleven days after the murder of his family, Billy underwent hypnosis to try to recall some clue to the killer's identity. He remembered that from inside his sleeping bag, he had heard his two sisters being shot. Then the man had approached his room and he had hidden deeper inside the bag. The killer left. Billy had seen nothing, so as much as the police fervently wanted to solve it, the case went cold.

Waitress Marlyss Wohlenhaus had also been killed in Minnesota that same year. Another area waitress, Diane Edwards, was murdered three years later, in 1981. Ture was investigated for both crimes, but there was no evidence with which to bring charges. One investigator indicated that Ture had confessed to the Wohlenhaus murder and had described a family massacre, but a call to officials from the Ford Motor Company turned up work records that indicated that Joe Ture had been working at one of their plants at the time Marlyss Wohlenhaus was killed. Thus, he could not be a suspect. No one checked his description of the Huling home with Billy, or the fact the Billy's sister had worked as a waitress.

So two waitresses in the same area were dead. A third was also murdered, along with her family. There were no leads until Joseph Ture pulled a thirty-year prison stretch during the 1990s for three unrelated crimes and decided to talk. He offered a confession to the Wohlenhaus murder in trade for incarceration in a state mental hospital.

Leery of false confessions, cold case detectives asked Ford Motor Company to locate the actual time card for the date in question. It turned out that Ture's father, also named Joe Ture, had been working there at the time. There was no record showing Joe Ture Jr., at work. In fact, when he worked, he was on the night shift, which would have allowed him ample opportunity to have committed the murder anyway—so he had no alibi.

On the third page of his confession to the Wohlenhaus killing, Ture mentioned a little girl who had seen him. Although this was not a detail from that investigation, the police took notice. At the time of the Huling murders, they had taken a statement from an eight-year-old girl who had been walking by the entrance to their long driveway. She had seen a "cream color little car" race out in a manner that threw gravel all over her. It was a confidential detail, never published, and although Ture appeared to have confused two crimes, he was now implicated in the Huling murders. That statement made the detectives reexamine the contents of Ture's stolen car.

They tracked down Billy Huling and he identified the toy Bat Mobile as his. He had left it on the kitchen table the night of the murders and had not seen it afterward.

That was the link they needed. Now they had a suspected murder weapon as well. Dr. Michael McGee, medical examiner and forensic pathologist, was a specialist in pattern injury recognition. He examined an elongated bruise on Alice Huling's autopsy photos. It had a cylindrical or tubular appearance, along with a distinct upper and lower border. In the midst of it were small, punctuated areas of hemorrhage. This suggested to McGee that whatever object had struck her was long, probably metal, and had a rounded edge and a series of circular or oval depressions. He examined the vinyl-wrapped bar found in Ture's possession and saw that the small holes presented in the surface of the wrapping matched the small focal areas of bruising and the abrasion on the surface of the body.

In the case of the Huling family massacre, Joseph Ture was found guilty in 1999 on four counts of murder and sentenced to four consecutive life terms. Since there had been no deal offered on this series of murders, Ture ended up in prison for life.

2

Murder leaves telltale marks of any instrument used, whether hands, teeth, guns, knives, or blunt instruments. Forensic pathologists are trained to know the differences in terms of bruises and puncture wounds. They must find and confirm the cause and manner of death, and for that they need to be able to identify the telltale marks.

One case that involved the ability to read impressions on skin threw the emerging science of forensic medicine into a crisis, with experts challenging experts. On the afternoon of April 5, 1905, a woman brought to a hospital in Paris a baby that appeared to be suffering from recent suffocation. The child had been left in the care of Jeanne Weber, a relative. The doctor found a reddish mark on its neck, and he learned that four babies had died from apparent suffocation among relatives in the Weber family. Jeanne Weber, thirty, was always involved. Her own son and two daughters had died. Then it was found that three years earlier, two other children had died while in Jeanne's care. The diagnoses varied from diphtheria to convulsions to cramps.

But this time she was charged with murder.

In January 1906, Jeanne Weber appeared before a court known as the Seine Assizes, where Dr. Leon Thoinot, the government's pathologist and the person in charge of the exhumations of four of the children, was to give an assessment. He was considered a man of science and this was a moment where the examining magistrate expected science to deliver. He was aware of the past eighty years' study of the marks left by manual strangulation. In 1888, a Dr. Langreuter had opened the skulls of fresh corpses, scooped out the brains, and watched what happened inside as his assistant choked the corpses or used cords to strangle them. He recorded it all for other forensic physicians, and much was now known about the various types of indicators in this sort of crime. They could also determine when a murdered man had been hanged to make it look like a suicide. A victim of manual strangulation would show specific bruises on the neck and dotlike facial and muscle hemorrhages.

With all of this information available, and with the condition of the exhumed children, the examining magistrate felt certain that the famous doctor would provide more than enough evidence against the child killer. However, Thoinot reported that his tests on the corpses were negative.

This seemed to fly in the face of what witnesses and examining doctors for the children had indicated. All the circumstantial evidence pointed to murder, but forensic science apparently could not support it.

Weber was acquitted, and reporters hailed science as a means of victory for the innocent. It had shown itself superior to testimony and detective work. For the moment.

Under another name, Jeanne Weber went on to become governess to a man with three small children, and a year later one of them died from "convulsions." Yet the telltale red ring was clear around the child's neck. Jeanne's past was revealed and she was again arrested. Yet Dr. Thoinot still rejected the cause of death as strangulation, despite the inch-wide red marks on the dead child's neck. Jeanne was acquitted once again, and the scientists congratulated themselves.

Yet the next time, she was caught, quite red-handed as it were. In 1908, she asked an innkeeper if his son might sleep in her room, as she was anxious at night. After the boy went to her, the family heard him screaming and burst into the room to find him dead with blood streaming from his mouth. Jeanne was pacing the room, her clothing, hands, and face stained with the child's blood. The examining doctor was determined not to make any mistakes that would be caught by Thoinot, so his documentation via photography was exhaustive. He found the deep groove on the boy's throat that supported strangulation, as well as traces of fingernails digging into the skin. He also learned that not long before that incident, Weber had been dismissed by an employer for attempting to strangle another child. The examining doctor determined that the victim he had just seen had died from manual strangulation, assisted by a handkerchief twisted under the chin.

Now the people turned against forensic science, believing that if its leading figures could so badly mistake the clear indications of a serial murderess, they weren't much good. What the public did not consider was that sometimes an eminent doctor let his reputation, along with his pride, override what science was telling him. The

Jeanne Weber case created a crisis for this budding science in the courtroom.

Madame Weber did not get a new trial. Rather than admit to their earlier mistake, the doctors now decided that she had become insane from the stress of all the suspicions and had committed only the last murder; her motive—sexual ecstasy. She was committed to an asylum, where she died trying to strangle herself.

For forensic medicine, it was a sign that even the most trained scientist is fallible and that improvements had to be made. That is in fact what occurred, as biologists used better microscopes over the years to study the effects of strangulation in human tissues, even in the structure of the cells themselves. It was a daunting lesson.

3

Traumas to the skin are classified as either sharp or blunt, with blunt trauma further divided into non-firearms and firearms. Trauma may also be classed as either penetrating (gunshot, knife) or non-penetrating (collision, fall).

Not all gunshots are alike. Different calibers of bullets and different types of guns and rifles leave distinctive marks. A gun's distance from a victim can be calculated by examining for evidence of powder burns or stippling on the skin and the size of the entrance hole. Shotguns fired at close range make a single large wound, while guns fired from a distance leave pelletlike scatter wounds. Entrance wounds are typically smaller than exit wounds, unless the exit wound is shored or supported by firm material.

Knife wounds, too, carry a narrative. Superficial cuts, known as hesitation marks, can indicate a suicide attempt or a killer with no real experience—or even a struggle with the knife. The shape and depth of a cut can reveal whether the weapon had a single cutting edge or was double-edged; angle analysis can help to reconstruct the incident. Force is calculated by depth, and intensity of attack can be revealed in the number of stab wounds, as can intent to kill.

Ligatures and hands produce distinctly different bruise patterns on the neck and throat, and many ligatures show clear homogenous indentations. Even if the skin is not marked, bruising in the tissues underneath and the condition of the hyoid bone can still tell the tale.

Lacerations are broken skin made from some kind of cutting instrument or a very hard blow with a blunt object. They might reveal something about the instrument used.

Bruises, or contusions, occur from weapon blows that traumatize blood vessels beneath the skin. Their coloring can indicate how fresh the wound is, and the shape may be a guide toward identifying the weapon—especially if it's distinct.

Yet sometimes weapons are used that cannot be easily identified. An early episode of *Cold Case Files*, which involved a celebrity, showed how baffling that can be.

Victoria Berry arrived at the apartment of former *Hogan's Heroes* star Bob Crane, forty-nine, in Scottsdale, Arizona. The door was ajar that June afternoon in 1978, but it was dark inside. She found Crane on his blood-spattered bed, with the left side of his skull crushed in. An electrical cord was wrapped around his neck.

Lieutenant Ron Dean headed up the initial investigation. He saw a trail of blood down the hallway that led to the front door. Crane had not moved after being hit, which indicated that he had likely been attacked while he slept. The killer had probably been someone who had access to the place and was familiar with the apartment.

While Dean was there, the phone rang and the person calling was a man named John Carpenter, a close friend of Crane's. He called twice more within three hours, but never asked why a police officer was in the apartment. On a hunch, authorities impounded Carpenter's rental car. There appeared to be drops of blood inside, and a blood smear on the door panel. These were tested for blood type, which matched Crane's type B. Only 10 percent of the population has this type.

Investigators reviewed Carpenter's relationship with Crane, which involved the two men in what appeared to be a playboy lifestyle. They picked up women together, but Carpenter seemed to be clinging to Crane. One woman indicated that Crane was trying to change his lifestyle and that Carpenter was not happy about it. During the evening before Crane's death, witnesses say they had argued at a club.

But blood spots in a rental car, which could have been made by any number of other customers, were insufficient evidence. Just as problematic was the difficulty with identifying the murder weapon. Crane's skull had been crushed with a blunt instrument that had left an injury impression not clearly recognizable by those who were experienced with pattern injuries. In fact, he had been hit twice with this instrument. Nothing in the apartment could be matched to it, and there were no other leads, so the case went cold.

Then in 1990, detective Jim Raines was assigned. He wanted to analyze the blood spots for a DNA profile, but since the biological evidence had not been refrigerated, the analysis was inconclusive. Next, he turned to the wound analysis. Since there were clear bloodstain patterns on the sheet next to Crane, Raines considered that the weapon may have been placed there after hitting Crane, so he asked a bloodstain expert to compare the autopsy photos of the wound impression to the stains. From the elongated and rounded shape, the expert identified the murder weapon as possibly being a camera tripod—an item that was missing from Crane's apartment. If delivered with sufficient force, it could have produced the long, deep laceration on Crane's skull that had resulted from the initial blow.

Investigators also found photographs of the inside of the rental car and saw what appeared to be human tissue—not just blood—on a door panel. While there was no tissue in the evidence bags stored with the case, the photograph was proof that brain matter had been inside the car. They arrested Carpenter for murder and obtained the testimony of five pathologists to the effect that the item in the photo was human tissue.

The trial lasted seven weeks, but due to lack of actual physical evidence, Carpenter was acquitted.

4

Besides weapons, some attackers bite their victims, and forensic bite mark analysis involves the ability to make comparisons of skin impressions with a set of teeth. Bite marks in human tissue vary in the quality of the defined area, especially if the bite was not hard or the victim was in motion. Biting into fatty areas leaves a less defined impression than biting into skin over muscle. Bite marks made before death will have a different appearance than postmortem impressions, which have no associated bruising.

An early bite mark case that came into court in 1968 set the precedent for admissibility.

Linda Peacock was a fifteen-year-old schoolgirl from Biggar, Scotland, and she had not come home. Officials discovered her body in the local cemetery. She had been strangled and beaten, and her bra and blouse were in disarray. On her right breast was an odd bruise. Since the bruise appeared to have been made in the struggle, numerous photographs were taken of it. Analysis indicated that whoever had killed the girl had bitten her hard. Investigators brought in Dr. Warren Harvey, an odontologist, and he confirmed that this mark was indeed a bite-shaped bruise from teeth. A closer look indicated that there was some unevenness to the killer's teeth, which could assist in identification.

A systematic search was undertaken to eliminate townspeople, and then police went to a detention center for young males, where nearly thirty of the inmates were asked to provide dental impressions of their teeth to compare to the bruise. Dr. Harvey studied them all, eliminating most and narrowing the suspects to five. Each was asked for another impression. At this point, pathologist Keith Simpson joined the team. Together these men studied all the impressions and came up with a single suspect: seventeen-year-old Gordon Hay.

Hay had been brought in for breaking into a factory. He submitted to yet one more dental impression procedure, which showed that one of his teeth was pitted in two places by a disorder known as hypocalcination. The pits matched the impressions made on the victim's breast.

As part of his presentation in court, Harvey made an examination of the teeth of 342 young men who were soldiers. Only two had pits of any kind, and none had the two pits that shaped Hay's teeth. From his analysis, he concluded that Hay's teeth were unique, that it would be virtually impossible to find another set of teeth that could come as close to the bruise impression.

At his 1968 trial, Hay claimed that he was in the dormitory at the detention center at the time of the girl's death, so he could not be the person they were looking for. However, another inmate claimed that Hay had actually come in later than he told the court and there was mud on his clothes.

To clinch it, the prosecution introduced the dental evidence. Since it was so unusual, the defense asked that this evidence to be ruled inadmissible. When the judge allowed it, they brought in their own dental expert to refute it, or at least to confuse the jury with dueling experts. The jury accepted the evidence, however, and convicted Hay of murder.

Still, the defense did not give up. They appealed, arguing once again against the bite mark evidence. However, the court upheld the judgment, which meant that other cases could now introduce bite mark testimony.

An odontologist examines such injuries under a magnifying glass. The site is then swabbed for traces of saliva (which can help to prove it's a bite mark) and photographed with a small ruler, called a scale. Then an impression is made with dental material that will yield a permanent stone cast. If a suspect is available, his or her teeth are cast and applied directly to the bite mark for comparison. The bite mark may then be excised to be examined under a microscope. Prints get made of the photographs and of the suspect's cast. Clear plastic sheets are placed over the prints for tracing exact shape and position of the teeth. Traced replicas of the teeth are laid over the bite mark prints to establish a correlation, and the two patterns—victim bite mark and suspect's bite—are compared. If saliva is present, DNA, blood type, and microorganism analysis can tie the impression to a suspect as well.

In January of 1978, Karla Brown's fiancé found her murdered in the basement of the home into which they were moving. She'd been strangled, beaten about the head, and stabbed, and there was blood on the doorknob. There was also bruising around the woman's neck, but no one took photographs. A neighborhood man was developed as a suspect, but there was no evidence against him. The case went cold.

Investigator Don Weber refused to give up. Two years went by before he met Dr. Homer Campbell, an expert on the computer enhancement of photographs. Campbell took a look at the autopsy photos and pointed out the fact that some of the bruises on the victim were bite marks. This stunned Weber, who had known nothing of such evidence. Campbell said that they were good enough impressions to be able to match to a suspect. It turned out, however, that the photos weren't clear enough, so they decided to exhume the body to get another look.

Four years after the murder, the remains of Karla Brown were exhumed. The skin was still intact and investigators were able to get a good impression of the bite mark on her neck. It soon came out that shortly after the murder a man named John Prante had talked about the fact that Karla had been bitten on the shoulder. He quickly came under suspicion and was forced by warrant to give a dental impression. His impressions and those of two other men were submitted, along with the new set of photos of the bite mark, to Dr. Lowell Levine, an odontologist at the New York State Crime Lab. Prante's teeth matched perfectly and he was arrested. Dr. Levine testified about his procedure and Prante was convicted.

Sometimes, even a good match is not good enough. In the following case, from *Cold Case Files* "Mark of a Killer," the odontologist figured out a unique way to meet the court's requirements.

On the evening of January 12, 1991, in Hartford, Connecticut, twenty-eight-year-old Carla Terry went out, but never came back. She was found in a bag on a snowbank, beaten and strangled. Bruises around both breasts were identified as human bite marks. She did have a lack of defensive wounds, often present on hands or arms when a person wards off an assault, which led police to believe that she might have known the suspect. Two days into the investigation, Inspector Steve Kumnik of the Connecticut Division of Criminal Justice received a phone call from a woman who said she had seen Carla Terry in a bar, teasing a guy named Al, a black male in his forties.

Investigators tracked down Al Swinton and searched his home and car. In his Chevy Chevette, they found a brown plastic bag the same color, size, and manufacturer as the one that had encased the dead woman. In his basement police found a black bra that Terry's family identified as hers.

Now the warrant was for bite samples. Swinton's eyeteeth were turned inward, making his bite unique. He submitted to having his teeth cast, and forensic odontologist Lester Luntz compared the plaster mold and impressions to the bruises found on Terry. He believed they were a match.

Yet a judge ruled that the state must prove the marks were made at the time of Terry's death. He ordered Swinton be released and the investigation went cold.

As Hartford police did an analysis, they found eleven more murders stretching from 1988 to 1992 that had an MO similar to Terry's. Most were prostitutes. A task force was formed, but did not generate new leads, although a reporter confirmed that Swinton had known five of the victims.

In 1998, cold case detectives reexamined the bite mark evidence. And while the crime scene photos themselves had not changed, the way detectives viewed them had. Lucis, an image-processing software that could differentiate fine contrast variations, enabled them to see image detail that would be either difficult or impossible to see otherwise. Its pixel digital image contains about 255 levels of contrast, which is quite a step beyond the eye's 32 levels.

Major Timothy Palmback and forensic odontologist Gus Karazulas began work on the Carla Terry bite, scanning the photo into the computer and adjusting the contrast levels. Dr. Karazulas made a transparent copy of Al Swinton's teeth from the plaster moldings made in 1991 and laid them over the enhanced picture. It was a perfect match. But that had already been done. They still needed to establish just when the bite had been made in relation to Terry's death.

Karazulas approached the problem armed with the knowledge that when an individual's heart stops, the healing process stops, and from her color, they could tell that between the time Terry had been murdered and the time she was found, no changes had taken place on her body. The bruise color represented a fixed point in time—the approximate time of Terry's death. Starting with that premise, the odontologist attempted to replicate the color of Carla Terry's bruises by taking the upper and lower plaster cast of Swinton's teeth and clamping them onto his own arm. Taking a constant stream of pictures to verify his work, he timed how long it took for the color in his arm to return to normal, for the arm in effect to heal itself. He observed that from fifteen to twenty minutes after it had been made, the bite mark disappeared. From the color of the strangulation marks on the victim, the color of the bite marks on her breasts, and the color of the bite mark on his arm, the odontologist determined that Terry had been bitten about ten to fifteen minutes before she was strangled. He repeated this test more than fifty times, with the same results. That effectively put Swinton with Terry at the approximate time she was strangled.

Alfred Swinton was arrested once again. His defense counsel decided to conduct a test in court on his own arm, but when he was done, he declined to show the jury the result. Apparently, the implication was clear. Two days later Al Swinton was convicted and sentenced to a term of sixty years.

5

Footprints, too, leave an impression that can assist in a crime analysis. These can be made by bare feet, sock-covered feet, or footwear, and they might be visible or latent, full or partial. As people walk around, their feet, shoes, and boots pick up debris in the form of such things as dust, dirt, oils, and moisture. This debris can leave a residue wherever they walk that, if latent, may be detectable with an oblique light source, or picked up as a distinct pattern by an electro-static dust lifter or with a powder and an adhesive lift. A footprint made in blood but cleaned up can be detected with chemicals such as luminol or another appropriate reagent. These are examples of two-dimensional impressions.

Three-dimensional impressions occur when people step into a soft surface such as mud or snow and leave a distinct mark that can be photographed with examination-quality photography, preserved, and collected for later comparison with a suspect. Dental stone or sil-icone casting materials preserve prints in dirt, but snow poses a dif-ferent kind of challenge. Some criminalists use a spray wax product or darkening aerosol paint that will not melt or crush fragile snow.

Whatever print is left is a collection of class characteristics (lots of shoes are like this but only a particular brand) and individual charac-teristics (the tack stuck in the toe of this shoe makes it unique, or the way it is worn in certain spots). Yet sometimes the individual charac-teristics fail to register in the impression, so the print does not neces-sarily eliminate that shoe as a possibility. At the very least, the shape and size of the footwear can be determined, as can the number of per-petrators. Sometimes footprints help to track where the perpetrator went, as well as characteristics of the way that person walked or ran. That's what assisted in solving the case in *Cold Case Files* "Foot-prints in the Snow."

On December 23, 1987, in Mauston, Wisconsin, Tommy Bolchen, a developmentally disabled man, punched out where he worked as a grocery bagger. He went out for a beer and then started home. He never got there.

Tommy was found lying on his back. Around the pool of blood near him was a blood spatter that appeared as if someone had stepped hard into it. Three sets of footprints led toward the body, but only two headed away. To preserve and use these prints, detectives pho-tographed them with scales and measured them for later comparison. If they were clear enough and distinctly enough patterned, police might be able to tie them to a particular kind of shoe. Footwear databases for the types of soles made by different manufacturers can help, as can databases of actual footwear impressions.

One set of prints were Tommy's. They had no suspects yet for the other two sets. Detectives also noticed patches of snow stained with blood, as if someone had tried to wash his hands, and Tommy's brown billfold was missing.

Barbara Seifert came forward to state that her boyfriend, Kent Holzberger, the bartender at the bar where Tommy had been, had stayed with her that night and had dropped a brown billfold. She said he had borrowed her car and had been talking with Tommy in the bar. But Kent denied this.

Detectives got search warrants. When they popped the trunk on Seifert's car, they found a hammer stained with what looked like blood and thought they saw blood on Holzberger's boots. They sent these items for testing.

Holzberger was arrested and booked for the murder of Tommy Bolchen. Barbara then added that Kent had taken her to the crime scene, handed her a hammer, and threatened to frame her. However, her credibility diminished when it was established that she had been intoxicated the night of the murder. Then test results came back to indicate that there was no blood on the hammer or boots. On the eve of the trial, the State dropped the charges and Kent Holzberger went free.

Then Seifert offered another story. She now claimed to have stumbled upon a party in the park. Twenty people led by Kent Holzberger had crowded around the dead body of Tommy Bolchen. Seifert added that a gang of men had forced her to perform sex acts on Bolchen's lifeless body, then on four other men, including her brother.

No one believed her, but they could not figure out why she would lie like that.

For eight years the case was cold.

In 1995, agents Rick Luell and Eric Szatkowski were handed the Bolchen file. They read all of Seifert's strange stories and believed that, taken together, they represented attempts at deflection. Each time her brother, Danny Buttner, became a focus of the investigation, she would offer another story that sent police in a different direction.

They looked at Buttner more closely. His shoe size was right for one of the sets of prints found near the body. He used drugs and drank heavily, and he had also needed money. They talked with him, but he repeated his sister's tale that he had gotten drunk and Kent Holzberger had lured him into a sex orgy. However, this tale contradicted the evidence. Crime scene photos showed not fifteen or twenty sets of footprints but three—including some that could well be his.

Buttner admitted to robbery, but stopped short of a murder confession by pinning it on his brother-in-law, Glenn Michael Jones. Conveniently, Jones had been killed in a car crash in the early 1990s.

Investigator Tom Sipin reviewed Tommy's injuries and spotted a pattern—a circular bruise on his forehead that appeared to have been made by the butt end of a nun-chuck, a rather unusual weapon. He believed the nun-chucks homemade and thus unique. Sipin's description fit a pair of nun-chucks that had been seized from Buttner. It was the final link detectives needed.

Daniel Buttner was arrested and charged with first-degree murder, and on November 1, 1997, a jury returned a guilty verdict. Impressions from footprints and nun-chucks had made the case against him.

While impression analysis is generally made by visual inspection, some items collected from a crime scene require the chemist's expertise.

NINE

Chemical Detectives

1

Within a year in California's San Mateo County, eleven newly constructed homes were burned to the ground. Messages had been scrawled on some of the charred walls, indicating that the fires had been deliberately set. The crimes became more serious when one of the torched homes turned out to have been occupied early by the homeowner, who barely escaped with his life. Yet the arsonist eluded investigators' best efforts to find him or her, and the case went cold. Whoever had done these destructive acts had left no clues.

To determine that an accelerant has been used, fire investigators look for the seat of the fire at its lowest levels, where they are alert for depth of charring, telltale odors, characteristic burn patterns, and other factors. They may use hydrocarbon detectors or an arson detection dog to locate high concentrations, and then remove contaminated material, if possible, in sealed containers for lab analysis.

In San Mateo, there was no doubt after analysis that these crimes had been deliberately set. And while the arsonist had left no leads to his or her identity, he or she had also not been careful—but in a wholly unexpected way. One day a boy found an army jacket lying along the freeway, wrapped around a videocassette tape. When he viewed it, he saw images of the local arsons, with excited voice-over commentary from someone enjoying the spectacle. The boy's father turned it over to investigators, who compared it against their own videotapes of the fires. They hoped to identify some of the homes in their jurisdiction, but they got more: Arson Inspector John Dellinges realized that the videographer, who sounded like an adolescent boy, had stood very close to where the inspector himself had stood when he made his own tapes of one particular scene. That helped to affirm the location, as well as the potential for using the tape as evidence. The boy had called out to someone named Omar, and that was the investigators' first real clue.

The task force asked the crime television show *Unsolved Mysteries* to air the suspect video. The program did so and received more than eighteen hundred calls. Those of interest were the five that came from San Mateo County. Doris Lantz called in to describe a seventeen-year-old neighbor named Omar, so the investigators questioned him. Under pressure, he implicated a friend. Just as investigators were about to go question him, the garage at his home burned down and gave them a free look inside. They found what they viewed as clear indications of a troubled boy with an inclination toward violence: a cutting table, bloody knives, Halloween masks, satanic literature, and evidence that animals had been cut up.

Under questioning, the boy admitted that he'd committed serial arson. He even had a collection of newspaper articles on the fires. His real motive for burning the homes, he said, was to protect a park area in which he and Omar played army games.

2

Investigation of a fire scene relies on scientific principles, notably from physics and chemistry, to find the origin and cause of the fire, in particular noting whether there may be more than one point of origin—which signals the probability of arson.

Arson is the intentional destruction of property by burning for some improper or illegal purpose. Motives vary, but self-enrichment from insurance money and destruction of evidence from another crime top the list. Some people—including disturbed fire officials—do it for the thrill. In any event, arson is a crime. When it becomes a pattern or involves several buildings within a limited area, a serial arsonist may be on the loose, and such a person may not stop until he or she is caught.

All fires offer clues about the heat source that started them. Generally, high-temperature fires that burn quickly are ignited with liquid accelerants, most commonly gasoline or kerosene, which may also be used to spread the fire, thus making a characteristic pattern or burn trail. Sometimes an ignition trigger device is used.

Fire burns upward and outward, so the seat is likely to be at the lowest point in the place most damaged, and that's where the search begins. Certain patterns are also indicative of the seat, and they're influenced by how available oxygen and combustible materials are. An inverted V pattern points to a seat at the apex of the V, and the depth of charring indicates the point of most intensity. Chipping and splintering (spalling) are caused by hot spots on a wall or floor. Wood beams or floors tend to carbonize into a pattern that looks like alligator skin, with the progressively smaller scales pointing to the seat.

Since newly started fires need a source of fuel, investigators look for what it might be, and since different types of fire burn at different temperatures, they also burn with different colors of flame and smoke. Cooking oil causes a yellow flame and brown smoke; gasoline yields a yellow or white flame with black smoke; phosphorus has both a white flame and white smoke; and wood and fabric fires burn with reddish-yellow flames and gray or brown smoke. However, some substances share the same colors.

Fire evidence is collected into metal cans that resemble paint cans, with the same kind of sealed top. These cans are handed over to chemists in the crime lab. Their tool is the GC/MS (gas chromatograph/mass spectrometer), which breaks chemicals down into charged particles, accelerates them in a magnetic field, and records the ratio of a charge to the mass as a spectrum. That's a visual representation of the chemical's composition. The test sample is shown as a "peak" on a graph or chart, and for identification it's compared against the GC/MS readings of known samples.

Liquid accelerants are grouped into one of five basic classes. Light petroleum distillates include such things as pocket lighter fuels or rubber cement solvents. Gasoline would include any brand of automobile gasoline and some camping fuels. Medium petroleum distillates are paint thinners and charcoal starters. Kerosene is diesel fuel or number two fuel oil. The final class, the heavy petroleum distillates, includes alcohol, turpentine, and lamp oils.

3

For five years, Barbara Martineau worked as a chemist at a private testing laboratory, National Medical Services in Willow Grove, Pennsylvania. She applied her background in chemistry to different types of analysis, from arsenic poisoning to drug identification. "The majority of learning in this field," she says, "is on-the-job training." An area she found most interesting was the testing for the presence of fire accelerants she did on samples brought from fire scenes.

"The first thing I would do was open the can and gently sniff at the sample to see if there was anything obvious. Then we'd do an activated charcoal carbon test. Essentially, we took a strip of the carbon and placed the sample inside a can, put the lid on, and heated it. Any accelerants that were present on the debris would get soaked into this strip of carbon.

"We'd then remove the strip and soak it in carbon disulfide, which would pull everything off the strip and into the liquid. We would inject that into a GC/MS and we'd use pattern recognition and ionic extraction to look for the specific accelerant. We'd look for the different classes of compounds commonly found in accelerants, one of which was alkanes. The majority of the accelerants have certain patterns, so when you have gasoline injected in the machine, it will show up on a chromatogram differently than the pattern for kerosene does. That would be our first clue, and then we'd break it down further, looking for specific components of the accelerant. We'd have to have the whole list of components to say conclusively that that accelerant was present."

She notes that preservatives in carpeting and wood floors can sometimes complicate the tests, so the analyst would only indicate that the accelerant was present or absent, not provide quantitative information.

"We tried to get as much detail as possible about a case to try to help us to figure out what we were dealing with. The investigators did not usually tell me specifically where they thought the fire had originated, but they would say which room the debris was from—the kitchen, the bedroom, the hallway. They would give me a layout of the house or facility. Then as the results come out, we could see where things may have happened. But that was never our determination. We just said whether the accelerant was there or not, and then it was their job to figure out where it originated and what the circumstances were.

"The actual testing would take about an hour and a half, from start to finish. Then the interpretation would take anywhere from half an hour to three or four hours to break down everything and try to pull out information. We encouraged them [the investigators] to get us what we considered a control sample—something that they thought would not have the accelerant in it. So maybe from a house, they would give us a piece of carpeting from under a piece of furniture, or something that was out of the way, so we could use that for comparison purposes. It didn't always work. Sometimes I've gotten a control sample that had an accelerant in it. It wasn't foolproof, but it would help us to work backwards and try to pull some things out that may have already been in the carpeting or in the varnish from a wood floor."

Unlike fire investigators, the chemists do not have to learn about the physics of fire. "It was a lot of chemistry training. I'd taken a seminar in hard-core chemistry that was pretty grueling. I learned which different components are involved in gasoline and kerosene, and what they look like, and weathered versus non-weathered, and how they start to break down. It was intense. The chromatograms looked very different from what I was used to with drug cases. With a drug case, you'd get maybe two peaks [on the readout]. Here's your cocaine and maybe something else. Whereas with arson tests, you would get five hundred peaks. You'd have to go through the layers of the peaks to figure out what they were. I'd draw structures on different pieces of paper and stick them up on the wall, and maybe have fifteen papers taped around me to try to piece it all together."

The experience was humbling to Martineau because she was always aware that someone's life might hang on her conclusions.

At one point, she decided to really work on the accelerant odors. "I used to go out in a warehouse where they had a lot of chemicals and cleaning products. I'd start sniffing stuff. I would take a lot of those items and test them, so that I would have a basis for comparison. I created a library of different chemicals to build up the arson department. I wanted to be able to distinguish by smell the differences between kerosene and gasoline and learn things that would quickly tip me off to what an accelerant could be. I wanted to develop a finer sense of the variations."

The more experience Martineau got, the more she realized how important it was for investigators in the field to learn the correct procedures for this specialized kind of evidence collection and preservation. "A lot of the investigators had no idea what scientists in the lab were capable of doing, so they would not collect the sample properly. I recall one investigator saying he considered the lab to be like a magic box—you send a sample in and get results out. We owe it to the case to each have a basic understanding of what the other is doing. Sometimes investigators assumed, for example, that if they didn't smell something, it wasn't there, so they wouldn't bring us a sample. Some guys would bring me samples in a paper bag that had been sitting in the sun for a couple of days, which made it useless. They never had the training and didn't understand what we needed. So I would go out and do training to teach the proper way of collecting and preserving samples. I think that giving the investigators a better idea of our job and what we can do makes for better investigations."

For Martineau, the driving force is passion for the work. "Some of it gets tedious, but that doesn't mean that it's less important. I also learned that you always have to keep an open mind. You can't just let your knowledge and logic lead the way, but must use them as tools while letting the samples guide you."

For example, several samples were once brought to her from a house fire. One was labeled "the origin," which was the living room. Other samples were from the doorway, hallway, and one other room. After testing, Martineau found no evidence of accelerant at the origin, but she did detect an accelerant in the other samples. She informed the investigator of her findings and he was baffled. He was so positive of the origin that he went back to the place to resample it. Once again, the results again came back negative. After discussing the case together, they found that the fire had burned very hot for a long time, thus burning off any accelerant that would have been at the origin. Because the fire was put out before other spots had the chance to burn it off, they still retained traces.

"After that case," says Martineau, "I encouraged investigators to bring samples from the 'edge of the fire,' the area where the fire burned pretty strong, but had been extinguished. That case really proved to me that it was important to have some knowledge of case history and fire, and to keep an open mind."

Chemical analysis at potential crime scenes is used for explosives as well, and also for detecting the presence of blood. But blood requires an entirely different kind of protocol—especially when it's invisible. It took a while for detectives in the *Cold Case Files* episode "Secret in the Cellar," but they finally found it.

4

In South Portland, Maine, Pearl Bruns, forty-eight, was missing. On August 13, 1991, her daughter, Elaine Woodward, reported it. She was concerned that Pearl's husband, Bill, might have done something to her. Police looked into it and found blood in the bedroom of Pearl's home, as well as on the cellar steps. Nevertheless, they decided that she had probably just left—though her suitcases were still in the home.

Elaine kept the pressure on for over a year before investigators finally questioned Bill Bruns. While his manner was oddly detached, they had nothing to prove that he'd committed any crime. A team did bring in a cadaver dog, who came alert in the cellar, but digging there produced nothing.

Then Pearl Bruns's purse was found a hundred miles north in New Hampshire, near where Bruns made trucking runs. Investigators searched the area on the suspicion that he might have killed his wife and moved the body, but they still found nothing.

A few months later, in December, they returned with a blood-detecting chemical called luminol (3-aminophtalhrdrazide).

In looking for blood evidence at a potential crime scene, a presumptive test is followed by a confirmatory test. The first procedure involves the use of a powerful light moved across every suspected surface. If nothing is seen, but there is reason to suspect blood was once present and has been cleaned up, luminol is sprayed across the scene to make the invisible blood luminescent. Luminol reacts to the hemoglobin in red blood cells and can detect one part per million. The procedure requires that the room be darkened to bring out the faint bluish glow, and the intensity of the glow increases proportionately to the amount of blood present. It works even with older bloodstains or diluted stains, and can illuminate smear marks where blood has been wiped away. However, luminol can also destroy blood properties, so its use is limited to proving only that blood residue is present. (Another chemical, flourscin, can also be used, but it only fluoresces under UV light.)

The Kastle-Meyer Color Test (in the catalytic color test category) is another investigative tool for the presence of blood. It relies on a solution of phenolphthalein on a piece of filter paper or a swab that has been rubbed on the suspected bloodstain. Then the investigator adds a drop of hydrogen peroxide. If the paper or swab picked up any blood, it turns bright pink. However, it also turns pink in the presence of potatoes or horseradish, so care must be taken at the scene. (There are other presumptive tests as well, but they work under the same principles.)

Each of several confirmatory tests applies a chemical to the suspect sample and heats it. If it's human blood, crystals will form.

At the Bruns home, investigators sprayed luminol in several rooms and within short order saw how a brutal assault had taken place. There were also bloody footprints across the floors, and a blood trail that led out of the residence and into the cellar. On the cellar floor, the shape of a body, illuminated by luminol, came out in stark relief.

Bruns said he did not know what could have happened.

Investigators knew they would need either a confession or a body, so they turned to the technique of ground-penetrating radar. The technicians who went over the cellar floor with their machine located an anomaly where the hard clay below the dirt had suddenly changed. That meant that either the soil had been disturbed or something buried there was absorbing the radar waves. The investigators started to dig and soon struck a plastic bag. In short order, they removed it from the hole and found the remains of Pearl Bruns inside.

Bill Bruns pleaded guilty to manslaughter.

Despite how well the crime scene may get cleaned up, even the finest trace of blood can be detected and further tested. It is often the case that while the perpetrator may scrub down the obvious places, he or she can still miss spots.

In Lansing, Michigan, Rose Larner, eighteen, had been dating John Kehoe, but was also friends with Bill Brown, and the three of them became inseparable. Kehoe eventually tired of Rose, and she was devastated. On the night she disappeared in December 1993, she said she was going to a friend's house, but she never showed up. Since she was on the wild side, the police believed she might have just left.

After two weeks, they undertook an extensive search for the girl but did not find her. John Kehoe admitted that he had spoken to her on the night she disappeared, but he was with another girl. He had an alibi.

The case went cold. More than two years went by and no one who knew Rose had heard from her. Rose's mother tried to keep the case alive, and she urged the state police to revisit what they knew. They decided that Kehoe was still a prime suspect, since he and Rose had had a volatile relationship—even after they broke up. Kehoe was also believed to be involved in drug dealing with Bill Brown, and they had been together that night. Investigators leaned on Brown to get him to talk.

He finally relented. He told police that John Kehoe had killed Rose in his presence, and that together they had cleaned up the house where the incident had occurred. They had lured Rose to the car with the promise that they would all have sex, but then they took her to the home of Kehoe's grandparents, who were away. They all showered together, but Rose refused to participate in a menáge à trois. So Kehoe strangled her and slit her throat there in the shower stall. Once she was dead, he proceeded to cut her body into pieces. Brown was horrified, but he helped to clean the place up. Once that was finished, the two men went to a cabin belonging to Kehoe's family and burned Rose's body parts in a campfire ring. Then as they drove away they spread her ashes along the highway. Brown feared that Kehoe would murder him if he told anyone about what they had done.

The police were convinced, but they needed evidence. They went to the home where the murder had occurred and sprayed the rooms with luminol, which picked up blood on a carpet that suggested a ring, such as the bottom of a bucket might make. However, there was not enough of it at that time to perform the type of DNA tests used then. Kehoe and Brown had done a thorough cleanup job, and it looked as if the case was going to stall once more when someone noticed a spot on the wallpaper that was not part of the intricate pattern. It was the right color for dried blood.

Technicians performed a phenolphthalein test on it to determine if it was indeed blood. The test results were positive, but the origin of the blood had not yet been determined.

They managed to extract enough for DNA analysis, but had nothing with which to compare it. Then they learned that Rose had had a blood test after she'd once reported a sexual assault. Testing indicated that the odds that the blood spatter on the wall could have come from anyone but Rose Larner were one in more than 700 million.

Investigators also checked the basement sump pump where the young men had dumped bloody water and went through the ashes in the fire pit where they had burned Rose's remains. With ultraviolet light, scientists analyzed fragments from both locations that appeared to be bone, knowing that bone chips would glow. A few small bone fragments were then magnified and found to be human, specifically from someone fairly young. That corroborated Brown's story.

In 1996, police arrested John Kehoe. Although he tried to finger Brown, he was convicted of first-degree murder. He went to prison for life.

5

The analysis of the properties and effects of serums is called serology. Blood is among the included substances, and even a single drop can help to solve a crime. Blood evidence found in crimes of violence may be in one of several forms: fresh liquid, coagulated, dried, or as a small drop or stain. Among the early breakthroughs in forensic science was the recognition of different blood types in 1875, and a quarter of a century later, in 1901, Austrian immunologist Karl Landsteiner named and standardized the various groups.

Red blood cells carry a substance called an antigen, which produces antibodies to fight infection, and there appeared to be several different types. In a centrifuge, Landsteiner separated the red blood cells from the plasma—the watery serum in which they are carried through the body. Then adding red blood cells from other subjects, he found two distinct reactions—clumping and repelling. He labeled them types A (antigen A present, anti-B antibody present, but antigen B absent) and B (antigen B present, antigen A absent). Then a third reaction was labeled C (both antigens A and B absent), but was relabeled later as O. A year later, another type of serum was discovered, and this fourth type was labeled AB (both antigens present). More testing indicated that types A and O are the most common in the human population, with AB the most rare (4 percent).

Thanks to Landsteiner, not only were blood transfusions made safer, but with the ABO test people could be eliminated as suspects if blood linked to a crime was not their type. Today, blood typing includes different enzymes and proteins that perform specific activities in the body, which further individualizes the blood. (More than 150 serum proteins and 250 cellular enzymes have been isolated, as well as many more antigens. Over a dozen blood-type systems are available.)

Yet just because blood is present at a scene or on someone's clothing does not make it human. Another discovery, also publicized in 1901, helped investigators to make that distinction.

German biologist Paul Uhlenhuth, barely thirty, discovered while searching for a serum to fight hoof-and-mouth disease that if he injected protein from a chicken egg into a rabbit, and then mixed serum from the rabbit with egg white, the egg proteins separated from the liquid to form a cloudy substance. He called it precipitin. In other words, the rabbit's immune system formed an antibody. In fact, as he worked at it, he found that the blood of each animal had its own distinct protein. Injecting human cells into the animal made this test applicable to humans. A coroner asked him to test dried bloodstains from both animals and to see if his method could accurately identify them. The serums worked, even on minuscule samples. Then a particularly brutal crime brought the test into the forensic spotlight.

The murder and dismembering of two young boys on the island of Rugen, off the coast of Germany, turned the authorities' attention toward Ludwig Tessnow, a carpenter from Baabe. The year was 1901, just four months after Uhlenhuth's discovery, and the two boys had failed to return from their play, so a search was organized. It wasn't long before their parts were found scattered over a wide area in a woods, their heads shattered, and the heart of the eight-year-old missing. A bloodstained stone proved to be the murder weapon.

Earlier that day, Tessnow had been seen talking to the boys, and although he denied any involvement, a search of his home turned up recently laundered clothing that bore suspicious stains. He claimed that they were from wood dye, which he used almost daily in his profession. This had long been the dilemma of law enforcement—proving that stains on clothing were even blood, let alone human. The police left Tessnow alone . . . until a magistrate recalled a similar crime.

Three years earlier, in Osnabruck, Germany, two young girls had been found in the woods, butchered and disemboweled in a style not unlike the boys. The man seen loitering near the woods, his clothing stained, was Tessnow. At that time, too, he had claimed that the stains were from wood dye.

The local prosecutor then heard a farmer's report that a man who looked like Tessnow had been seen fleeing from his field, and the farmer then found seven of his sheep slaughtered. Their legs had been severed and tossed about the field. Tessnow was brought in for a lineup and the farmer had no trouble picking him out.

Still, the police needed better evidence to tie Tessnow to the murders. Then they heard about the test that Paul Uhlenhuth had developed that could distinguish blood from other substances, as well as mark the difference between human and animal blood. Uhlenhuth had published a paper in February, 1901, with the title "A Method for the Investigation of Different Types of Blood," and the word about it had spread far and wide. If his claim were true, it would change law enforcement dramatically, making it much more difficult for violent criminals to get away with their crimes.

Tessnow's clothing and the bloodstained stone were given to Uhlenhuth for thorough examination. He applied his test to more than one hundred spots. While he did find wood dye, he also detected traces of both sheep and human blood.

With this evidence, Tessnow was tried, convicted, and executed.

Shortly thereafter, forensic blood analysis became a standard tool in police investigations. In the modern forensic test for human blood, either a sample of the suspect blood is put over the rabbit serum in a test tube or it's used in the "gel diffusion" test, where it's placed in gel on a glass slide next to a sample of the reagent (anti-human serum). When an electric current is passed through the glass, the protein molecules filter into the gelatin and toward each other. If a line forms where they meet—called a precipitin line—that means the sample is human blood.

Using synthetic antibodies has taken the test from the lab to the field, where a blood analysis can be done right away.

In 1925, another blood-related discovery important to criminal investigation was made. Around 80 percent of people in the human population were found to be "secretors," which means that the specific types of antigens, proteins, antibodies, and enzymes characteristic of their blood can also be found in other bodily fluids and tissues. In the case of a secretor, investigators can tell the blood type by examining the saliva, teardrops, skin tissue, urine, or semen. In a rape case, for example, where the perpetrator is a secretor, potential suspects can be narrowed down more easily through blood type analysis.

Just because science proved it did not mean the court accepted it. Even fourteen years later, juries rejected the proof from saliva removed from cigarette butts that implicated Joseph Williams for a murder in England in 1939. Williams's fingerprint matched a print from the crime scene as well, but he had been a friend of the victim's, so that was not compelling. That he had suddenly come into money on the day after the murder also did not move the jury, but the defense attorney was most adamant about the physical evidence. He launched an all-out attack against the saliva evidence, and the jury bought it. They acquitted Williams, and that very evening he confessed to a reporter that he was indeed guilty.

These days, thanks to discoveries in 1985, DNA technology has replaced the tests for specific enzymes and proteins. It's more accurate to match DNA from a blood sample at a crime scene to a source than to draw up an entire blood profile. However, blood still has plenty of value to crime scene reconstruction.

Before moving on to DNA analysis, there's one more aspect of the analysis of blood evidence that must be explored.

TEN

What Blood Reveals

1

Sam Sheppard, thirty, was a prominent osteopath working in Bay Village, Ohio. Sam and Marilyn had been high school sweethearts, and after they married, they had a son, Sam Reese Sheppard, known as "Chip."

In the early morning hours of July 4, 1954, someone bludgeoned Marilyn to death in her upstairs bedroom. There were blood spatters throughout the room, blood smears on the sheets where she lay, and a blood trail leading through the house. The police arrested Dr. Sheppard and charged him with murder, but he claimed that a "bushy-haired stranger" had invaded their home, killed Marilyn, and attacked him twice. His account had glaring holes, including lies about his extramarital affair, and the jury returned a verdict of second-degree murder. The judge sentenced Sheppard to life in prison.

While serving his time, he recruited attorney F. Lee Bailey, who filed a motion with the federal district court to overturn the conviction based on prejudicial pretrial publicity. The U. S. Supreme Court ruled that Sheppard should get a second trial.

In this trial in 1966, Sam did not testify, and the culprit was no longer a bushy-haired stranger but neighbors, the Houks, whom Sam had called right after the murder—before he called the police. Bailey's theory was that Marilyn had been involved in an affair with Spencer Houk, the part-time mayor of Bay Village.

For the blood evidence, Bailey called as an expert witness Dr. Paul Kirk, who had done extensive analyses of the autopsy photos and the blood spatter at the crime scene. Dr. Kirk testified that the killer had been left-handed, which would exclude the right-handed Sam. He also testified that the apparent blood spatter found on Sam's watch was a transfer stain resulting from incidental contact with Marilyn's body while he tried to find her pulse. In addition, Kirk stated that in the bedroom where the murder took place there was a spot of blood that had come from someone other than Sam and Marilyn. It was type O, the same as Marilyn's, but of a different composition, which eliminated her as its source. To determine this, Dr. Kirk had performed an unprecedented test, claiming that one of the stains reacted slightly slower than the others. Thus, he could conclude that the slow-reacting stain was type O blood from a source other than Marilyn.

"There was a problem with this," says former FBI profiler Gregg McCrary in his analysis in *The Unknown Darkness*, in which he describes his involvement with the case as it was going to court a third time. "Unlike true science, which demands repeatable experiments and replicable results to validate new procedures and novel discoveries, neither Dr. Kirk nor anyone else was ever able to repeat this alleged test."

The important point for Bailey was that Sheppard was type A, not type O, and therefore could not have been the source of what Kirk was calling "the killer's blood." Bailey concluded that a left-handed woman had struck Marilyn "lightly" but repeatedly and was bitten during the attack, resulting in the blood trail throughout the house. It is undisputed that Sam had no open wounds, cuts or scrapes of any kind when the police arrived to investigate.

After a short deliberation, the jury returned a verdict of not guilty. Sam was a free man, but he became an alcoholic and was dead by forty-six.

And the murder was still technically unsolved.

Late in the 1990s, Sheppard's son, Sam Reese Sheppard (referred to here as Sam R.), decided to sue the State of Ohio in civil court for the ten years his father had been in prison, demanding $2 million in damages. The theory that he and his attorney, Terry Gilbert, offered was that a former "window washer" with a criminal record named Richard Eberling was the offender. They even claimed they had a DNA match that would prove that he was their man.

The plaintiff's attorney proposed that Eberling had two primary motives: unbridled sexual lust for Marilyn and a virulent hatred for Sam. Based on tool marks on a cellar door mentioned in a Cleveland police report, they theorized that he had entered the house through the outside cellar doors, made his way upstairs, raped and murdered Marilyn, and then assaulted Sam. They also theorized that Marilyn bit him and made him bleed at the scene.

McCrary's job was to assess the crime scene from photos and reports to determine whether a stranger could have committed this brutal murder. Among the many problems he spotted were issues with the bloodstains.

"Crime scene analysis is based in part on the transfer theory," he says, "which postulates that any two surfaces coming into contact leave trace evidence behind on both. This is especially true with wet blood, which is incredibly adhesive."

Given how much blood there was around the bedroom, he believed that the killer would have been soaked in it. Sheppard had stated that he had grappled with this man, yet he only had a small spot of blood on the knee of his pants. He also claimed he had checked his wife's pulse twice, but despite her blood-spattered body, he somehow got no blood on his hands. Nor was there any blood on the furniture that the murderer supposedly had ransacked after the killing, and no indication that he had cleaned up before doing that.

However, there *was* blood on the face of Sheppard's watch—tiny elliptical drops. This is a spatter pattern, generally from cast-off blood from a weapon hitting someone, not smear from contact with the body when checking for a pulse. How did that get there?

In addition, blood patterns on the bed indicated that Marilyn had lain in one position as blood pooled and then had been moved to another one, leaving a smear. From what McCrary could tell from this evidence and other problems with Sheppard's inconsistent statements, he believed this crime was a domestic homicide that had been staged to look like a home invasion and a stranger murder.

In court, the plaintiff's side believed they had the trump card with the DNA evidence, but it turned out that their expert had not done a basic ABO blood typing test on the blood he had analyzed for DNA. He ended up being embarrassed in open court when it turned out that the chief suspect's blood type did not match the sample that supposedly contained his DNA—a biological impossibility.

The jury decided that the State of Ohio owed Sam R. nothing. Even in a civil venue, he had failed to make a convincing case.

2

Paul Leland Kirk, the very expert who expounded on the Sheppard crime scene at the second trial, was the person who coined the term "blood dynamics" for the scientific approach to bloodstain pattern analysis. He once wrote, "No other type of investigation of blood will yield so much useful information as an analysis of the blood distribution patterns." The areas of this expertise include evidence collection, pattern identification, incident reconstruction, experimental design, research, and testimony. Bloodstain pattern interpretation generally involves teamwork, with different specialties concentrating on different types of blood behavior, from drops to smears to arterial spurts.

At the scene of a violent crime where blood is spilled, the shape, size, and position of the stains—or blood spatter—can assist investigators in putting together a narrative about what occurred there.

In 1975, a massacre in Winter Garden, Florida, was solved based mostly on bloodstains, blood typing, and careful logic. On Christmas Eve, businessman Tommy Zeigler called police to say that he had been shot during an attempted robbery. When police arrived, they found a wounded Zeigler, shot in the stomach, and four other people lying dead in his furniture store—his wife, her parents, and a black man, Charles Mays. Zeigler claimed Mays was part of the gang that had tried to rob him.

Yet a bullet-cracked clock indicated that Zeigler had waited two hours to make his call, and a background check turned up marital problems for the Zeiglers and a recent hefty life insurance policy taken out on the dead wife.

Internationally renowned bloodstain pattern analyst Herbert Mac-Donell worked the scene. He had testified in the assassinations of Robert F. Kennedy and Martin Luther King Jr., and had been consulted in numerous other high-profile cases. Using information about the postures of the victims, blood type, and whose blood was on whom, he managed to show that the wife was the intended victim and had died first. The parents had likely stumbled into the murder inadvertently, and Mays had been set up. Zeigler had shot himself, but investigators had found no blood at the places where he said, which was a clear indication of his deception. Mac-Donell proved that Zeigler had in fact shot himself while standing by the phone.

A jury convicted Zeigler of quadruple homicide.

When wounded (while the heart is still pumping), bodies leak or spray blood, and the behavior of blood in flight tends to remain uniform. When blood flies through the air, the pattern in which it lands can determine its track, as well as the location and position of the weapon that inflicted the blow. When layered, one spatter atop another, it can also provide an estimate of how many blows were struck and how much momentum a murder weapon may have been given. The width of a blood path can offer information about the kind of weapon.

Blood pattern experts examine many different things, including the type of injuries on a body, the order in which the wounds were received, whose blood is present and in what locations, the type of weapon that caused the injuries, whether the victim was in motion when struck, whether the victim was moved from one spot to another, and where blood spray or drops landed in terms of travel distance and patterns.

While blood spatter interpretation is not a science like a DNA analysis, and while experts can vehemently disagree with one another (and do), there are some areas listed in the textbooks that seem to be in accord.

The most essential aspects for interpretation of the bloodstains at a scene are size of spots and velocity of drops at impact with a surface that can record them. Blood may be dripped out, sprayed from an artery, oozed out through a large wound, smeared, or flung off a weapon raised to strike another blow. In the 1930s, Scottish pathologist John Glaister classified blood splashes into distinct categories—based on the energy needed to disperse the blood, and on projectile angles—which many experts still rely on today, and several books on the subject offer the following guidelines:

■ Circular marks come from blood ejected with relatively little force that strikes a surface at right angles to it.

■ Crenellated marks are made by blood flying at a high velocity or falling a distance to a surface below.

■ Elliptical blood drops strike a surface at an angle, and their degree of elongation can help to calculate the angle from which they came.

■ Splashes with long tails come from blood flying through the air and hitting a surface at an angle of thirty degrees or less. The tail points back in the direction from which the drop came.

■ Pools around the body indicate where the victim lay while alive and bleeding out.

- Spurts that come from a major artery or vein produce a strong blood spray.

- Smears caused by pressing a bleeding object against a surface leave a transfer pattern.

- Trails may take the form of smears when a bleeding body is dragged, or droplets when someone wounded walks or is carried for some distance.

Assuming that blood generally moves in a straight trajectory, with a slight arc, and that a fine mist indicates more force than large droplets, bloodstain patterns can assist investigators in figuring out the positions and the means by which the victim and suspect interacted and possibly struggled through a crime scene. The patterns can be used to reconstruct events, or to support or undermine a statement of events.

In Brownsville, Texas, Susie Mowbray was convicted in 1988 of murdering her husband, who was shot once in the head. Expert Herb MacDonell said that the wound pattern revealed a tight shot close to the head, which should have sprayed high-velocity spatters onto the nightgown that Susie had been wearing, as it had against the sheets and bed board. He believed the man's death was a suicide. His analysis was ignored, as was a banker's statement about Mowbray's despondency, and she went to prison for nine years. Her attorney contacted MacDonell, and in a second trial in which all the evidence came out, Susie was acquitted.

Choosing several stains at strategic points, and using basic trigonometry from the point of convergence or origin, enables investigators to develop a three-dimensional recreation of the area in which a bloodletting event occurred. Computer programs are available for a simulation.

Blood pattern analysis is a complicated discipline and requires experience with many different situations to learn to do an accurate reading. While there are formulas and guidelines for common incidents, there can also be exceptions, and all interpretations are contingent on the factors that influence the context of the crime scene. We can see that in the *Cold Case Files* episode called "Man's Best Friend."

In Vernon, British Columbia, Dan Schrader's house burned with him inside early in 1991. Yet investigators soon realized that he had been beaten to death before the fire, as was his dog, which was discovered in a shed on the property. Schrader was eighty-one, and the chief suspect was Billy Faulconer, who had once lived there with him. But Faulconer had an alibi for noon, the approximate time at which the coroner estimated the death had occurred. With no other suspect and no way to definitively link Faulconer to the victim, the investigation lost steam.

Six years later, new detectives on the case wondered if the estimate for the time of death had accounted for the effects of the heat from the fire, which likely had raised the body's temperature. The coroner admitted that he had not thought of that and was willing to revise the estimate, as long as they could figure out when the fire had started.

At the RCMP Forensics Lab, they looked through films taken of the fire, and four minutes into the video, as well as later, the frames indicated that a clock inside the burning home had stopped at 6:12 A.M., the time the power had gone off. Investigators believed this indicator put Schrader's time of death around 6:00 A.M., six hours earlier than the previous estimate and at a time when the suspect had no alibi. Yet they needed more than that.

Among the evidence items was a pair of jeans stained with blood and found in the garbage outside Faulconer's home. In 1997, DNA matched the blood to Dan Schrader. But Faulconer had lived in Schrader's home, so he might have had contact with Schrader's blood. Looking more closely at the test results, investigators realized there was another kind of DNA present. The detectives had taken samples of the dog's blood at the crime scene, and the lab compared them and found a match to the blood on Faulconer's jeans.

With that knowledge, they had a way to do a thorough reconstruction. They returned to Schrader's home to analyze the blood there—a mix of dog and human blood. From the spatter patterns, they were able to conclude that Faulconer had killed the dog by swinging its head against the fireplace. He had then killed Schrader in his wheelchair.

In 1997, Faulconer pleaded guilty to manslaughter and was sentenced to ten years.

3

Many criminals do attempt to clean up the blood, but they may very well miss a spot. Detectives might do so as well, unless they're thinking about every possibility. Even evidence that has been moved can assist in proving that a crime took place, which is what happened in the following case in Ridgefield, South Carolina, the subject of *Cold Case Files* "The Missing and the Dead." The case involved many different areas of forensic science, but the crucial evidence came from a blood spatter.

On November 7, 1989, a navy seabag held the body of a young woman, burned beyond recognition and dumped. The bag had been doused with gasoline and set afire, burning everything but the woman's legs. From these parts investigators knew she was a white female.

The Naval Criminal Investigative Service (NCIS) began to search for the young woman's identity. The body had been bound hand and foot and clad only in a nightshirt. The skull had been crushed into more than 120 separate fragments. Large portions of the front teeth and surrounding bone were missing entirely. The coroner, Martin Sauls, found some portions of teeth and bone in the corpse's stomach and lungs. He estimated that the woman had been in her early to mid-twenties and saw evidence that she was a recent mother. Investigators sent the crushed bits of skull to a specialist at the University of South Carolina.

Ted Rathbun, forensic anthropologist for the university, first classified the fragments according to anatomical function, then glued the skull back together. One area beneath the nose was missing—a key feature for indicating how far out the nose projects. Rathbun believed the victim was of European descent. From the rebuilt skull, an artist reconstructed and sketched a likeness of her face, which was published and distributed, but it failed to spark a lead. Finally, the victim was buried.

Yet she was not forgotten. Eighty miles away in Charleston, South Carolina, a young woman had gone missing, and her best friend, Kathi French, was desperately searching for her. She knew that Annie Tehan, twenty-four, was in a difficult relationship and Kathi had not been happy about Annie's last call to her, a call that said that Annie was scared.

Although he was married to another woman, United States Navy Chief Petty Officer Michael Paalan was Annie's boyfriend, and they had just had a baby. Annie believed Michael was going to take her child away from her, so she had called Kathi, who had wired money to her. Annie promised to call back but never did. Kathi learned that Annie's phone had been disconnected. She called Paalan's mother, who told her that Michael was serving on a tour of duty and that Annie had abandoned him and her newborn. Kathi did not believe it.

Berkeley County Detective Pamela Lee picked up the case. She learned that Annie, the mother of three children, had met Paalan in Maine in 1988. They had some trouble and when her six-month-old daughter perished in a fire that broke out mysteriously in their apartment Paalan was a suspect. When no evidence was linked to him, investigators came to a dead end and dismissed the fire as having an unknown origin. But nothing clearly indicated more recently that anything violent had happened to Annie. She was just gone.

The case went cold for everyone except Kathi. For five years, she worked the phones up to eight hours a day, searching for Annie. She ran up phone bills in excess of $15,000 as she called every law enforcement agency, hospital, and morgue on the East Coast, as well as every missing persons center around the nation.

In September of 1993, Detective Lee turned to the NCIS for assistance, and NCIS Special Agent Jim Grebas picked up the Tehan file. Grebas reviewed the physical evidence in the case and conducted a search of Michael Paalan's former apartment and car, but could not generate new leads. Then he sent NCIS agents to Hawaii to question Paalan, who reiterated that Annie had simply disappeared.

While flipping through some missing persons information, Grebas came across a sketch of a young girl who had been found in Jasper County the day after Annie disappeared, the sketch prepared for Ted Rathbun at the University of South Carolina. Grebas believed this was Annie. He pulled the dental records from this Jane Doe and sent them to a forensic dentist. It turned out that Tehan had retained a baby tooth that fell out and left a space. The shape of her molars and the bowing of the roots and the molars that could be seen on the X-ray were also unique. The dental restorations matched identically.

Two cold cases suddenly became one—and warmed up.

NCIS Special Agent Peter Hughes joined Grebas, as they pulled the case file from Jasper County. Detectives went to Paalan's former apartment and looked for trace amounts of blood. The unit appeared to be clean. They then reviewed Paalan's personal records. His gas credit card had been used on November 6 and 7, about twenty-five miles from where the body had been dumped. Paalan had also made a call that day to Savannah, Georgia, at five o'clock in the morning, to his mother. Detectives tracked down Paalan's now ex-wife, Enete, and pressured her until she finally yielded.

Late in 1989, Enete reported that she had driven to the Springhill apartment, where she had seen Annie dead on a mattress and their baby covered with blood. She said that Paalan intended to give the baby to her (although the child ended up with Paalan's mother). She helped Michael drag Annie into a back bedroom and put her into a seabag. The following day they headed into South Carolina, where Paalan poured gasoline over the body to burn it.

The investigative team returned to the apartment for a closer inspection. With Paalan's ex-wife as a guide, they focused on specific areas where detectives believed Tehan had bled out and died, and did a phenolphthalein test and an immunoblot assay for the presence of protein found in the blood. The tests indicated a large area on the floor where blood once had pooled. Then in Enete's statement they noticed that she had mentioned an old television set in that room. The detectives felt that Paalan, who had been described to them as being extraordinarily cheap, had probably sold it.

In 1995, NCIS agent Charles Reno tracked down Raymond and Cindy Gantts, who had purchased the television. He found it in storage and delivered it to the crime team. Agent Peter Hughes said, "You can look for reasons not to chase down leads or you can look for reasons why you should, and I think that's the approach that we took in this investigation."

Just inside the front panel of the TV speaker they found nine separate bloodstains. Although too degraded for DNA testing, they formed the smoking gun NCIS agents had been searching for. The stains indicated trauma to the victim, from which blood flew and landed so forcefully against the television that it went into the speaker. There it stayed until quick-thinking detectives found it.

Confronted with this evidence, Paalan pleaded guilty to the murder of Annie Tehan and was sentenced to thirty years. Kathi French was sad but relieved to finally see justice done for her friend.

4

The history of forensic science is rich with innovative thinking that has advanced its techniques. Like any discipline, it has suffered from established ideas that resist change, but those who have honored the ideals and ingenuity of science have persisted and ensured that new methods get attention.

In England in 1949, a man's dismembered torso was found in a bundle in the marshes. By this time, forensic pathologists were often called to such scenes, and Dr. Francis E. Camps was the one who answered the call. He concluded that the corpse had been in the water approximately three weeks and had been placed there around two days after the murder by stabbing. He removed the skin from the hands for fingerprint analysis. The deceased was quickly identified as Stanley Setty, forty-seven. He'd been missing for two and a half weeks, since right after he had cashed a large check in London.

It was clear from an autopsy that one of his stab wounds had produced a large amount of blood, so wherever he had been killed should yield bloodstain evidence. Setty also had postmortem injuries that indicated he'd fallen from a great height—like a man whose parachute had failed.

Checking small airports, investigators learned that a Donald Hume had hired a sports plane around the time in question, and had loaded two large packages on board. A check of the plane revealed bloodstains inside, and an investigation turned up a link between Setty, the dead man, and Hume.

Under questioning, Hume said that two men had hired him to fly the parcels over water and drop them. It was a preposterous story, but the Scotland Yard detectives had to prove otherwise. They went to Hume's apartment, and learned from a housekeeper that Hume had worn out the cleaning implements. Camps went in to look for traces of blood, and Dr. Henry Smith Holden, a chemist and expert in serology, accompanied him. They knew that Setty's blood group was O, and on three floorboards and in several rooms Holden soon found bloodstains of that type, which proved to be of human origin. The floor had been refinished, however, so Camps and Holden found only a few visible spatters. Yet there were cracks between the floorboards. They looked down into them and saw what appeared to be blood, so they ripped up the floor and discovered altogether about a cupful. In order to compute how much blood had been spilled to leave that quantity of coagulated blood inside the cracks, they replicated Hume's floor in the lab and poured varying amounts of blood over it. Keeping careful measure, they determined that three pints of blood had been spilled in that area alone. It was much more than someone having an accident or nosebleed would lose. Adult humans have about ten pints of blood. Losing three pints is quite a lot.

Had Setty bled this much through the parcels that Hume had supposedly received, he would have noticed—yet he had said nothing of the kind. The case was a struggle in court. The scientists proved that a bloody corpse had been in Hume's home, but could not prove that he had done the killing, so he was sentenced as an accomplice. Then when he got out of prison, he sold his confession to a tabloid, saying that he had indeed killed Setty exactly as the scientists had described.

It was cases like this, with the need for increased specialization, that inspired experts in various branches of forensic medicine to set up councils or coordinated teams with representatives from each of the various relevant branches. Blood pattern analysis began to take on an increased significance and called for refined expertise.

Wounded people do leave blood behind and sometimes in such an amount that one could only say that person is no longer alive. Deciding if a sufficient amount of blood is present to make that decision involves a blood volume test. Volume of blood is a time sequence indicator. In other words, blood running in sufficient quantity to make a pool takes time and indicates that a victim lay in one place for a while—especially if the blood was only seeping from the injuries. The larger the pool, the more likely it is that the loss of blood had a negative impact on the victim's vital functions. A person can survive a 25 percent loss if leakage is slow and replacement occurs quickly, before anything malfunctions. A rapid loss will have a more harmful effect, and a 33 percent loss, without restoration, is considered a potentially fatal amount.

Irregular pools indicate faster bleeding and possible arterial damage, with a round pool suggesting a slower seepage. No matter what kind of stain is found, it's an important source of information, especially if the victim is not present.

Caren Campano was missing from Oklahoma City, but there seemed to be nothing sinister in her home . . . at first. Her husband, Chris, admitted that

they'd had a fight just before she disappeared on July 1, 1992. He offered to let investigators look around, which was his first mistake. A huge brownish patch on the bedroom carpet alerted police to the possibility that it was blood. They used a presumptive test that came up positive.

With luminol, investigators found spatters on the walls, doors, and even across the ceiling. A blood trail also ran through the house and down the outside steps in back. Piecing a narrative together from the spatter patterns, investigators believed that the victim had received numerous blows to the head with a blunt object, which collectively would have been fatal. But they did not have a body.

On the same rug but in the lab, they poured the amount of blood that would have been needed to make a stain the same size as the one they had found, and then estimated that a person the size of Caren Campano would have lost at least 40 percent of her blood. She could not have survived that.

Although Caren's father was deceased and they had no samples of her DNA, investigators took blood samples from numerous members of her family, hoping for a partial match with all of them. Finding it, the police had enough for an arrest on the suspicion of murder.

It was unclear whether they would get this conviction without a body, but a year after her disappearance, Caren's remains turned up, though by this time they were mostly skeletal. The dental records matched and a story of great trauma was revealed in the multiple fractures to the skull. She had been beaten to death.

Chris Campano was convicted of the murder of his wife.

In a 1991 case from Texas, *Cold Case Files* "Blood Trail," no body was ever found, and the only possible way to prove a murder was to rely almost entirely on the blood volume test.

It began when Jim Dunn received a call from Leshia Hamilton, his son Scott's girlfriend. She was searching for Scott and appeared to be worried. She said she had not heard from him in three days. Nor had he shown up for work, although his car was in the parking lot.

Jim filed a missing persons report for Scott, twenty-four, and heard from Leshia that a large piece of carpet had been cut from the

living room floor in Scott's apartment and replaced. The police looked
into it. The replaced area was outlined with duct tape and appeared to
have blood on the edges. Lifting it showed the presence of blood
underneath in the padding. Tests showed that there was also a substantial amount of dried blood on the walls and ceiling. The apartment
was declared a crime scene and treated with luminol. Investigators
found an abundance of luminescent areas, along with wiping stains.
Another test proved that it was Scott's blood and detectives believed
he'd been murdered. When the spotlight turned on Leshia, she fingered a neighbor, Tim Smith, twenty-eight. He had followed her
around like a stalker, she claimed, and records showed that he had
failed to report to work on the last day that Scott was seen alive.

Detectives talked with Smith and spotted a roll of duct tape in his
home. They confiscated it and the crime lab found carpet fibers on it
consistent with those in Scott's apartment. Some human hairs were
also stuck to it, which were consistent with Scott's. Smith looked like
the culprit, but Scott's father, Jim Dunn, believed Leshia knew something more, so he invited her to dinner. She talked as if she knew that
Scott would not be back, and Dunn decided that she had conspired
with Tim Smith to kill his son.

But they did not have a body, and in Texas, they needed one. So
the case went cold.

Then Jim learned about the Vidocq Society.

It was an organization of mostly retired law enforcement and
other forensic professionals founded by William Fleisher (former FBI
special agent), Frank Bender (forensic sculptor), and Richard Walter
(forensic psychologist). They had banded together to use their extensive and varied experience to help other agencies brainstorm about
cold cases. The organization had grown over the years to having representatives from eleven different countries.

They met for monthly luncheons in the Public Ledger Building,
near Independence Hall, in Philadelphia, Pennsylvania. While dining
in a refined, wood-paneled atmosphere, they listened to invited
guests—usually a police officer at a dead end—present the gruesome
details of a case, to which they would offer suggestions about how

an investigation might be advanced. They took on cases as a public service, and those with the relevant skills volunteered their input.

For example, in the decades-old stabbing death of a fast-food restaurant night manager, one of the Vidocq members asked whether anyone had checked the knife handle for DNA. No, that had not been done. Ten years earlier, the technology had been expensive and not always accessible. Now they could have another look. In the case where a murder victim was found barefoot, a suggestion to look for suspects with foot fetishes gave investigators a new direction. They found a security guard with a compulsion about women's sneakers. A third case had resulted in the linking of a double homicide with two other murders, and a conviction in all four.

The founders named the club after François Eugène Vidocq, a brilliant French police spy during the eighteenth century who mingled so well with the criminal element that no one suspected he was responsible for a spate of arrests. Once they caught on, he continued his work in disguise; his skills derived, in part, from having been a criminal himself. In 1811, he became the founder and first chief of the Sûreté, an elite undercover unit that rapidly gained international fame. Vidocq is considered the father of modern criminal investigation. Among his accomplishments was the introduction into police procedure of many of the basic methods of criminalistics, including document examination, casting of footprint impressions, and firearms analysis.

Since the Vidocq Society can't accept every cold case out there, they follow a specific protocol: Only a family member of the victim or a police officer may bring a case before them, and the victim cannot have been associated with high-risk activities, such as drug dealing. They also focus mostly on homicides, not missing persons cases. While they have no law enforcement authority, the impressive array of expertise in this group, from U.S. Marshals to FBI Behavioral Science Unit members to attorney generals, gives them the force of perspective and collective experience. Their suggestions have helped with leads that resulted in convictions in many cases, but they've also helped to free the innocent.

Jim Dunn decided to take his son's case to the society. He talked with Bill Fleischer in June 1992, and Richard Walter agreed to look into it. They went together to Lubbock, Texas, and Walter viewed the crime scene with one question in mind: Is it consistent or inconsistent with life?

With the help of Richard Shepherd, a forensic expert from Scotland Yard, they came to the conclusion that the measurable amount of blood in Scott's apartment was inconsistent with his survival. Thus, they had a "body" and they knew it was Scott's.

While the DA accepted the blood volume measurement, he said he needed proof of the suspects' involvement. They had the hairs and fibers from the duct tape, and also had hair found on the piece of carpet that had replaced the missing section in a failed effort to cover up the crime scene. These were sent to the FBI lab. Some of that hair was consistent with both the neighbor and with Leshia, placing the two side by side at the crime scene. They also had letters from Leshia that hinted at getting rid of Scott.

Both were indicted on November 20, 1996. At trial, blood spatter expert Tim Bevel testified about the way the blood told a story of impact and being cast off from a weapon. With that, the blood volume measurement, and the trace evidence, both defendants were found guilty of murder.

While many areas of forensic science such as blood pattern interpretation have made great strides in this century, none has been more profound than that which arose from the science of genetics: DNA identification.

ELEVEN

The DNA Revolution

1

In July 1993, forty-seven-year-old Joseph Buglia was found stabbed to death in his bloodstained pickup truck, which had been left near a mine reclamation area in Pennsylvania. The wounds were centered mostly on his arms and torso. Technicians went to work to collect the biological evidence in the hope that, as is often the case, the killer might have cut himself in the stabbing frenzy and left his own blood behind.

An investigation turned up a suspect, William Huth Sr., a convicted killer, based on a witness who claimed that Huth had talked about how it might feel to be stabbed many times. He'd also had a cut on his leg, which he had told others had occurred from falling onto some glass, but, even collectively, that was not enough to charge him with this murder. The case went cold.

Five years later, Huth was convicted of third-degree murder in that same county, which strengthened the case against him. He was already in prison. Detectives reexamined the evidence and decided to run DNA tests on the blood samples taken from Buglia's truck.

In 2003, a DNA analysis of the blood found in the truck turned up two sources of origin. One was Buglia and the other, with a stated probability of 1 to 98 trillion against two people having the same DNA, was Huth. He was arraigned on charges of murder, evidence tampering (for moving the body to a location different from where the murder had occurred), robbery, and aggravated assault.

For crime investigation, DNA identification has been the most revolutionary discovery since fingerprinting, and it's only getting better.

"It's become the smoking gun," says Detective Richard Peffall, lieutenant of major crimes at the Montgomery County Detective Bureau in Pennsylvania. "In the past, prosecutors wanted us to have either a confession from suspects or a smoking gun in their hands. Substantial DNA evidence is just as good. It's such an exact science that it's not open to interpretation."

2

Investigators now actively search for DNA-based evidence, aware they can find it many places, such as in saliva on a licked stamp or in skin cells that were rubbed off when tying a ligature—genetic samples the size of a pinhead.

Its many benefits were demonstrated in the very first case, making DNA technology among the fastest forensic techniques to be developed and accepted in the scientific community.

It happened in Narborough, England, during the 1980s, when two fifteen-year-old girls were raped and murdered almost three years apart, along similar village pathways, not far from each other. In both cases, a semen sample identified the killer's blood type as A. There were no witnesses and no fingerprints. After the second murder, a kitchen porter with mental illness was arrested as a suspect, and during an intense interrogation he confessed to the second incident but denied the first one.

Then the investigation stalled when police could find no evidence beyond the confession to tie the suspect to the crime. They kept him imprisoned, but looked for something stronger. The year was 1986.

Less than ten miles from this village, in Leicester, geneticist Alec Jeffreys had recently mapped a person's unique profile via genetic markers in specific regions of the DNA. He had also discovered the profile's consistency across different types of body cells, from blood to saliva to skin, and he named his discovery DNA fingerprinting.

DNA was first detected in 1868, but its actual structure was not figured out until James Watson and Francis Crick identified the double helix in 1953. Individual cells contain two types of acid in the nucleus: ribonucleic acid (RNA) and deoxyribonucleic acid (DNA). Within each cell's nucleus are twenty-three pairs of chromosomes that are made of DNA, which acts as a blueprint to dictate our physical functions and characteristics. The "instructions" are issued in a genetic code transferred from our parents, and these are unique to each person.

DNA is made up of deoxyribonucleotides, each of which contains a sugar, a phosphate, and a base. There are four different kinds of nucleotide bases: adenine (A), guanine (G), cytosine (C), and thymine (T). They join to form the rungs of what looks like a ladder—the double helix.

When strung together in these paired chromosomal strands, A always aligns with T, G with C, and so on, to form the protein and enzyme makeup of our cells. A segment of DNA that arranges the amino acids into protein is called a gene, and when scientists refer to our entire collection of genes, they use the term genome. The genome tells the body what to do.

While most of these instructions are universal for all humans (species-specific—two eyes, two legs, etc.), certain sections of the gene (about 0.01 percent) contain the codes for individual uniqueness. These variations in base sequence are called polymorphisms, and the polymorphic DNA regions continually repeat. The base pairs in these regions are called variable number of tandem repeats, or VNTRs, and they provide the possibility for genetic identification.

By looking at the parts of the DNA that make a person unique, experts can determine whether a particular strand of DNA found in a biological specimen is indistinguishable to an overwhelming statistical probability from the DNA of a particular person. Some people call that making a match, but since it's stated as a statistical probability, the "match" is not entirely exact.

To make this unique discovery, Jeffreys had made the genetic markers radioactive and then X-rayed them. Once the X-rays were developed, he saw the patterns of gray and black bands, which looked like grocery store bar codes, that would soon be recognized as the genetic signature. This is what he called DNA fingerprinting (although experts since then have decried this term, since identical twins—who have the same DNA coding—still have unique fingerprints). Others have referred to it as the DNA profile or genetic identification.

The process that Jeffreys used came to be called restriction fragment length polymorphism (RFLP). By the time he had patented and refined it, and had made the published claim that no two people (besides identical twins) would have the same DNA fingerprint, he was ready when the local police came calling.

The Narborough investigators had heard about Jeffreys's work and approached him for help. He wasn't sure. He'd used it successfully in a paternity suit, but not in a criminal case. Yet the police felt certain that the suspect's semen would prove their case, as well as affirm the technique's viability, so he went ahead and tested a sample of the suspect's blood.

To everyone's surprise, there was no match between the hapless kitchen porter and either of the samples taken from the clothing of the murder victims. The test was done again, and once again proved negative. Despite this man's initial confession, he was not the offender in either of these assaults. The DNA test had probably saved him from punishment for something he had not done. Indeed, he became the first person in criminal history to be exonerated based on a DNA test.

When asked later why he had confessed, he said that he'd felt pressured. Yet the police countered that he had known unpublished facts. In light of the conflicting evidence, investigators decided that the man had probably come upon the body, enabling him to use what he had seen to give them the impression that he knew more than he should have if he were innocent. Based on what he had said about it, they had simply worked him into a confession. Now, given what the scientific evidence told them, they released him from custody—a bold move in light of the relatively untested methods.

Yet they still had a killer at large, with no leads—except that Jeffreys had confirmed that the same person had raped and killed both girls. They did have a way to test every man in the area, so this set of crimes also inspired the first wide-scale DNA dragnet. All the men of Narborough and the villages nearby who had type A blood were asked to voluntarily submit to a DNA analysis. Thousands did so and were cleared, but the object was to find any man who did not willingly submit, because that could indicate he had something to hide.

That man was soon revealed. Colin Pitchfork, who had once been arrested for indecent exposure, had persuaded a friend to go to the test site in his place. Pitchfork provided his friend with a false passport, but the friend had a big mouth. When he bragged about what he had done, a woman who overheard him told the police. That placed the spotlight dead on Pitchfork. After questioning, he confessed, and his genetic profile proved to be statistically indistinguishable from that of semen samples from both crimes. In 1987 he became the first person to be convicted of murder based on genetic fingerprinting.

It was a momentous case, and media the world over picked it up. A person's unique genetic profile could be revealed from a small sample of his or her cells and compared against biological evidence from a crime scene. If this was a surefire technique, as it certainly appeared to be, that meant a complete transformation in crime scene analysis. And not just in the future. Those cases that had stalled but that still had preserved biological evidence could also be revisited for possible resolution. All that was required was to have the proper lab techniques and a suspect against whom to compare the evidence.

3

The rush was on to apply DNA technology to more crimes, but without safeguards in place for proper scientific examination, the challenges from defense attorneys came just as fast. Barry Scheck and Peter Neufeld cofounded the DNA Task Force of the National Association of Criminal Defense Attorneys. Their goal was to debunk DNA typing in courts across the country, or at the very least to limit its application. They evaluated laboratories and evidence technicians and offered support to any attorney faced with this evidence in the courtroom.

A case in New York in 1989 poked a hole into DNA evidence handling, and it had significant repercussions. A woman and her daughter were stabbed to death in their home and a speck of blood was found on the watch of a neighbor named Castro. The blood was tested, along with that of the victims, and it matched one of them. However, in the course of a twelve-week hearing, the defense pointed out that the lab had made a technical error, which made the DNA results invalid (although the defendant later pleaded guilty).

Thanks to cases like this, and to misquoted statements in 1990 by prominent scientists against the use of DNA testing, the courts backed up, allowing the use of DNA to *exclude* suspects as the source of origin but not to make claims that the suspect's DNA was a match for the collected evidence. Prosecution experts had to work hard to prove that DNA evidence and analysis could perform as they claimed.

Improved methods over the next few months increased testing accuracy, and strengthened the technology that could demonstrate that the chance a sample matched a particular person showed statistical odds so overwhelming that the courts allowed it for stronger claims. In 1992, the National Research Council Committee of the National Academy of Sciences affirmed the use of DNA but recommended tight regulations over collection and analysis, and that testing be done by those with no stake in the outcome.

Challenges are now limited to the credibility of the lab, human error during evidence collection, or new techniques.

National Medical Services, one of the country's private testing labs, points out that current controversies surrounding DNA analysis center on evidence integrity. "Tampering with evidence is relatively easy," runs a statement on their Web site, "and should be a major concern in today's judicial system." Tampering and contamination is detectible via the presence of varying amounts of blood anticoagulants in a biological sample. This lab offers a protocol for making those determinations for blood evidence. They examine stained and unstained areas of an evidence item to ensure that the test is not picking up compounds present in low levels in the environment, and the testing is done in such a way as to conserve the DNA for later testing.

To properly analyze it, DNA must first be extracted from the surrounding cellular and environmental materials. What happens next depends on which test is used. Since 1985, the use of DNA fingerprinting, profiling, or identification has taken one of two basic directions. The first is the restrictive fragment length polymorphisms (RFLP) used by Jeffreys, and the second is polymerase chain reaction, or PCR.

In RFLP testing, the extracted DNA is mixed with a substance called a "restriction enzyme" that "digests" or cuts the DNA strand in different areas. Those fragments are then covered in a gel to separate the double-sided fragments into single strands, and an electrical current is applied (electrophoresis). The negatively charged fragments move through the gel at different speeds toward the positive pole, with the shorter pieces migrating faster. The end result is that they line up according to size.

The scientist then takes the pieces from the gel with a nylon membrane called a Southern Blot, and through heat or air-drying the DNA fragments get fixed to the membrane. The A, T, C, and G bases of the strand are exposed. They get treated with a radioactive synthetic genetic probe—a DNA fragment that acts as a sort of sleuth. The single-strand probe seeks out and binds to its complementary base, revealing a pattern. (The multi-locus probe binds to multiple points on multiple chromosomes, while the single-locus probe focuses on a region within one chromosome.)

The radioactive probe identifies specific parts of the DNA that complement the nucleotide sequence of the probe, as revealed by an X-ray (autoradiograph or autorad) of the membrane. The responding DNA segments are visualized as dark bands. Then a print is made of the polymorphic sequences, which can be compared (visually and by computer) to prints made from other specimens. (Chemical luminescence may be used instead of radiation, taking much less time to illuminate the pattern.)

While that method was in use for over a decade, it had some drawbacks: It required a considerable amount of DNA material to work with (a semen stain the size of a nickel, for example), and it did not do well with degraded samples.

The PCR method has been hailed as an even greater breakthrough. This method requires only a minute amount of DNA, because it works by mimicking the cell's ability to replicate DNA. It can also work with degraded specimens. PCR extracts the DNA and heats it in a thermocycler to make it split. The temperature is lowered and raised multiple times to replicate the DNA into millions of copies.

The PCR method most commonly used these days is STR, short tandem repeat. In 1999, the FBI mandated that state labs switch to this system, which meant they had to convert all of their RFLP-based samples and revise their lab protocol.

STRs are regions of a DNA molecule, also known as variable micosatellites, which have short segments of two to seven repeating base pairs that are less susceptible to degradation than the longer segments used for RFLP, and more easily replicated or amplified. When the DNA is amplified via PCR, it's separated in an electrophoretic gel or a capillary device. There are hundreds of different types of STRs in human genes, which means that the lab tech can extract and amplify a number of different DNA markers in a single analysis.

Another DNA test that works on even smaller samples—as few as fifteen to twenty cells—is the LCN, or low copy number test. It's time-consuming, expensive, and thus far available to very few labs. While it may enable forensic scientists to do more with less, there's a problem. The analysis must increase in sensitivity, which also increases its vulnerability to contamination. A single foreign cell introduced at any step of the way can affect the results.

Theoretically, DNA analysis can distinguish between all human beings alive now and all who have ever been alive. Its development has occurred before a broad and varied scientific forum, scrutinized by biologists, geneticists, and statisticians, which has provided a firm theoretical base. The National Institute of Justice issued a report to the effect that "DNA has had an intensity of scrutiny far greater than other methods of criminal investigation . . . The scientific foundations of DNA are solid."

4

In May of 1976 in Lynnwood, Washington, twenty-three-year-old Donna Morris arranged for her sister, eighteen-year-old Kim Kuntz, to babysit her three-year-old daughter, Melissa. Just before 2:00 A.M. Donna came home but could not get in, so she called the police. What happened next became the Cold Case Files episode "Blood Relations."

Inside, Detective John Szalda found Kim dead from repeated stabbing to the chest, and there was also evidence that she had been bound with adhesive and raped. Thankfully, Melissa was still alive. Donna asked Melissa if "Daddy" had come to see her. Melissa nodded, so Donna surmised that her former husband, James Stephens, who had assaulted her just weeks before, had murdered Kim.

The police found him at a roadside motel in Bellingham, Washington. Stephens had scratches on his neck and chest, as well as rug burns on his elbow, and a patrol officer who spoke to Stephens shortly after the murder remembered seeing a roll of athletic tape in the backseat of Stephens's car.

At the crime scene, detectives found semen, and a serology test indicated it might belong to Stephens, but it was from the same bed on which his ex-wife said he had raped her, so it could not be proven that he was a killer.

The investigation went cold.

Nothing happened for the next two decades, but by the time detectives looked at this case again, DNA was in use for crime scene investigations. In November of 1997, Detective Jim Rider happened upon the T-shirt Kim Kuntz had been wearing when she was raped and killed. If the sample had been properly dried, he knew, there was still the possibility of extracting DNA from it. Brian Smelser, with the Washington State Crime Laboratory, scanned the T-shirt with varying wavelengths of intense light and found two or three areas that glowed. He lifted a sample from the shirt and treated it with a chemical re-agent. The chemical reacted with some of the acid phosphatace in the semen stains and changed the color of the sample area. A second test further defined the area that could possibly contain semen, and he managed to extract a DNA profile.

Police got a warrant for a sample of Jim Stephens's blood, and within six weeks, they had a match. He pleaded guilty to murder and was sentenced to a maximum term of thirty-five years.

Criminal investigations often rely on blood samples from the accused and from the victim, but they may also use other biological products such as hair follicles, saliva, semen, tissue, or urine. The estimate of any two people having the same DNA can be as high as one in several billion.

But the statistical measure of a DNA match has also been controversial. In 1996, the National Research Council supported expert statements that DNA from a sample was a "match" to an individual if a minimum number of VNTR loci (where DNA sequences punctuate the chromosomes) had been analyzed—the number being set at nine. With STR markers, thirteen is the national standard for a DNA profile, wherein the odds of a random match can reach one in several hundred million times the Earth's population. In 2000, the FBI authorized their experts in court cases to declare that they were 99 percent certain about an accurate source determination in the context of the entire country's population.

Some crime labs are increasing the number of loci for DNA identification to sixteen as a means of tightening procedures and raising standards, because several labs have come under fire for shoddy practices.

But it's not just human DNA identification that's solving crimes. DNA can distinguish animals from one another, as well as bacterial strains, and even plants within the same species.

The first time plant DNA was used as evidence in a criminal case occurred in 1993 in Phoenix, Arizona. Denise Johnson was found on May 2, 1992, strangled and left nude near a cluster of palo verde trees in a remote part of Maricopa County. She had been bound in several different ways, with a cloth tied around her neck. A pager belonging to Earl Bogan was found nearby and a witness had seen a white truck leave the area—the same type that was driven by Bogan's son, Mark. The truck was seized for a search, which turned up seedpods from a palo verde tree. Bogan claimed he'd picked Johnson up and had consensual sex, but had dropped her off after they argued. He denied being anywhere near the area where she had been found. She had stolen his pager, he insisted, so that's why it was found near the body.

Dr. Timothy Helentjaris, a professor of molecular genetics, agreed to test the pods found in the truck. Using a process developed in the 1980s called randomly amplified polymorphic DNA, he compared the various trees in the area against one another and was able to match the crime-related pods to a specific tree, which tied Bogan's truck to the place where this plant grew—exactly where the body was found. That same tree had a gash in it that fit nicely against the truck, as if Bogan had backed into it. With all this evidence, Mark Bogan was convicted of first-degree murder.

An appeal, based on challenging the fact that this DNA method had not been used before in court, failed in 1995 and the conviction was upheld.

Another type of DNA analysis, used when there are no nucleated cells available, is called mitochondrial DNA, or mtDNA. This substance is found in the cytoplasm of most cells, and it's different from that found in the cell's nucleus. For one thing, it does not degrade through decomposition as the cell nucleus does, and it can endure in bones for centuries. For another, it stays the same in a family for generations and it's only inherited through the maternal line. That means when a J. Doe is being identified, DNA can be extracted from living relatives or descendants on the mother's side. They will possess an identical mitochondrial DNA type. Sometimes that's the only way to identify someone, as happened in *Cold Case Files* "Deadly Lies."

For six years, Kent Hill had been the number one suspect in the disappearance of Frank Ross because Hill was seen leaving a bar with Ross. In 1992, Kent Hill's recent ex-girlfriend said she knew the truth about Ross. After stabbing Ross, Hill had dragged his body into the nearby woods. Then, feeling pressured by police questioning, he had moved the corpse to Claremore Lake.

From skeletal remains found previously in the lake, investigators extracted a sample for mtDNA testing. Scientists also took samples from Frank Ross's surviving family members. The results confirmed that the remains were those of Frank Ross.

During another round of interrogation, Hill broke down and claimed he had strangled Ross in self-defense. He pleaded guilty to a charge of manslaughter. On April 26, Kent Hill was sentenced to twenty years, and Ross's family had closure.

Once DNA testing was accepted and widely used, the next step was to collect samples from people already convicted of certain felonies, like sexual assault, so that they could be matched against other crimes. In 1998, the FBI launched the National DNA Index System (NDIS), a national computer database that could link to databases around the country. It is the capstone of the Combined DNA Index System (CODIS), which uses a multilevel software package designed to facilitate computerized cross-checks. All states have profile databases of specific types of convicted felons, and the FBI's CODIS is a vast DNA profile index to which participating labs can submit samples for electronic comparison. CODIS uses two indexes to generate leads, the Convicted Offender Index and the Forensic Index, which contains DNA from biological crime scene evidence. During its initial experimental phase over a three-year period, the FBI used CODIS to link nearly two hundred crime scenes to felons.

A database search that uses only a crime scene specimen and turns up a match is known as a "cold hit," and such searches are solving both recent and past cases, as in the next *Cold Case File*, "Texas Drifter."

On July 31, 1993, in Granbury, Texas, seventy miles southwest of Dallas, two sisters, ten and eleven, sat under a bridge. A dark-haired man approached them with a knife and forced each girl to watch as he sexually assaulted the other. When he was done, he let them go, and they ran home to call the police. But the man escaped, and aside from semen samples there was little evidence to track him. And there were no DNA databases in 1993, so without a suspect, there was no way to make use of the samples.

Several other small towns reported similar incidents, but each case went cold.

Four years later, the authorities acquired the ability to link into the Texas CODIS program. Under state law, any convicted sex offender had to submit a blood sample for a DNA profile to add to the database. It could then be compared in seconds to any and all existing crime scene samples.

Without a clear suspect, Detective Bruce Espin submitted samples from the case of the two sisters in Granbury. On June 6, 1997, they got a cold hit: Lester Don Parks, who lived in Coleman, a hundred miles east of Granbury. The other similar cold cases hit on his name as well. He was a serial rapist. On June 5, 1999, he was convicted of indecency with a child.

Some states have even sworn out warrants on genetic codes alone, as a way to beat statutes that placed time limitations in which certain crimes must be reported. Increasingly more states have expanded the types of criminals from whom DNA samples are mandated.

Yet CODIS is controversial. How far do we go with genetic sampling? Is it a violation of the right to privacy? Does individual privacy outweigh community safety?

In England, genetic sampling via a noninvasive saliva swab is part of the booking procedure for offenses as innocuous as shoplifting. Some states in the U.S. want to expand their sampling law to cover even nonviolent crimes, but the issue remains controversial. While critics raise privacy issues, law enforcement hails the database as a tremendous asset.

In addition, even the collection of DNA from a suspect raises civil rights issues, and police procedures have had to be evaluated in court.

On November 18, 2003, a judge in Seattle, Washington, ruled about a police ruse to acquire DNA in a cold case. Authorities had tricked John Nicholas Athan into licking an envelope so that they could make a determination as to whether his DNA matched that in an unsolved rape-murder case. In 1982, Kristen Sumstad, thirteen, had been found strangled and dumped in a cardboard box. Athan, then fourteen, was her neighbor, and on the same night her body was found he was seen pushing a hand truck carrying a large box. Under questioning, he claimed that he had been stealing firewood.

Police could not crack the case until they mailed Athan a document that involved an invitation and a return envelope. Athan licked the envelope and sent it back, and the crime lab matched the DNA from his saliva to the semen sample taken from the victim. Athan's defense lawyer made a motion to have this evidence thrown out because it was gained through deception and by detectives who had illegally posed as attorneys. Athan's rights were violated, he said.

But the prosecutor maintained that the police have often used such ruses to collect evidence. The judge ruled that the police did not break the law and therefore the DNA evidence was admissible and the defendant would stand trial. On January 21, 2004, Athan was convicted of second-degree murder.

5

As good as DNA analysis is, and even eliminating the problems with contamination, there is still one key issue that it faces: the fact that identical twins share the same DNA. This means other evidence must be processed as well to ensure that the right person is convicted of a crime. It reminds law enforcement officers that DNA does not solve crimes; it only contributes to a resolution. In the *Cold Case Files* episode "Evil Twin," they found themselves confronted with just such a situation.

A cocktail waitress was found raped and stabbed to death in her apartment on January 2, 1990. Fifteen deep stab wounds suggested a high level of anger, yet there were no clear suspects, so the case went cold.

Four years later, Detective Mike Ring reexamined it. Investigators looked up people who had been around that apartment complex at the time and requested their cooperation. More than 150 men provided samples for DNA analysis, but the police received none from the tenant in apartment 4453, Brian Calzaecorto, whose window had a view of the victim's door. They did a background check and found that he was a suspect in his father's 1986 murder in Pennsylvania. But when they returned to question him, he was gone.

Eventually the police found him in Florida and interrogated him. He refused to give a sample for analysis. Since they had no probable cause for a warrant, they had to come up with another way. They went through Calzaecorto's garbage and found hair and cigarette butts from which they could extract a DNA reading. The profile matched the DNA extracted from semen in the victim. But then police found out that their suspect had a twin brother, Alfred, who also lived in Tampa. That meant they had to eliminate the brother. So they went through his trash as well and found a toothbrush. The profiles were identical.

Brian had no alibi, but Alfred said he had been working on the day of the rape-murder, and his boss affirmed it.

Brian Calzaecorto was arrested, tried, and convicted for the crime.

*   *   *

In all cases where there is a developed suspect, the value of DNA lies not just with evidentiary support for a conviction, but also with suspect elimination. A case of serial murder from the 1960s, still unsolved, has nevertheless generated an entire industry of amateur sleuths, and in the process, many suspects have surfaced.

Between December 1968 and July 1969, two couples from Vallejo in northern California were attacked, and of the four people, only one young man survived. Then the editors of three San Francisco papers received a strange letter from a man claiming to be the killer in Vallejo. Police noted that he used more than the necessary postage on all of the envelopes.

His message, sent in three parts, one to each paper, consisted of a printed cryptogram composed of symbols. The Vallejo murderer signed the letter with a crossed circle symbol. A teacher cracked the code, which translated as:

I LIKE KILLING PEOPLE BECAUSE IT IS SO MUCH FUN IT IS MORE
FUN THAN KILLING WILD GAME IN THE FORREST BECAUSE
MAN IS THE MOST DANGEROUS ANAMAL OF ALL TO KILL
SOMETHING GIVES ME THE MOST THRILLING EXPERIENCE IT
IS EVEN BETTER THAN GETTING YOUR ROCKS OFF WITH A
GIRL THE BEST PART OF IT IS THAE WHEN I DIE I WILL BE
REBORN IN PARADICE AND THEI HAVE KILLED WILL BECOME
MY SLAVES I WILL NOT GIVE YOU MY NAME BECAUSE YOU
WILL TRY TO SLOI DOWN OR ATOP MY COLLECTIOG OF SLAVES
FOR AFTERLIFE. EBEORIETEMETHHPITI

Thus began a game of cat and mouse, and in a later letter, the killer named himself the Zodiac.

Then on September 27, 1969, Cecelia Ann Shepard and her friend, Bryan Hartnell, went for a picnic at Lake Berryessa, where a man approached them. He wore a black executioner's style hood with four sharp corners at the top. It hung down to his waist and had an odd symbol on the front. He appeared to be around six feet tall and to weigh over two hundred pounds. On his left side hung a knife, on his right side an empty gun holster, and he held a semiautomatic pistol. He stabbed Shepard and Hartnell, attacking the girl repeatedly. When he thought they were dead, he called the police to report it. Cecelia died but Bryan recovered.

Then the Zodiac struck again, two weeks later, killing cabdriver Paul Stine and leaving two fingerprints in blood.

Soon after, the *San Francisco Chronicle* received a letter addressed "Please Rush to Editor." In this one, the killer threatened to shoot schoolchildren. He also included a piece of a bloody shirt, which was identified as a torn piece from cabdriver Stine's shirt. Although the police went to great lengths to find fingerprints using a toxic chemical called Ninhydrin on the letters, they found none.

More letters followed with more pieces from the shirt, and threats to build a bomb.

Some people believed the Zodiac was linked to an earlier murder of a girl, Cheri Jo Bates, in Riverside, California. Six months after the murder, the local *Riverside Press Enterprise* ran a story on the case. The very next day, the police, the paper, and Cheri Jo's father Joseph Bates all received handwritten letters from the killer. Each simply said "BATES HAD TO DIE   THERE WILL BE MORE   Z."

A handwriting expert confirmed the link between the letter and the Zodiac confessions.

Throughout his years of terror the Zodiac killer kept in contact with the San Francisco Police Department, as well as the *Chronicle*. He (or someone imitating him) wrote letters from 1966 to 1984. He used codes and symbols, and his handwriting was precise and descriptive. But his killing seemed to have come to an end.

Originally, when the Zodiac investigation began, there were 2,500 suspects. Over the years, the police narrowed their search down to a handful. The number one suspect was Arthur Leigh Allen. He had gone scuba diving in Lake Berryessa on the day of the attack there and returned that evening covered in blood, with a knife on the front seat of his car. He said he had killed a chicken. Allen had spoken often of the "most dangerous game" and "man as true game"—phrases the Zodiac had used in his letters. In November 1969, Allen's sister-in-law saw him with a letter that appeared to have symbols and lines written on it, and Allen remarked it was the "work of an insane person."

When Allen's trailer was searched, police found mutilated bodies of rodents in the freezer and the hearts and livers of small animals. His fingerprints were taken, and although they did not match the prints from Stine's cab, the police believed that false prints could have been left to deflect investigators.

The Zodiac was ambidextrous, as was Allen. He was seen on many occasions wearing a Zodiac brand of watch. Like the Zodiac, he used double postage on his letters. Most importantly, of all the suspects in the case, Allen could be placed at the scene of all the Zodiac murders. He attended the same college as Cheri Jo Bates in 1966, lived near several of the other crime scenes, and was even given a speeding ticket in the Lake Berryessa area only moments after the attack on Hartnell and Shepard.

He was a former navy man with knowledge of codes and ciphers, as well as explosives—while in prison on a child molestation charge, he was caught assembling a bomb believed to be meant for a break-out. At the time the Zodiac was making his threats against school-children, Allen was working in a school as a custodian. Mageau, one of the early victims who survived, also identified Allen as the man who had attacked him.

In short, he was a very good suspect.

Then Allen's death in 1982 ended the possibility of a confession. Police were hopeful when a videotape was discovered postmortem that was labeled with the capital letter Z, but it contained no additional evidence. When Allen died, the police retrieved tissue samples for a DNA analysis.

Eight years later, the SFPD assigned the case to an active homicide team. They decided to look at the envelopes, hoping to lift some saliva off the stamps that would enable them to get a DNA profile. They chose letters that they considered to be genuine—such as the one that had arrived with the piece of Stine's bloody shirt.

They managed to pull off a partial profile. It was not enough to conclusively identify someone, but they knew it was possible to use it to eliminate suspects. So they compared it to the frozen brain tissue from Arthur Leigh Allen.

It was not a match. At least, he was not the person who had donated the biological material found on the stamp (meaning someone else might have licked the stamp).

So investigators had another idea. They looked for a palm print from where a letter writer rested his palm on the paper. They found one, but again, there was no match. Finally, after he was dead, Allen was cleared of suspicion—just as he had always claimed he should be. It was frustrating, but may also prove to be a step toward eventually solving the case.

A couple of other suspects were eliminated this way as well. DNA undermined a few theories, but it brought truth and a bit of closure to one aspect of the case.

Even more important is the elimination of a suspect who has actually been wrongfully convicted, as some cold case files portray.

6

On January 16, 2004, Nicholas Yarris became the first person on Pennsylvania's death row to be exonerated with DNA. He had been in prison, awaiting execution, for twenty-two years. Convicted of a rape-murder in Philadelphia, he had often sought DNA testing, but getting it proved to be a long, difficult process. Finally, a federal judge ordered a new trial, a county judge overturned Yarris's conviction, and after much consideration (and more months in prison), the original prosecutor freed him.

This has been a similar story for more than 130 men, many of them on death row, exonerated by DNA since post-conviction testing began in 1989.

Officials at the New York–based Innocence Project rely on DNA evidence testing to help the innocent prove they are. The project,

founded by Barry Scheck and Peter Neufeld, is based in the Benjamin
N. Cardoza School of Law at Yeshiva University. Scheck and Neufeld
were the two attorneys on the DNA Task Force for the defense attorneys' association who had worked hard to bring accountability into
evidence handling. Under the auspices of the task force, they set up
the Innocence Project, a pro-bono advocacy group. They evaluate
requests from prisoners or families of prisoners, read through court
transcripts and other reports, and determine whether biological evidence from the case has been sufficiently preserved for a DNA extraction. If the case fits all their criteria, and they see problems with the
investigation or prosecution, they take it on. Thanks to their work,
other lawyers have followed a similar pattern and many more such
projects have been set up around the country.

**Ronnie Bullock was arrested in Chicago on May 5, 1983, for the rape of
an eleven-year-old girl. He had a criminal record and he fit the suspect
description. The victim even picked him out of a lineup. At trial, he was
found guilty, although he continually proclaimed his innocence. For this
crime, he was sentenced to sixty years in prison.**

**In an act of uncanny prescience, he made a request to the court to
preserve key evidence, in case there might be a time in the future when it
could be revisited. He'd been in prison ten years when he met a new
lawyer who accepted his case. Now it was the 1990s and DNA analysis
was available. The lawyer got the DNA from the rape sample tested, and it
did not match Ronnie Bullock. After all those years of serving time in
prison, he was exonerated.**

Barry Scheck states that many prosecutors have resisted the idea
that DNA results can conclusively establish someone's innocence, but
in 2000, when Illinois Governor George Ryan learned that thirteen
men on death row had been exonerated by DNA testing, he placed a
moratorium on the death penalty in his state and mandated a redesign
of the system. He was shocked that innocent men might be executed,
and everyone wondered if some already had been. Thirty-seven other

states allow the death penalty and it is no secret that court proceedings are not always about justice. Even when they are, many convictions rely on eyewitness testimony, which has proven in some cases to be notoriously unreliable. Lack of funding, legal misconduct, and bad lawyering also top the list of reasons why someone might be falsely convicted. Whatever the reason, DNA testing can provide a way out—but it is not always accepted without a fight. Many states have resisted postconviction testing.

Scheck has said that many of the cases he takes on are "literally wars." To assert that an innocent person has been convicted is tantamount to an attack on the justice system.

Janet Reno took note of this situation, and in 1996 she called together a Commission on the Future of DNA Evidence. Everyone who attended agreed that postconviction testing ought to be available.

In 2003, the U.S. House authorized more than $1 billion to expand the use of DNA evidence in criminal cases. Seven hundred and fifty-five million dollars over a period of five years will go to the states to reduce the backlog of cases that have gone, or soon may grow, cold. Nationwide, there are some 350,000 DNA samples, mostly from rape cases, waiting to be processed. The rest of the funds will pay for postconviction DNA testing for inmates who meet certain guidelines.

While humans are the primary investigators in a crime, they have their limitations. There is also a science of the nose, and for that, we must turn to man's best friend.

TWELVE

Odor Detectors

1

In Fenton, Michigan, in 1983, Doug Wright was gunned down in the driveway of his home in what appeared to be an execution-style hit. Bloodhounds led police officers on a scent trail directly to a nearby woodpile, where they found several spent shell casings. It appeared that the shooter had stood there waiting for Wright. The dogs took off into the woods, but the scent trail suddenly ended, as if the shooter had entered a vehicle and left. But the dogs had made a potentially significant find. Even so, Wright had no obvious enemies and there was no weapon against which to compare the casings, so without immediate leads the case grew cold. The shell casings were filed away for a future suspect comparison.

Yet the investigators did not forget. Eventually, they interrogated three different suspects who offered information that helped them to zero in on the main perpetrator. Fifteen years after the incident, Wright's wife, Kimberly, admitted that she had wanted the life insur-

ance money and did not want Wright around, so she had hired someone to find a hit man.

In the end, she was the only one convicted. If the dogs had not
found the physical evidence—the shell casings—essential to making
the case, she might have gotten away with murder. Instead, in this
cold case file, a dead man received justice.

2

Bloodhounds have been used in hunting for centuries—and since
the sixteenth century in tracking humans. The sense of smell in mam-
mals correlates with the number of receptor cells found in their noses
and olfactory bulbs. Dogs are believed to have five to six times more
receptor cells in their nasal cavities than humans—around 100 million for bloodhounds—and their sense of smell is thousands of times
more acute. In fact, it's so much more sensitive that they not only can
detect odors humans cannot, but can also detect them from greater
distances and for longer periods of time. On a search, they will identify the odor of a fresh body before it becomes strong enough to alert
humans to its presence.

Smell receptors bond to molecules in the air, and these pass over
the dog's olfactory neurons, triggering a reaction in the brain that
guides the process of sniffing. The dog then utilizes a different route
of airflow than it uses for breathing. During sniffing, dogs draw more
air over the neurons, so they can make sense of odors and can follow
a pattern of increasing concentration.

Complex scents contain many types of odorant molecules, each
of which causes a different neuronal firing pattern, and the total odor
has its own unique pattern. That makes it possible to train dogs to a
specific type of scent, so they can focus on and respond to that scent
alone, despite the presence of others. Dogs can sniff past concrete,
packed dirt, solid walls, deep snow, bodies of water, and layers of
thick material. Some dogs can even detect different types of skin cancer on a human.

Dr. Arpad Vass, a researcher at the Body Farm in Tennessee, is hoping to develop an electronic detector that will respond to the same scents that attract cadaver dogs. It's an artificial nose that pulls air through a tube into a spectrometer chamber. When there's an ongoing project (a corpse), the researcher assigned to it makes a precise digital record at regular intervals of the disintegration process, and uses the "nose" to record changes in the various odors. This machine will isolate the specific chemicals given off by the more than 450 volatile fatty acids of the human body that offer a "fingerprint." Vass hopes to pinpoint specific molecules for this artificial nose and then make the unit portable for police use. He also wants to develop sprays that can be used to train cadaver dogs.

While bloodhounds have been bred specifically for scent capabilities, no single breed shines under every condition, and sometimes crossbreeds make excellent detector dogs.

When dogs come upon the odor that they are trained to find, they alert their handlers by indicating with a specific trained position, such as lying down or barking. They generally associate the scent with a game—they want to "possess" it—and the best dogs show strong stamina and persistence.

Not all dogs trained for forensic work do the same type of job. Many are trained to specialize in a specific type of search: explosive devices, arson accelerants, land mines, narcotics, or human decomposition. Some can also track down the living, following their odor for miles, simply from sniffing something the target subject wore or handled, while other dogs may be involved in search and rescue operations.

Locating the remains of a deceased missing person can be a serious challenge. Sometimes a death was brutal, or the body is dismembered or that of a child, or sometimes the victim has been missing for a long time and the remains are in bad condition. Occasionally the terrain to be searched is difficult to navigate or the corpse has been carefully hidden in an enclosed area. One dog located a girl who had been wrapped in a blanket, sealed inside an airtight coffin, and buried under successive layers of concrete, dirt, wood, and more concrete.

Another found a woman missing for over a year buried in a thirty-five-foot-deep well that had collapsed in on itself. Yet another talented canine detected several sets of remains in Canada that dated back 175 years, to the War of 1812.

It was the presence of decomposition odor that led cadaver dogs in Philadelphia in August 2001, to the body of Kimberly Szumski, thirty-six, a woman who went missing from her home three months earlier. She'd been wrapped in plastic and duct tape, buried under cinder blocks, and cemented into a wall reinforced with steel bars. Nevertheless some odor had escaped, and because the dogs signaled the presence of decomposition, the walls were torn down and the body was located. The discovery threw suspicion on the estranged husband, Tom, who had done construction work in that building. Authorities believed that Tom Szumski had killed his wife, but he died in his home from a drug overdose, so he was not investigated.

Unlike trailing scent dogs that stick with an odor on the ground, cadaver dogs may find it in the air as well and track it via patterns of increasing concentration to its source.

The use of such specialized dogs in police work began in 1974, for multiple victims that had been buried in a forest. A yellow Labrador retriever was brought from Texas to New York for the task, and her first "hit" was a college student buried four feet down. Now many police agencies train dogs for this purpose, and there are more than one hundred volunteer search dog teams around the country as well.

3

We saw in Chapter Two, in the cold case file "Reconstructing Murder," how a revolutionary way of creating a facial sculpture helped police to identify the missing Mwevano Kupaza in Baraboo, Wisconsin, who had been dismembered, beheaded, and skinned.

Once she was identified and linked to a suspect, it was a human remains sniffing dog that helped the police to locate important physical evidence of the murder.

Mwevano's cousin, Peter Kupaza, had told acquaintances that she had returned to her home in Tanzania. Yet her Tanzanian family believed she was still in Wisconsin. The more time that passed, the better for her murderer, who believed that even if she were found, she could never be identified.

He was wrong. On July 31, 1999, she was found, and the following year she was identified. Authorities did background investigation on Peter Kupaza and learned that he had raped Mwevano in 1997, and when she became pregnant, he had forced her to get an abortion. Kupaza was arrested and charged with killing the young woman.

However, he insisted that Mwevano's father in Tanzania had assured him in April of 1999 that she'd arrived home. So detectives contacted the father, but he said he had not heard from his daughter since June 1998. Nor had he spoken to Kupaza in over two years.

A search of Kupaza's apartment turned up possessions belonging to the victim, including her Bible, clothing, jewelry, and purse—things she would not have left behind. In addition, there were garbage bags in his place similar to those that had been found wrapped around the dismembered body parts. Yet investigators could not determine just where Mwevano had been so brutally killed and cut apart. The likely place was Kupaza's home.

To search for hidden evidence, the police turned to a detection dog handler. Sandra Anderson from Michigan brought in Eagle, her scenting dog, a mixed breed of Doberman pinscher and German short-haired pointer. Anderson had been involved in over one thousand cases, both forensic and historical, and had used Eagle to find human remains in Panama, Mexico, and many areas around the United States. Certified by several forensic organizations and approved in courtrooms in over twenty states, Eagle had a stunning track record. Anderson was told nothing about the Kupaza case, as was her custom, so that she could work "blind" and avoid subliminally directing Eagle to specific areas.

Eagle was taken into the Kupaza apartment and allowed to do his work. He soon alerted investigators to the presence of decomposition— a minute amount of blood—behind a baseboard in the bathroom. The apartment quickly became the suspected murder scene, and DNA analysis later matched the found blood to the missing woman. Eagle also alerted investigators to several more spots—places where the lab had already found blood, as well as locations where they could not visually detect anything. In a garage that housed twenty-eight cars, Eagle immediately alerted on Kupaza's.

Peter Kupaza went on trial, and his former wife testified about his abusive behavior. She stated that they had discussed his background in Tanzania, where families often butchered their own livestock, and he had said that he knew his way around slaughtering techniques. Added to that was a demonstration for the jury of how cadaver dogs worked. The prosecution's team stained one cloth with beef blood, another with pig's blood, and still another with a drop of human blood. They even washed this latter cloth in cold water. They then placed these cloths in brown paper bags and put them in different areas of the courtroom. Eagle was let in. He ignored all of the bags in which were cloths stained with animal blood and came alert only on the human blood. The demonstration not only affirmed his ability but showed the jury that he would only alert in the presence of human remains.

Kupaza was convicted of hiding a corpse and of first-degree intentional murder.

Eagle was also involved in a case in which Azizul Islam, a physician, was suspected of killing his wife. The woman went missing on December 20, 1999, and two days later, female body pieces were found in a Dumpster and a field. Nevertheless, Islam willingly allowed a search of his home, and the police called in Anderson and Eagle. Anderson noticed strong bleach odors and she feared that this would hinder Eagle's work. However, the dog immediately alerted on a paint roller and soon indicated that there was something associated with human decomposition on the floor that the doctor had recently painted. Tests showed that blood was present in the paint, and it matched the DNA found on the missing woman's toothbrush. Islam was arrested and convicted of murder.

Sandra Anderson got her start as a forensic dog handler during the mid-1980s, when she watched news reports of how dogs were being used to find missing victims in the aftermath of a major earthquake in Mexico. Interested, she began attending seminars and taking classes devoted to the topic of training such dogs. Some cadaver dogs, she learned, would alert on any form of decomposition, animal or human, but others could be trained to do a more refined search on only human remains. She started into this work as soon as she felt her dogs were ready.

Eagle was her third dog to specialize in human remains. She took him on cases and to seminars, where she showed students in various forensic areas what Eagle could do. To continue her own education, she worked closely with anthropologists, pathologists, coroners, and medical examiners around Ohio, Michigan, and Wisconsin. Asked what traits she looks for in a dog with potential for this work, she lists the following:

* *A good temperament.* "I don't have the time, energy, or respect for a dog that is unsociable or shows any aggressive qualities."

* *High drive to hunt.* "If I throw a ball in some tall grass and the puppy won't come back until he finds that ball—-even at eight weeks of age—he'll make a good search dog."

* *Focus.* "While he's hunting for that ball, if a car backfires or I clap my hands, he won't care. He's got a job to do."

* *Will retrieve a toy.* "That tells me the dog has possessive qualities. And though I still need to teach the dog to possess scent, I

have a head start because he's already showing me that he has that quality."

▪ *Methodical.* "I don't like a dog that's hyperactive. I may choose the puppy that I notice is always sniffing around on the ground versus bouncing off the walls."

▪ *Observant.* "I like the dog that's sitting under the table watching everything. There's a lot going on with a dog that watches other dogs."

▪ *Desire to please.* "A dog needs to want to give his best effort."

▪ *Intrinsic interest.* "They do it for the joy of doing it."

To test for these traits, Anderson will do several different things. "Naturally we'll use a toy like a ball to test for hunt drive. We'll walk among the puppies and clap our hands, and if any run away or don't hunt for the ball, we put them aside. They won't have the traits we're looking for. If any puppies are shy, they won't have it. We can't make that better. Once we get the litter down to one or two—and sometimes none—we bring out a box containing very smelly human remains in some state of decomposition. Then we watch the dogs for a certain attraction or for being averse, which a lot of puppies are. We won't even look at a dog like that again, because it's not going to outgrow its aversion. If we have a dog that smells the box and that doesn't want to leave it, even if we make noise or walk away—if he's obsessed with it—we probably have a winner."

While she may acquire remains from an anthropologist for the purpose of training, Anderson is aware that many trainers prefer to use synthetic cadaver scent. "I think that until we're out there looking for pseudo-people, we're kidding ourselves with those chemicals. I have a real problem with it, and I think that a lot of dogs have problems in training because we've become such a fast-food society: Whatever is the quickest way to train the dog is the way we go. That's not a good idea. I know, from experimenting with numerous dogs over the past decade, that if I put out cadaver chemical pseudo-scent and I have an arson dog along, the arson dog will find it. That tells me that something's wrong."

She wants a dog that will develop into a human remains specialist. "So in the training program and throughout our lives together, I'm not going to let him down by not being a specialist, too. That means he will only detect human remains and not something else. Nothing else is satisfactory."

The way she gets a dog to imprint on a specific type of scent is to fall back on the Pavlovian technique of association and reward.

"The puppies are in a crate," she says. "It's time to eat. Twenty minutes before they're due to eat, we bring human remains out in a sterile paint container or jar, and put it on the crate. It doesn't take long for them to associate that smell with getting fed. Once we've got that down, then the puppies get fed regularly. But then we get a new toy. It might be a towel or a squeaky ball. Ten or twenty minutes before we let them out to play with it, we bring out the scent. This will go on for about six or seven months. Then we begin to teach them the search process. That means they have to hunt for it and then something good happens."

In about a year, she will imprint them on skeletal remains. "Then at two and a half, we start imprinting blood and trace evidence. That's it in a nutshell. It's a very basic procedure."

When on a case, Anderson takes the dog out and looks for specific behaviors that indicate the dog has found the target scent. "I expect a bark. If I don't have a bark, he's not on the target. That's key to everything. Excitement levels dictate the strength of the odor. It's like a good hunting dog. A big bird excites the dog more than a small one. Dogs are honest creatures. They can't contain their excitement if the smell's really good. Then there's also the ease with which he works on a problem; if he goes into a room and within two minutes he can tell me there's scent, I know there's probably a great deal of odor present. If he's working hard, then there's not a lot. With skeletal remains, because we teach the dog that he can only possess the scent and not the object, he'll go down [adopt a prone but alert position]. He knows he can't touch anything, so he has to go down because that's how he controls himself. Preservation of the remains is everything, so they have to be able to hold the point. But he's got the scent and the anticipation of 'What are we going to do now?' "

These dogs are in constant training. "It's obsessive. There's no end. There's scent work, and then work on obedience and manners, and also handling planes, trains, and automobiles. He has to learn to be a good dog while someone's eating dinner, and when a place is noisy. There are so many parts to the training process."

Given how complex and demanding the training is, inevitably there are problems.

"Most dogs fail the program because they can't differentiate. At around one year of age, we start introducing distractions, sometimes earlier, depending on the dog's progress. Some dogs just like dead raccoons better than bodies. Some would rather find food than a body. Some would rather find a tennis ball. So when we encounter any of that, that dog's probably not going to make it through the training. Usually if a dog's in the program as long as a year and a half, we know he's good to stay."

And then there are the handlers. They, too, must be trained.

"It can be difficult. A lot of them don't do it as a career. They might do it because they're on a search and rescue team and they want to get called out with their dog once in a while. Yet I've met numerous passionate individuals who work very hard at it and are able to accomplish some very good work with their dogs. They're the kind of people who are willing to say, 'The victim deserves better than adequate. If this dog doesn't make the cut, I'll get another dog.' At no time do we look at our partners as pets; we see them as friends and as working associates."

She uses an expression for this: "We share the nose." By that, Anderson means, "We translate. We're the communicators. The training process is one in which the dog handler learns how to read the dog. The dog builds the work ethic. The dog learns what the game is. We're sharing the nose in that the dog has to communicate its abilities to us. We're the folks who are trying to transfer what the dog is telling us to the public at large."

During training, some people "clue" the dog, or give signals to point the dog in a certain direction.

"If a dog can be clued," Anderson says, "it's already the wrong dog. If you have a dog that we call a deceiver or a dog that is more involved in getting the toy or pleasing the handler than in hunting, you already have the wrong dog and you need to find one that is honest, confident, and above all else loves hunting and the odor of human remains.

"If you look at a really good hunting dog, there is nothing in the world that is more important to that dog than finding that pheasant or quail. You could have a tennis ball fall from heaven, but nothing is more important than finding the bird. We're hunting human remains, but we still have to have all the same energy and desire as those hunting dogs."

Eagle's first case, when he was just over ten months old, was finding a drowning victim in Michigan's Muskegon River. "The only reason he was used is that the dog I had then was older and getting tired. We'd been out for three days, and the sheriff asked if I could use Eagle. I said he was only a pup, but he figured we had nothing to lose. Within about fifteen minutes, Eagle had run up this trail to this little cliff, literally jumped off the cliff, and dropped about twelve feet into the river and started barking. And there was the body. At that moment I thought, wow, he's really good! In water, he was a natural."

When asked to explain how a dog can scent a body in water, Anderson says, "We have to remember that the oils from the body come to the surface. As it decomposes, there's a great deal of odor that comes up, and at some point the decomposition gases began to rise. If there's been a stabbing, we even have blood odor."

In the following *Cold Case Files* episode, "Lady in the Box," Anderson brought Eagle three separate times, and each time produced something that confirmed what the police believed or knew about a suspect.

4

In 1991, Betty Fran Gladden Smith went missing from West Windsor, New Jersey. Her family members were convinced that her secretive and erratic husband of sixteen months, John Smith, was somehow involved. He claimed that Fran—who had a broken hip— had told him she was leaving for a few days. He did not seem concerned. He only filed a missing persons report when pressured to do so, but failed to mention that he'd twice tried to leave his new wife. He also failed to mention his longtime girlfriend, living in a home he had purchased while married. When Fran's relatives asked for assistance, he ignored them or deflected them with the wrong information. Everyone was suspicious, but Fran's relatives felt stymied.

Knowing next to nothing about Smith except that he often acted impetuously, Fran's daughter, Deanna Weiss, and her sister, Sherrie Davis, began to piece together the past. They discovered a prior marriage in Ohio that had ended in 1974 with a divorce. Weiss and Davis began a search for Smith's first wife, Janice Hartman. They hoped she might have something to tell them about the man.

In March of 1992, they started dialing numbers and eventually tracked down Janice's brother, Garry, who startled them with his own bad news. Janice was also missing, and had been since a month after her divorce from Smith. Fran's relatives brought this information to West Windsor detective Mike Dansbury, who reviewed both files and then obtained a warrant to search Smith's home. He found nothing suspicious, but when he talked with Smith, his instinct said that something was wrong.

Nevertheless, the investigation into John Smith grew colder and stayed that way until the FBI took an interest.

Special Agent Bob Hilland brought Smith in for questioning, but he just stared in a blank way at each question. When the agents asked about the effect of the disappearances on Smith's family members, he began to crack. He even gave an odd shriek at one point, but he still offered no information.

FBI agents in Ohio began to question those family members,

especially John's younger brother, Michael, whom they knew had warned women away from John. A profiler had told them that of all the relatives, Mike would be the one who would respond to an appeal to conscience. At first, he refused to talk, but eventually he told them a strange story.

One day he went to John's trailer home in Montrose, Ohio, to help him take bags of women's clothing out, which Michael assumed had belonged to Janice, who had recently divorced John. They placed these in the garage where their grandfather lived in Seville, Ohio. Shortly afterward, Michael came out to the garage to find John constructing a long wooden box. Next to the box were the clothing bags. He saw John rolling the clothes to place them in the box, and he appeared to be agitated and angry, so Michael left him alone.

He forgot about the mysterious box, which lay undisturbed in the garage for five years. Then in May of 1979, Michael and his grandfather opened the box and discovered Hartman's mummified remains. Her hair, Michael remembered, was oddly multicolored, and her legs had been cut off below the knees. He asked John about it, but John denied responsibility for the box's contents. He came up with an elaborate story that no one quite believed, but Michael Smith and his grandfather agreed to keep quiet. John shoved the box into his car and disappeared with it. He told Michael that he had thrown it into a field to let the animals take care of it. Michael surmised that the box had been taken either to Indiana or to an apartment building in Seville that at the time was under construction, with concrete about to be poured in the garages.

Two decades after his discovery, Michael contacted agents at the FBI to tell his story. At their request, Michael agreed to participate in a phone sting, but John was too clever to incriminate himself. Investigators had to come up with another angle.

In May 1999, detectives summoned Sandra Anderson to bring Eagle to Grace Lane Apartments in Seville. Her associates, forensic anthropologists Frank and Julie Saul, came as well, in case remains were found that needed to be identified. There were several dozen garages for this complex, so the investigators hoped that Eagle could make the job easier for them. It wasn't long before he gave a signal near one garage, barking to be let in. But before he was allowed any farther, a team went in with a ground-penetrating radar device to locate anomalies beneath the concrete. They plotted what they found on charts but did not tell anyone until after Eagle was allowed to do his work. Once inside, he went to a specific location near the middle and lay down. It was the same spot where the engineers had located an anomaly.

An FBI evidence recovery team came to cut away the concrete and dig for remains. Two feet down, they found pieces of two teeth. The Sauls identified them as human. The team also found fibers, but no more remains. However, the teeth fragments were not those of Janice Hartman. They were also not a match for Fran.

In 2000, Sherrie Davis got on the Internet and downloaded addresses for all the sheriff's departments and coroners in the state of Indiana, and Detective Brian Potts sent out letters. A call came in from Detective Gerry Berman in Morocco, Indiana. The Indiana lawman told Potts a story about a five-foot-long wooden box found abandoned in the weeds of an Indiana cornfield back in 1980. Inside the box, investigators found clothing and a soiled quilt, and when they moved some of it, they discovered the skeletonized remains of a young woman. Upon examination, it turned out that her legs had been cut off below the knees, and those bones were missing. An anthropologist determined that she had been petite and in her early twenties. To them, she became the "Lady in the Box." They kept the sawed leg bones, the clothing, the skull, and the box, and buried the unknown woman. They hoped that one day someone would offer information that would give her an identity.

Detective Potts secured a court order to exhume the Lady in the Box. He also gathered the remains that had been kept aside. At the Lucas County Coroner's Office in Ohio, Dr. Frank Saul did a detailed examination of the bones and determined that they were from a human female in her twenties and that the skull belonged to the body, but he could not determine a cause of death. The legs had been sawed, just as Michael Smith had described, so Saul referred the team to Dr. Steven Symes, an anthropologist whose expertise lay in identifying specific saw markings on bone. He determined that each leg had been individually cut with a serrated knife, and with a great deal of force.

Now they needed more corroborating evidence for court. Detective Potts called Anderson back into the case.

"They had me search the outside of this building," she remembered, "and then they brought me into this alcove area between the garage and house. I didn't get anything, so we went into this garage. They filmed it. I let Eagle go around, and he kept going up to this one wall and indicating. There were boards there and they asked if I thought Eagle was responding to the boards, so we moved one and he was still indicating at the wall. I moved another board and he still indicated. So I said it wasn't the boards. I told them that all along the cinder-block wall, he's indicating. They thanked me and sent me home. A couple of days later they told me I had confirmed what their witness had said. He had told them that he'd seen a body in a box for an extended period of time at a specific spot in a garage. That's where Eagle had indicated."

In early spring of 2000, a DNA sample from Janice Hartman's mother was also collected and compared against a sample drawn from the bones of the corpse. The reason for the rainbow-colored hair, it turned out, was that clothing in the box had released dye as the body fluids had soaked into it. In fact, the dye had bled so much that an impression of the victim's face could actually be seen in some of the clothes that had lined her coffin.

On April 24, 2000, twenty-six years after she had disappeared, mtDNA analysis confirmed that the Lady in the Box was Janice Hartman, which was sufficient evidence to arrest John Smith. Using the independent but corroborating evidence of Michael Smith's recollections and Eagle's detection, the prosecution developed a case—based on the theme that Smith had cut off his former wife's legs as a symbolic gesture that she would never walk away from him again. But the search was not yet over, because one former wife was still missing.

Inside a storage facility near Wooster, Ohio, was a locker once used by John Smith. Anderson and Eagle also went there. But Eagle did not indicate on Smith's former unit. Instead, he alerted outside another one, so the police got permission from its owner to go inside. The place where the wall met the floor interested Eagle, and he lay down in a specific spot. A crime scene technician poked into the cracks and retrieved several charred bone fragments and a piece of dried skin. Investigators submitted these discoveries to Dr. Saul, who informed them that the pieces were from the top part of a human skull. Yet DNA testing established that the skull did not belong to John Smith's other missing wife, Fran Gladden Smith.

Fran's family believed they might have discovered a potential answer to this riddle. In researching John Smith's background they happened across an old briefcase he once had owned. When they opened it, they found some financial papers in it along with pictures of four women. One was Janice Hartman. The second was Fran Gladden Smith. The other two pictures, older snapshots, were of John Smith with two unidentified women. One of the women was subsequently identified and accounted for. The other remained a mystery.

The fate of Smith's second wife, Fran Gladden Smith, remains unknown. Her body was never recovered. The source for the human bone fragments and the teeth recovered in Ohio also remains unknown.

John Smith was found guilty of Janice's murder and sentenced to fifteen years to life. Later, in New Jersey, a civil court judge awarded the family of Francis Gladden Smith $1 million from John Smith for expenses and damages in their wrongful death suit.

When we speak about the science of cold cases, DNA springs most quickly to mind. Along with that comes toxicology, fingerprints, and other areas of investigation that are processed in a lab. Yet there are times when physical evidence is not available or not clear. Sometimes the science of the crime scene involves the mind, and that's where psychology comes in. While many forensic professionals object that it's not a science, a good psychological analysis at a crime scene, based on what is known about criminal behavior, can make an important contribution to getting the crime solved, and that's often admissible in court.

THIRTEEN

Reconstruction and the Criminal Mind

1

Helen Dean, ninety-one, had just had surgery and was doing fine. She returned to the nursing home from the hospital but died shortly thereafter. That was in 1993. Her son, Larry Dean, felt certain that someone had caused her death, and he distinctly recalled that she had said that a male nurse had "stuck me" with a needle, although her records indicated that no one had prescribed medication by injection. An autopsy was ordered, along with toxicology reports, but nothing sinister turned up.

Nevertheless, Dean spent until his death in 2001 investigating the mystery of his mother's demise. Then late in 2003, male nurse Charles Cullen, who had worked at the hospital where Mrs. Dean had her surgery, confessed to having killed as many as forty patients over the past sixteen years with an overdose of the heart drug digoxin. In Helen Dean's case, no one had thought to test for that. Cullen, who moved around to at least ten different facilities, had been under investigation at other hospitals, and was finally stopped with murder charges in one in New Jersey. In April 2004, in seperate plea deals, he admitted to killing seventeen people, Helen Dean among them. He may yet include more.

While physical evidence was lacking in the Dean case, those who study the behavior of these so-called "angels of death" could have pointed out the constellation of red flags that followed Cullen wherever he went: secretive behavior, history of depression, suspicions from colleagues, disempowerment in all significant areas of his personal life, remarks about which patients would or would not "make it." Such professionals, from FBI profilers to forensic psychiatrists/psychologists to criminologists, have studied psychological indicators of criminal minds and can offer information that helps narrow down leads. They're available not only to law enforcement but to other institutions as well. Psychological assessment addresses many different areas, although profiling is probably the most well known.

2

Criminal profiling falls within the area known as forensic psychiatry or psychology. Wherever the legal system and psychology intersect, you have forensic psychology. Forensic psychologists (or psychiatrists) may advise in criminal investigations, assess threats of violence in schools or workplaces, determine the fitness of a parent for a child's guardianship, develop specialized knowledge of crimes and motives, evaluate the effects of sexual harassment, or conduct forensic research. In short, they are consultants within the legal system who possess more in-depth training in human behavior than police officers or detectives.

For the court, they're often asked to evaluate a person's present psychological state for the competency required to participate in the legal process. They may also evaluate a defendant's mental state at the time he or she committed an offense. In addition, psychologists generally appraise behaviors such as malingering, confessing, or acting suicidal. They can assist in understanding domestic violence or discuss the contributing factors to poor judgment that leads to crime. If they gain experience in investigation, they may also offer a criminal profile, either to help narrow leads or to explain a suspect's motivation, as in the following *Cold Case File,* "Murder Illustrated."

On February 11, 1987, in Fort Collins, Colorado, Detective Jim Broderick found a body in a field on the edge of town. A blood trail indicated that the victim had been dragged. The victim was thirty-seven-year-old Peggy Hettrick, who was last seen six hours earlier, leaving a bar. She had been attacked in a blitz fashion, stabbed once in the back, and her vaginal area had been mutilated. The coroner's report showed that two different knives were used in the attack, a scalpel and a larger knife.

Clyde Masters and his fifteen-year-old son, Tim, lived in a nearby trailer. Tim admitted he had seen a body that morning but did not report it. While several knives were found in his bedroom, none could be linked to the murder. Yet more than fifteen notebooks full of his writing were discovered, along with sketches depicting decapitation, death, and dismemberment. Police discovered hidden in a closet a homemade mannequin, used for sexual purposes. Tim clearly had a problem. He was brought to the police station for questioning and he failed a polygraph. But without physical evidence tying him to the victim or the crime scene, the police could not make a case, so the investigation went cold.

Nine years later, cold case detectives tried again, but this time they were armed with a forensic psychologist. Detective Broderick reviewed the file with Dr. Reid Meloy, an expert in the pathology of sexual homicide and author of *The Psychopathic Mind.* In his eighteen years of doing this kind of work, he said, he had never seen such a voluminous production by a suspect. Tim's deviance, his writings, and his admission about seeing the body, along with strong psychological testimony from an expert, finally combined to bring him to trial in 1999.

Dr. Meloy focused the jury's attention on two sketches in particular. The first depicted a figure being dragged across the ground—just as the victim had been. Tim Masters had admitted to drawing the

230 THE SCIENCE OF COLD CASE FILES

picture the day after Hettrick was killed. Meloy then moved to the second drawing, dated the month prior to the murder. Its details closely resembled the victim's sexual mutilation. Meloy said that it represented a rehearsal fantasy of the way in which Masters wanted to sexually mutilate the victim. He explained that many rapists and killers mentally act out a fantasy before actually doing it and that their subsequent actions are generally guided by the fantasy. The prosecutor held up a photograph of Peggy Hettrick's mutilated vaginal area. Then he placed Masters's drawing next to it. The resemblance was uncanny.

On March 26, 1999, thanks largely to a psychological evaluation that linked the boy more clearly with the crime, Masters—now a young man—was found guilty of first-degree murder.

A good profile is an educated attempt to provide investigative agencies with clear parameters about the type of person who committed a certain crime, based on the idea that people tend to be slaves to their psychology and will inevitably leave clues. Psychologists look at personality traits that are evident from behavior. From a crime scene, they can assess whether the person is an organized predator who planned and arranged a crime, or instead someone who committed an impulsive crime of opportunity. They may also observe if the offender used a vehicle, is criminally sophisticated, or is enslaved to a sexual fantasy. They look at the weapon used, the state of the crime scene(s), the type of wounds inflicted, the risks an offender took, his or her method of committing the crime and controlling the victim, and evidence that the incident was staged to look like something else. In addition, there may be indications that the offender did not act alone.

Profiles work best when the offender displays obvious psychopathology, such as sadistic torture, postmortem mutilation, or pedophilia. Some killers leave a "signature"—a behavioral manifestation of an individualizing personality quirk, such as staging the corpse for humiliating exposure, frenzied stabbing in a specific area, or tying ligatures with a complicated knot. This helps to link crime scenes and alert law enforcement to the presence of a serial rapist or killer. Sometimes the signature will also alert them to other types of behaviors to look for.

What a profile can offer that tends to be helpful are the offender's general age range, racial identity, ideas about the modus operandi, estimates about living situation and education level, travel patterns, the possibility of a criminal or psychiatric record, and probable psychological traits. A profile may also describe a fantasy scenario that drives the person, or even pinpoint an area where he or she probably resides. A responsible profiler will always caution the investigators that profiles are valuable but limited. They are based on known data from *other* similar crimes, and there is always some chance of anomalous human behavior. No one can predict everything a person is capable of doing.

The earliest profiles were drawn up by psychologists and psychiatrists before the FBI developed such a program to teach to law enforcement under its own auspices. By virtue of their expertise on human motives and behavior, some mental health professionals have done a surprisingly good job in offering specific details about a potential suspect. Yet with the popularity of profiling, thanks to movies and television, it's been relatively easy for charlatans to pose as profilers and for the media to evolve the idea of a behavioral profile to fit its own agenda. Hence, there has been much misunderstanding of the subject.

The most common error is the idea that profiling is a sort of blueprint or set list of traits for certain criminal categories, against which one can measure people to see if they might be viable suspects. For example, the media might ask, "What is the profile of an 'angel of death' and does Charles Cullen fit it?" But that's the wrong question. More accurately, law enforcement should ask, "From what you see at this [or these] crime scene[s], what traits or behaviors in a person might we be looking for?"

Each case is unique, and the decisions made about whether and how to use a profile are generally specific to that case. A profile is one of many tools in use when trying to solve a crime, and its primary function is to help prioritize leads. The profiler usually states that suspects should not be eliminated just because they don't match some specific trait, such as race or age.

A behavioral profile is based on the available behavioral evidence, and faulty information can guide the profile in the wrong direction. For example, in the case of the Canadian killing team of Karla Homolka and Paul Bernardo, several witnesses "saw" two men in a Camaro pick up a missing girl who was later found murdered. All of them were mistaken about both the car and the kidnappers, but until the police realized that, the eyewitness information affected how the profile was devised.

Tunnel vision in an investigation can also hamper behavioral analysis. If investigators decide that a set of crimes was committed by a white male, they may disregard witness reports that a black man was seen lingering in the area. Thus, the only information they will offer to an incoming profiler is whatever is consistent with their own hypothesis about the crimes.

Yet no profile is static. With additional information, it can evolve.

The first recognized profile was done by Dr. Thomas Bond, a surgeon, based on the five murders done in London in 1888 by the man who came to be known as Jack the Ripper. The murders had escalated in brutality and were clearly sexual in nature, with an intense element of rage against either women or prostitutes. Except for the last one, they were clean, quick, and out in the open, often disemboweling the victim in some manner. Dr. Bond had assisted in the autopsy of the victims. The police, desperate to catch this maniac, requested his expertise in addressing how much the killer knew about surgical procedure, but Bond offered much more.

He said that all five murders had been committed by one person alone who was strong, cool, and daring. Bond thought the man would be quiet and inoffensive in appearance. He would be middle-aged and neatly attired, probably wearing a cloak to hide the bloody effects of his attacks. He would be a loner, without a real occupation, eccentric, and mentally unstable. He possessed no anatomical knowledge—could not be a sur-

geon or even a butcher. Bond thought the offer of a reward would garner clues from people who knew the man.

3

Throughout the first half of the twentieth century, some mental health professionals made a study of murderers and through their published works, the motives and background were often clarified. Psychiatrist Karl Berg questioned German serial killer Peter Kurten in prison in 1930, after he was charged with numerous counts of assault and murder. James Melvin Reinhardt, a psychiatrist and professor, published his interviews with spree killer Charles Starkweather in 1960. But perhaps the most famous profile by a psychiatrist to that point was the one developed by Dr. James Brussel during the 1950s, who provided so much accurate detail about the offender from crime scenes and notes the man had written that when the police arrested George Metesky as Manhattan's "Mad Bomber" in 1957, the written portrait bore an uncanny likeness to the man. Brussel offered Metesky's motive, prior employment, living circumstances, state of health, temperament, religion, and ethnicity, and even precisely how he would dress.

Brussel also went on to profile the man who was committing a series of sex murders in the Boston area from 1962 to 1964, but others had done so as well and it became clear from the many diverse opinions that the area of criminal profiling was not an exact science—not even close. Learned men openly contradicted one another in their assessments of the Boston Strangler, and the police were back at square one. Brussel wrote about his approach in a book about his cases, which caught the eye of Howard Teten, an FBI agent who was teaching a course in criminology at the National Academy.

While J. Edgar Hoover had firmly resisted psychology of any kind in the FBI's agent training, he died in 1972, opening the way for Teten to develop a program based in part on what he was learning from Dr. Brussel. Teten met with Brussel to compare their approaches, and, with Patrick Mullaney, he designed a method for analyzing unknown offenders in unsolved cases. He would look at the behavioral manifestations at a crime scene for evidence of aberrant mental disorders and other traits, and use that information to make specific deductions.

The Behavioral Science Unit began to form from a handful of agents interested in different areas of criminal psychology, and as they went out to local jurisdictions to teach, they began to help solve cases. Soon requests for consultations started to come in from police departments around the country, so more agents were trained, and that became the Crime Analysis and Criminal Personality Profiling Program. By 1977, the unit had a clear identity. It changed its name several times, and in 1985, it came under the auspices of the FBI's National Center for the Analysis of Violent Crime (NCAVC). It's now known as Behavioral Science Services, with an Investigative Support Unit offering the Criminal Investigative Analysis Program (CIA).

This is a multifaceted approach to many types of crime. CIA divides an investigation into four clear stages:

1. Determine that a crime has been committed.

2. Try to accurately identify the crime.

3. Try to identify and apprehend the offender.

4. Present evidence in court.

Profiling takes place during the third stage.

To develop this comprehensive approach, the early profilers not only worked on crime scenes but also collected data from imprisoned offenders who were responsible for some of the country's most heinous crimes. The early BSU instructors trained local law enforcement to work with a profile, taught psychological analysis to hostage negotiators, and offered specialized crime analysis for other arms of law enforcement, such as the Bureau for Alcohol, Tobacco and Firearms (ATF).

They utilized a computer database known as VICAP that collects data from police departments around the country on solved, unsolved, and attempted homicides; unidentified bodies in which the manner of death is suspected to be homicide; and missing persons cases in which foul play appears to have played a part. With serial crimes, the key was crime identification and linkage analysis—finding the commonalities among crimes that suggested they had been committed by the same offender. Sometimes those links jump right out, but as occurred in *Cold Case Files* "Diary of a Serial Arsonist," sometimes they first require winnowing out a large body of suspects.

On January 16, 1987, in Bakersfield, California, police responded to a call about a fire in a fabric store. In the middle of the store they found an incendiary device, which consisted of three matches and a cigarette. Folded inside was a piece of yellow legal paper held together by a rubber band. A second call came in, and then a third—both involving craft stores that were burning, with the fires ignited by similar devices. Ironically, at the center of the arson activity sat a fire investigators' conference in Fresno. A check showed that fifty-five of the participants had traveled through the fire areas to get to the conference.

A latent print was lifted off one incendiary device, but it was too faint to make a clear determination during comparisons, so the investigation went cold.

Two years and another symposium later, arson fires again broke out in the area. When the symposium roster was cross-referenced against the 1987 list of fifty-five, ten names stood out—all of them among the top fire investigators in the state. Comparisons against the latent print again turned up no leads.

Then two years later, stores in Los Angeles began to burn. The five fires were within a few miles of each other, all were in commercial department stores, and all were close to a California freeway.

Jerry Taylor, a criminal profiler for the ATF, believed that California had a serial arsonist, responsible for over two dozen fires. He wanted the fingerprint examined with the latest technology, so it was submitted to the lab. Using advanced photography and colored filters, the technicians enlarged and enhanced it. The print was then run through California's fingerprint database, where it was compared against criminal records as well as prints taken from members of law enforcement. The search registered a hit: John Orr.

He was a top arson investigator with the city of Glendale, California, and his print had been compared and cleared two years earlier. But a mistake had been made, based largely on the difficulty of reading the latent print. The ATF began to investigate, and they learned that Orr was considered a man who possessed an almost supernatural ability to pinpoint the cause of a fire, often within minutes.

That was a red flag. Now he was a good suspect.

Cold case detectives constructed a time line to establish Orr's whereabouts during each of the fires. It turned out that he had been operating in an unmarked law enforcement vehicle, which could cross any jurisdictional line. He worked in plain clothes and there was no record of his whereabouts when the fires started. Yet the odds that one person could be within an hour of thirty fires were near impossible.

Orr was arrested and charged.

In support of the profile, which outlined his obsession with fire, among Orr's possessions the team found an extensive collection of home videotapes of the very fires he was charged with setting. But there was something more: a draft of a novel written by Orr about a firefighter turned serial arsonist. The manuscript paralleled many of the actual fires—which was good psychological evidence of his strong personal connection to them.

A federal jury found Orr guilty on three counts of arson. In the second federal case Orr pleaded guilty to three additional counts and was sentenced to thirty years in a federal penitentiary. However, as detectives read Orr's manuscript further, they realized that perhaps it was a blueprint for more than just arson.

In 1984, an Ole's department store had burned to the ground, fed by polyurethane foam in the building. In his novel, Orr described an almost identical fire set in a fictional store called Cal's. In real life a two-year-old boy and his grandmother, along with two employees, perished in the Ole's fire. The boy's name was Matthew. Orr's novel described the death of a fictional grandmother and her three-year-old grandson, Matthew. Investigators believed that there was at least one telling detail in Orr's chapter that only the arsonist could have known. He described the grandmother deciding to take her grandson for ice cream. The grandmother who had died in the Ole's fire had promised her grandson a mint chocolate chip ice cream cone at Baskin Robbins. It was a bit too coincidental.

On September 17, 1998, in state court, Orr was convicted on four counts of murder.

4

At times, a suspect has already been developed but the case has stalled. In such instances, a profiler or a consulting forensic psychologist can offer information about the suspect's motivation and weakness. These experts base their analysis on crime scene information, along with police reports and other documentation—anything that offers psychological clues. Armed with that, investigators can plan a way to acquire information, even a confession, from the suspect. That's what they got in the next Cold Case Files episode, "Pride and the Fall," by using psychological maneuvers.

In April of 1993, Robert and Donna Spangler were hiking a remote trail in the Grand Canyon when Donna fell to her death. After an investigation, her death was ruled an accident. A year after the fall, Coconino detective Bruce Cornish learned about a second "tragedy" in Robert Spangler's past. In 1978, he'd had a wife and two teenage children who were killed in Littleton, Colorado. The conclusion of that investigation was that the case had been a double murder and suicide, with Nancy Spangler killing the children and herself, and leaving a note behind.

Suspicious about so much bad luck, Cornish shared his concern with Investigator Paul Goodman, who then reviewed the physical evidence from that case. Goodman began with the suicide note and the typewriter upon which it was written. Surprisingly, the note bore no fingerprints. Why would Nancy Spangler wipe it clean? As well, the typewriter appeared to have wipe marks on its surface. Next were the gunshot residue tests done on Nancy and Robert. Nancy's test was negative, but Robert's had revealed the presence of residue. Photos of Nancy's wound also showed an injury characteristic of an intermediate-range wound, which meant that the gun that killed her was held at a distance of three to ten inches from her head. Holding it at such a distance made the possibility of missing much greater than if the gun was in contact with the skin—which made suicide questionable. In short, the original investigation had serious flaws—possibly influenced by tunnel vision. It seemed more likely that Nancy had been murdered, and whoever did that had killed the children as well—a triple homicide.

Because the Grand Canyon was federal property, cold case detectives utilized the FBI in tracking down Robert Spangler. When they found him, he was resistant. In a ruse to draw him out, based on evidence that he was narcissistic and would like to be viewed as "important," Special Agent Lenny Johns told the suspect that if they could show he was a serial killer, a team of FBI profilers would study him. Hearing that, Robert Spangler agreed to talk. Taking the detectives back to 1978, he revealed the details of how he had murdered his family. But a triple murder would not be enough. They told him he'd have to confess to another murder to really be considered a serial killer, so he described how he had killed his second wife by pushing her off the cliff.

Spangler pleaded guilty to four counts of first-degree murder and was sentenced to life in a federal prison. He died in 2001.

5

As the first generation of FBI profilers retired, some became consultants, working alone or forming groups. In either event, they offer a long history of experience with crime investigation, along with an appreciation for the role of psychology in crime scene reconstruction. Both FBI profilers and forensic psychologists contribute to groups such as the Vidocq Society, and some have banded together in the Academy Group Incorporated (AGI), which was founded in 1989 by former chief of the Behavioral Science Unit Dr. Roger Depue.

Members of AGI include retired former FBI and Secret Service supervisory special agents, including those who helped to develop the National Center for the Analysis of Violent Crime (NCAVC). They consult with organizations on the motives behind different types of aberrant behavior, of employees, customers, and unknown adversaries. They also provide training and expert testimony.

Among their programs is CCAP, the Cold Case Analysis Program. Those consultants who work on CCAP offer their extensive experience in investigating sexual violence, mass destruction, threat assessment, fraud, and terrorism, to assist law enforcement in brainstorming older cases. On their Web site, they state, "AGI's goal is to serve the law enforcement community so violent offenders now must look over their shoulders and hear the approaching footsteps of today's enforcers, armed with new technologies. Our shared objective is to serve victims who can no longer speak for themselves, to include the victim's extended family, who continue to hope for closure and resolution."

The cold case team at AGI seeks to provide shortcuts, resources, experience, and knowledge to help determine whether or not a case can be solved, and with what means. They assist with crime analysis, the development of an offender profile, and post-offense behavioral issues. They may also offer interrogation techniques, prosecutorial strategy, and assistance with search warrants. In the following case for *Cold Case Files*, "The Nail File," they helped to clarify the nature of the crime, which provided a suspect.

On February 3, 1984, inside a Roy Rogers restaurant in Fairless Hills, Pennsylvania, twenty-five-year-old assistant manager Terry Brooks was found beaten, strangled, stabbed, and suffocated. A few feet from her body, detectives noted that the restaurant safe had been opened and emptied. They suspected the Freezer Bandits, a gang that had targeted fast-food restaurants in the area. Yet they had no evidence.

Over time, the case faded away.

In 1998, fourteen years after Terry Brooks's body had been found, criminalist Diane Marshall focused her attention on fingernail clippings taken from the victim during the autopsy. Under one fingernail she discovered something that looked like skin. She was able to isolate an unknown male DNA profile. The criminalist next tried her luck with a strand of human hair plucked off Terry's clothes—its profile was the same. Finally, Marshall examined the knife used to kill Brooks. Inside the knife's handle, visible after she took it apart, Marshall found the same unknown genetic profile. If investigators found a suspect, they could make a case.

They looked through the files and found a 1990 behavioral profile of the crime scene that AGI had developed for a private civil suit. AGI's conclusion had been that the murder was intensely personal. True, money was missing, but the dominant behavioral evidence consisted of the injuries to the victim and the stages of overkill. It was their opinion that the person who had killed Brooks knew her and had vented a lot of emotion in the process of committing the disorganized, unsophisticated murder. This led them to interview those closest to Terry Brooks. Included on the list was her former fiancé, Scott Keith. The answers Keith provided during an interrogation appeared to be lies.

Cold case detectives now dug further into Scott Keith's past, with particular emphasis on his relationship with Brooks. Witnesses had indicated that they believed Terry was planning to end the relationship. That was sufficient to make Keith a strong suspect. Now they needed a sample from him to acquire his DNA profile.

In the Commonwealth of Pennsylvania, if one puts one's trash out on the curb, it is anyone's domain. Detectives watched the trash collectors pick up the trash in front of the Keith residence. They then transferred the trash from the trash truck into a pickup and drove to the lab. Twenty cigarette butts bearing the brand Newport, Keith's smoke of choice, were recovered. The DNA type from the saliva matched the DNA from underneath Terry Brooks's fingernail, on the knife, and from the strand of hair.

Confronted, Scott Keith wrote out a full confession to the murder.

6

Sometimes law enforcement decides that showing a profile to the public will assist them in gathering information. They believe that someone out there may know something, and when that person hears the personality traits of the offender, he or she may come forward. Some crimes have been solved in exactly this manner, while others are awaiting resolution. On *Cold Case Files*, they select those cases that have some chance of gathering more information if offered to viewers. The following, titled "The Original Night Stalker," is one such case.

The man who came to be known as the East Area Rapist in northern California raped over thirty women in 1977 and 1978, but left no physical evidence that could be used for leads at the time. Sometimes he called to taunt his victims. Often he tied up the husbands and raped the women in front of them. There were indications in several rape-murder cases that he might have been involved in those as well. In 1979, the rapes stopped and the cases were eventually packed into storage.

In 1998, cold case detective Larry Pool called Leslie D'Ambrosia, a criminal profiler in Miami, for a crime scene assessment based on the similarities in the offender's behavioral patterns. She indicated that the offender was disciplined, intelligent, organized, planning, meticulous, predatory, and thought his victims were worthless. He specifically targeted affluent women. He liked to control and manipulate the male, as well as harm the female. His crimes were compulsive. He was a dominator. He was arrogant and superior and degrading. Since these traits would hold true for his sexual relationships, investigators figured someone out there would know him and would recognize his characteristics.

Twenty years after the East Area rapes, criminalist Paul Holes examined the preserved semen samples to extract and compare the DNA profile. He confirmed that the same man had engaged in all of the assaults. Then he contacted police officers from several California-based murder cases that had occurred during the 1980s committed by someone dubbed the "Original Night Stalker." The profile was the same, so the 1970s rapist had become a killer. He had killed at least ten people and raped more than fifty women, spanning half the state of California.

With the DNA profile in hand, investigators searched for suspects in the prison system, but were stopped when identified suspects refused to volunteer specimens. Investigators pressured for the laws to change to force convicted felons to give blood samples, but civil rights groups protested. Nevertheless, a bill was passed in 2002 that gave DNA collection from convicts more latitude, but as of this writing, no suspects in this case have been arrested. The investigators still hope someone will offer information to confirm whatever they might find or present new avenues of investigation. For the purpose of collecting information or getting new leads, they offer the number 1-888-390-CLUE.

Cold case squads have had a lot of success, but there are many cases that remain unsolved. To address this, various groups have gotten involved in coordinating investigations and calling on both professionals and laypeople with information to assist.

FOURTEEN

Solved and Unsolved

1

A skull found in Stanley Park in Vancouver, British Columbia, in 1997 showed evidence of blunt force trauma. DNA extracted from a tooth indicated a boy around age thirteen. Via dental records for two runaways who had disappeared in 1989, investigators found the parents and matched the DNA, giving the boy an identity, Ramsey Rioux. They then returned to the ten-acre forest with dogs and metal detectors to search for the other missing boy. Dental fillings were found near the skull location site but did not match that skull's teeth.

The police asked the public for help and soon learned that the boys had been seen on the streets with an older male. Then a man who lived near the park came forward to admit that he had picked up a skull because he liked how it looked and taken it home. Anthropologists determined that it had belonged to Kenneth Lutz, the second missing boy.

They did not find the rest of the remains or the killer's identity, but their appeal to the public had at least given the families closure and a way to bury the boys' remains.

Crimes involving children are especially difficult and they tend to haunt investigators. One such crime caught the attention of the Vidocq Society, and thanks to a public appeal, they believe they have come as close as possible to a resolution.

This story began on February 25, 1957, on the outskirts of north-eastern Philadelphia. In a weedy, trash-filled lot, a man peered inside a furniture box and found the malnourished and bruised body of a blond Caucasian boy, between the ages of four and six. Someone had recently—and amateurishly—trimmed his nails and hair. Someone had also caused his death from severe head trauma. Those who found him were horrified by his brief, brutalized life, but no one knew who he was.

Several clues made a quick identification seem likely: The box had held a bassinet purchased locally; a man's customized cap was found near the scene and traced to the seller; the boy's nude body had been wrapped in two sections of a distinctive blanket; he had seven scars from medical treatment and eight moles, and he might also have had an eye ailment.

Yet every potential lead dried up. Days turned into months, and months into years, without a resolution.

Haunted by the tiny victim, some investigators continued to search on their own time and at their own expense. Remington Bristow, from the Medical Examiner's Office, never ceased to check information, even after he retired. As long as he lived, this case was not going cold.

Then in 1998, the Vidocq Society adopted the case. They rechris-tened the boy America's Unknown Child. Sam Weinstein, an officer present at the initial crime scene, led their reinvestigation. Later, investigators Joseph McGillen and William Kelly took over. The boy's remains were exhumed for DNA testing and then reinterred in a bet-ter location in Ivy Hill Cemetery.

That same year, the television show *America's Most Wanted* aired a segment about the case, which inspired George Knowles, a private citizen, to get involved. When he was eleven, he'd seen a flyer about the crime at a local police station. He watched the program and then joined an Internet discussion group. Seven people from those discussions formed a private chat to examine the unsolved crime from every angle, and from that, Knowles's Web site devoted to the victim was born.

Word got around, albeit slowly. In June 2002, Kelly, McGillen, and a Philadelphia homicide detective interviewed a woman who had offered information through her psychiatrist. She described her abusive mother, who had purchased a toddler in the mid-1950s whom the family called Jonathan. The woman's parents had kept him in a box in the cellar, and her mother killed him when she banged his head on the bathroom floor. The woman recalled the blanket in which the mother had wrapped him and the box into which he had been placed. She herself had trimmed his fingernails, while her mother cut his hair. Her initial disclosures, the psychiatrist attested, had predated the AMW broadcast and the Web site.

The details were in close accord with what detectives knew, yet while neighbors from her former residence remembered the woman as a girl, which confirmed some of her story, no one recalled the boy. Since the tale is based only on the woman's memories, Philadelphia police will not officially close the case.

Nevertheless, those closely involved believe that their public appeal resulted in the best information they can expect for a case this old.

2

Since 1960, some 200,000 murder cases have gone unsolved in the U.S., and even more rape cases. Some forensic professionals who notice how families are deeply affected by lack of closure, or who believe the victims of these unsolved crimes should gain a voice, have developed programs to bring focus, information, and talent to the task. Similar to the Vidocq Society is the Institute for Cold Case Evaluations at the University of West Virginia (www.coldcases.org). They match forensic scientists with police departments that lack the means for forming cold case squads, offering a newsletter, cold case review, and Web site to facilitate the connections.

Cold case squads have discovered media outlets that can reach potential witnesses or people who did not know they had information until they saw a particular story on the news. Community publications, newspapers, radio, and television can all have a positive effect in gathering information. When a Canadian television station broadcast an hour-long program offering everything the police knew about the death of a kidnap victim, Kristen French, it alerted the killer's girlfriend to how accurate the behavioral profile was about his traits— especially his escalating abuse of her. She eventually turned him in, resolving three unsolved murders.

In 1985, Volith Long, only six years old, was found in a Dumpster. She had been strangled, sexually assaulted, and murdered. No witnesses came forward, and because she was Cambodian, the language barrier between the Austin, Texas, police and the girl's community made it difficult to learn much about the crime. The girl had been playing outside an apartment complex where she lived and had suddenly gone missing. A few suspects turned up, but nothing could be proven. Eventually, the police could do nothing more.

In May 2000, the Austin Police Department Cold Case Unit, which had been in place since 1999 and faced with some 130 unsolved homicide cases, ran a CrimeStoppers story in their local media about the incident, hoping to generate new leads. They also posted information on their Web page, and they soon received a call from an elementary school teacher who remembered the case. She had once had a Cambodian boy in her class who was arrested later that same year for murdering a woman. Since he was a juvenile, he had been released. The Cold Case Squad tracked him down and learned that he was now serving a life sentence in California for a double homicide.

The investigators ran a DNA test on the biological samples they had from the 1985 incident and compared them to specimens from the suspect. He proved to be a match.

Some police departments have set up a way to give regular notice to the public about difficult cases. A number of Web sites now devote themselves to such projects, and as mentioned earlier, even *Cold Case Files* runs an occasional story that is unsolved but that might benefit from being brought to the attention of the public, such as the following, featured in the episode "Unsolved."

On November 25, 1991, Cindy Wanner disappeared from her sister's home, leaving her eleven-month-old daughter in a high chair, which the family insisted she never would have done. Calls to friends and family turned up nothing. There were no signs of a struggle inside the house, as there would have been if an intruder had come in and abducted Wanner; she seemed to have simply vanished.

A stray cigarette butt was found on the walkway outside the Wanner residence, and since Cindy did not smoke, it was collected as potential evidence. Then, almost three weeks later, Cindy's body was discovered in the foothills of the Sierra Nevada Mountains. From the corpse, investigators picked up traces of green fiber and metal flaking. Nearby, detectives found a bag containing beer cans, a videotape, and a pornographic magazine. The bag also contained green fibers and metal flakes. Fingerprints were found on the beer cans and videotape, but when run through AFIS, no match was made.

Given the quality of evidence the police had, this case seemed solvable. Yet the question of who killed Cindy Wanner and why remained unanswered, and the case went cold.

Detective Bob McDonald had worked the Wanner case for almost ten years without success. One morning he attended a cold case seminar in which investigators could present their cases and get some benefit from the group's brainstorming. Jill Spriggs, a DNA expert who remembered the Cindy Wanner crime, was in the audience. She got involved, and used a laser light to search for traces of semen on the pornographic magazine. She also examined with a chemical test the bra Wanner had been wearing to try to pick up any trace of saliva. Spriggs came up empty, so she turned her attention to the beer cans found near the body, as well as a cigarette butt found outside the home. However, to date, no profile has been developed.

It was possible that someone might have overheard the murderer bragging about the crime, or that someone saw something that day that he or she did not realize was significant. It was also possible that the killer had a girlfriend who had since left the relationship and might be willing to talk. Perhaps his family knew something. Since police had fingerprints, a suspect lead would be valuable, but it appeared that they might only acquire that with public assistance, so *Cold Case Files* developed a program for that purpose. While the emphasis for the series is on the manner in which cold cases have been solved, for those unsolved cases in which solvability factors are high, the show's involvement may in fact bring about a resolution.

Among Internet resources for cold case resolution are:

▪ Veronica D'Amario's Web site, where she posts the details of some forty unsolved cases in the hope that someone will come forward with details that can help to close them. Unsolved-crimes.com began with the murder of twenty-two-year-old Jennifer Whipkey, who was last seen in May 2002 leaving a New Jersey restaurant. She was stabbed and dumped near a motel. D'Amario had known her and was friends with her mother. She wanted to help, so she created the Web site, and her oldest case dates back to 1961. She requests that people whose memories are triggered contact the relevant police jurisdiction.

▪ Crimelibrary.com offers a series of articles that detail cold cases, in the hope that someone with information can help to resolve them.

▪ The Doe network at doenetwork.org concerns itself with unidentified and missing persons from any place in the world.

▪ For nationwide assistance, statetostateunsolved.com offers resources listed for each state

▪ Cold Cases Yahoo Group is one of several chats on Yahoo that offer comfort and resources to those concerned with cold cases.

While resolving cold cases has become an area of focus during the past decade, should crime rates increase again, some of those resources may be reassigned. Raising public awareness while resources are available is key, and those people who care about the victims have learned that they can take an active part. All cold cases are under the auspices of law enforcement, and civilians should not try to solve these cases themselves, but good information can improve the solvability odds. Only passion and caring can generate the heat a cold case needs, and the victims depend on that.

Cold Case Files offers science, ingenuity, and intrigue as it presents cases from around the country that were sometimes merely stalled and sometimes seemingly hopeless, but which eventually were resolved. Highlighting the persistence and dedication of those who would not let a case rest, the show inspires hope that in the future more such investigations will bring peace to families and justice to victims.

References and Sources

Baden, Michael, with Marion Roach. *Dead Reckoning: The New Science of Catching Killers*. New York: Simon & Schuster, 2001.

———, with Judith Adler Hennessee. *Unnatural Death: Confessions of a Medical Examiner*. New York: Ivy Books, 1989.

Barrett, Sylvia. *The Arsenic Milkshake*. Toronto, Ontario, Canada: Doubleday, 1994.

Bass, Bill, with Jon Jefferson. *Death's Acre*. New York: G. P. Putnam's Sons, 2003.

Beavan, Colin. *Fingerprints*. New York: Hyperion, 2001.

Benedict, Jeff. *No Bone Unturned*. New York: HarperCollins, 2003.

Berlow, Alan. "The Wrong Man," *Atlantic Monthly*, November 1999.

Bowers, C. Michael, and Raymond Johansen. "Forensic Dentistry: An Overview of Bite Marks," in *Human and Animal Bitemark Management*. Forensic Mailing Services, 2000.

Brenner, John C. *Forensic Science Glossary*. Boca Raton, FL: CRC Press, 1999.

Britz, Marjie T. *Computer Forensics and Cyber Crime*. Upper Saddle River, NJ: Prentice Hall, 2004.

"Convicted by Justice, Exonerated by Science," The National Institute of Justice Report, 1996.

Dix, Jay, and Robert Calaluce. *Guide to Forensic Pathology*. Boca Raton, FL: CRC Press, 1999.

Douglas, John, Ann W. Burgess, Allen G. Burgess, and Robert K. Ressler. *Crime Classification Manual*. San Francisco: Jossey-Bass, 1992.

Evans, Colin. *The Casebook of Forensic Detection*. New York: John Wiley, 1996.

Fenton, John Joseph. "Forensic Toxicology," in *Forensic Science: An Introduction to Scientific and Investigative Techniques,* edited by Stuart H. James and Jon J. Nordby. Boca Raton, FL: CRC Press, 2003.

Fisher, Barry. *Techniques of Crime Scene Investigation*, 6th edition. Boca Raton, FL: CRC Press, 2000.

Fridell, Ron. *Solving Crimes: Pioneers of Forensic Science*. New York: Grolier, 2000.

Geberth, Vernon J. *Practical Homicide Investigation*, 3rd edition. Boca Raton, FL: CRC Press, 1996.

Gerber, Samual M., and Richard Safterstein, eds. *More Chemistry and Crime*. Washington, DC: American Chemical Society, 1997.

Goff, M. Lee. *A Fly for the Prosecution: How Insect Evidence Helps Solve Crimes*. Cambridge, MA: Harvard University Press, 2000.

Hammond, Robert. *Identity Theft*. Franklin Lakes, NJ: Career Press, 2003.

Houck, Max M. *Trace Evidence Analysis*. New York: Elsevier, 2004.

Houde, John. *Crime Lab: A Guide for Nonscientists*. Ventura, CA: Calico Press, 1999.

Inman, Keith, and Norah Rudin. *An Introduction to Forensic DNA Analysis*. Boca Raton, FL: CRC Press, 1997.

Innes, Brian. *Bodies of Evidence*. Pleasantville, NY: Reader's Digest Press, 2000.

———. *Profile of a Criminal Mind*. Pleasantville, NY: Reader's Digest Press, 2003.

James, Stuart H., and Jon J. Nordby. *Forensic Science: An Introduc-*

tion to Scientific and Investigative Techniques. Boca Raton: FL: CRC Press, 2003.

Lee, Henry C., and Howard A. Harris. *Physical Evidence in Forensic Science.* Tucson, AZ: Lawyers & Judges Publishing Company, 2000.

Lee, Henry C., and Frank Tirnady. *Blood Evidence: How DNA Revolutionized the Way We Solve Crimes.* Cambridge, MA: Perseus, 2003.

MacDonell, Herbert L. *Bloodstain Patterns.* Corning, NY: Laboratory of Forensic Science, 1993.

Manheim, Mary H. *The Bone Lady.* New York: Penguin, 1999.

McCrary, Gregg, with Katherine Ramsland. *The Unknown Darkness: Profiling the Predators Among Us.* NY: Morrow, 2003.

Miller, Hugh. *Proclaimed in Blood: True Crimes Solved by Forensic Scientists.* London, England: Headline, 1995.

———. *What the Corpse Revealed: Murder and the Science of Forensic Detection.* NY: St. Martin's Press, 1998.

Nickell, Joe, and John Fischer. *Crime Science: Methods of Forensic Detection.* Lexington, KY: University Press of Kentucky, 1999.

Nordby, Jon. *Dead Reckoning: The Art of Forensic Detection.* Boca Raton, FL: CRC Press, 2000.

Owen, David. *Hidden Evidence: Forty True Crimes and How Forensic Science Helped Solve Them.* Buffalo, NY: Firefly Books, 2000.

Platt, Richard. *The Ultimate Guide to Forensic Science.* London: DK Publishing, 2003.

Ramsland, Katherine. *The Forensic Science of C.S.I.* New York: Berkley Boulevard, 2001.

Randall, Brad. *Death Investigation: The Basics.* Tucson, AZ: Galen Press, 1997.

Rebmann, Andrew, Edward David, and Marcella Sorg. *Cadaver Dog Handbook.* Boca Raton, FL: CRC Press, 2000.

Rhine, Stanley. *Bone Voyage: A Journey in Forensic Anthropology.* Albuquerque, NM: University of New Mexico Press, 1998.

Saferstein, Richard. *Criminalistics: An Introduction to Forensic Science,* 7th edition. Englewood Cliffs, NJ: Prentice Hall, 2000.

Scheck, Barry, Peter Neufeld, and Jim Dwyer. *Actual Innocence*. New York: Random House, 2000.

Snyder Sachs, Jessica. *Corpse: Nature, Forensics and the Struggle to Pinpoint Time of Death*. Cambridge, MA: Perseus, 2001.

Taylor, Karen T. *Forensic Art and Illustration*. Boca Raton, FL: CRC Press, 2000.

Thorwald, Jurgen. *The Century of the Detective*. New York: Harcourt, Brace & World, 1964.

Trestrail, John Harris. *Criminal Poisoning*. Totowa, NJ: Humana Press, 2000.

Ubelaker, Douglas, and Henry Scammel. *Bones: A Forensic Detective's Casebook*. New York: M. Evans and Company, 1992.

Wambaugh, Joseph. *The Blooding: The True Story of the Narborough Village Murders*. New York: William Morrow & Co., 1989.

Wecht, Cyril. *Mortal Evidence*. New York: Prometheus Books, 2003.

Wonder, A. Y. *Blood Dynamics*. San Diego, CA: Academic Press, 2001.

Index

Katherine Ramsland, Ph.D., has published twenty-two books. She holds graduate degrees in forensic psychology, clinical psychology, and philosophy. Currently she teaches forensic psychology at DeSales University in Pennsylvania and consults on criminal investigations. She has written for *The New York Times Book Review, Psychology Today, The Philadelphia Inquirer, The Newark Star Ledger,* and *Publishers Weekly.* Her forensic studies positioned her to assist former FBI profiler John Douglas in writing *The Cases That Haunt Us* and to cowrite *The Unknown Darkness* with former FBI profiler Gregg McCrary. She also published *The Forensic Science of* CSI and *The Criminal Mind: A Writer's Guide to Forensic Psychology,* and she frequently contributes articles to Court TV's *Crime Library.*